More Than Meets the Eye

Portrait of Hans Christian Andersen at the age of thirty-one (1836) by C. A. Jensen. Reproduced in agreement with Odense City Museums, Denmark.

More Than Meets the Eye

Hans Christian Andersen and Nineteenth-Century American Criticism

Herbert Rowland

Madison • Teaneck
Fairleigh Dickinson University Press

Associated University Presses
2010 Eastpark Boulevard
Cranbury, NJ 08512

The paper used in this publication meets the requirements of the American National Standard for Permanence of Paper for Printed Library Materials Z39.48-1984.

Library of Congress Cataloging-in-Publication Data

Rowland, Herbert.
    More than meets the eye : Hans Christian Andersen and nineteenth-century American criticism / Herbert Rowland.
      p.   cm.
    Includes bibliographical references and index.
    ISBN-10: 0-8386-4092-3 (alk. paper)
    ISBN-13: 978-0-8386-4092-0 (alk. paper)
    1. Andersen, H. C. (Hans Christian), 1805–1875—Criticism and interpretation.   2. Andersen, H. C. (Hans Christian), 1805–1875—Appreciation—United States.   3. Scudder, Horace Elisha, 1838–1902.
I. Title.
PT8120.R65 2006
839.8'136—dc22

                            2005031858

Contents

Preface

THE TITLE OF THE PRESENT VOLUME PROBABLY CONTAINS A COUPLE OF surprises for the vast majority of readers, even the literary scholars among them. Longer than anyone can remember, Americans and other English speakers have associated the name of Hans Christian Andersen almost exclusively with fairy tales for children. Yet the title of this book indicates that critical study of Andersen, like that of Emerson or any other literary figure, is both possible and has actually been practiced in the United States. In Denmark and other parts of Scandinavia, indeed, there exists a long tradition of Andersen scholarship that continues to thrive to this day. In histories of Danish and Scandinavian literature Andersen occupies a position reserved for major writers, receiving, for example, chapters of thirty-two and seventeen pages each in two volumes of a recent standard work.[1] This recognition derives in part from the knowledge that Andersen's fairy tales are only a portion of a lifework that also includes several novels and travel books, many plays, a substantial body of poetry, and an autobiography. Andersen himself was offended by the suggestion that he wrote only, or primarily, for children. Significantly, many of Andersen's coevals in the United States were aware of his broader literary activity. Leading authors and critics commented on his works as they appeared in the country, establishing a respectable corpus of criticism, and one of them wrote a seminal essay that surpassed virtually all contemporary writing on him in any language. The basic purpose of this study is to trace and explain the course of American Andersen criticism from its rise in 1845 to its decline upon Andersen's death in 1875.

At this point I would like to thank personnel in the Interlibrary Loan Office of Purdue University, especially Kathy Walters and Suzanne Ward, for handling what must have seemed like an interminable number of requests for books and articles that were often rare or otherwise difficult to locate. Thanks also go to Anne-Mette

Kirkeby and Erik Schwägermann of the Royal Library in Copenhagen as well as to Ejnar Askgaard at the Odense City Museums for photocopies of material unavailable in the United States. Photographic images of Andersen and some of his American critics used in the book were graciously provided by Kasper Maaløe, also of the Odense City Museums, as well as by Emily Walhout and William P. Stoneman of the Houghton Library of Harvard University. Other photographic images were furnished by Photo/Digital Imaging Services at Purdue University. The publishing firm of Rosenkilde og Bagger in Gentofte, Denmark, was kind enough to grant me permission to quote extensively from their title *H.C. Andersen og England,* by Elias Bredsdorff. I would like to express special gratitude to Johan de Mylius, Director of the Hans Christian Andersen Center at the University of Southern Denmark and a leading Andersen scholar, for clarifying several matters for me. Portions of the present study are drawn from "The Image of H. C. Andersen in American Magazines During the Author's Lifetime," which appeared in *H. C. Andersen: Old Problems and New Readings,* ed. Steven P. Sondrup (Odense: University of Southern Denmark Press, 2004), 175–98.

More Than Meets the Eye

Introduction

IN HIS FIRST LETTER TO ANDERSEN, WRITTEN ON MARCH 8, 1862, CHIL-
dren's writer Horace E. Scudder relates that he had read the author's
stories as a child and adds that "all of us American children do."[1]
Born in 1838, Scudder thereby intimates the fact that Andersen
entered the American book market and reading public almost as
soon as he was translated into English. For English writer and translator Mary Howitt's earliest renderings of Andersen's works—*The
Improvisatore* (*Improvisatoren*) in 1845, a selection of the fairy tales and
stories entitled *Wonderful Stories for Children* in 1846, and *The True Story
of My Life* (*Mit egen eventyr uden digtning*) in 1847—were published
concurrently in New York or Boston as well as in London.[2] They
helped introduce a series of translations that regularly appeared in
both the United States and England over the next two decades. Viggo
Hjørnager Pedersen goes so far as to plea that Andersen be considered as an English writer, since "from the very beginning up to the
present day his works have appeared in English just as frequently,
just as quickly, and in some cases even before they appeared in
Danish. . . ."[3] As far as the provenance of the earliest translations is
concerned, Hjørnager Pedersen is entirely justified when he subsequently equates "English" with "British" from the point of view of the
mid-nineteenth century.[4] If one understands "English" to refer to a
linguistic community, however, one must conclude that "English"
means "American" as well as "British" and that it possessed this meaning from the very beginning of Andersen's entry into the English-
speaking world.

Taking the third quarter of the nineteenth century into account,
moreover, even provenance of translation ceases to be a consideration. Independent American translations and/or editions of Andersen's works began to appear in 1863 with the publication of *The Ice
Maiden, and Other Tales,* which was followed by new collections of the
fairy tales and stories in 1864, 1866, and 1869, and then by a seem-

ingly endless stream that continues to the present.[5] Indeed, the
English-language version of the novel *Lykke-Peer* (*Lucky Peer*) came out
in New York before being issued in London, and translations of
eleven of the fairy tales and stories as well as the final version of the
autobiography, *Mit livs eventyr* (*The Story of My Life*), appeared in the
United States before being published in England or even Denmark.[6]
The only collected edition of Andersen's works in English, the ten-
volume "Author's Edition," was edited by Scudder and published by
Hurd and Houghton in Boston and New York from 1869 to 1871.[7]

Certain aspects of the theme "Andersen and America" have already
received scrutiny, for example, Andersen's view of America and
Andersen scholarship in the United States.[8] However, Scudder's comment in his initial letter to Andersen suggests that the Dane was an
American writer not only, or simply, because his works appeared in
American bookshops but because he had become a cultural posses-
sion of Americans as well, early occupying a distinctive niche in the
national consciousness, and this central aspect of his presence in the
United States has gone virtually unnoticed to date.[9] The present
study seeks to rectify this state of affairs in two ways. On the one hand
it examines American commentary on Andersen from 1845, when
the first reviews appeared, to the period following his death in 1875,
which witnessed the subsidence of writing about him in forums
addressed to the general public. More specifically, it considers review
criticism in magazines and newspapers as well as writing, often both
general and critical, that appeared in these media as well as in books.
It thereby treats at once the most highly ideated means by which
Andersen gained access to the American national consciousness and
the most differentiated expression of that consciousness.[10] On the
other hand, the study outlines the position of the writers' commentary in relevant contexts within, for example, the history of literature
and literary criticism and sociopolitical history and thought.

Before considering the procedures used in the study, some observations concerning the materials on which it is based are in order.
Between 1825 and 1850 the young American magazine industry experienced what has been described as a veritable tsunami, the number
of publications rising, according to one estimate, from 100 to 600.[11]
By 1870 that number had doubled, and by the time of Andersen's
death five years later it was well on its way to the 3,300 it reached in
1885.[12] Unfortunately, less than a third of these magazines are more
or less readily accessible for study. The American Periodical Series,
published on microfilm by the University of Michigan, represents the

largest single source.[13] However, it does not include a subject index, a practical necessity for research of this nature. Moreover, *Poole's Index to Periodical Literature,* for over a century the standard tool in the field, encompasses only a small percentage of the magazines. Although it includes many of the most important ones, Sitzfleisch reveals that it is neither exhaustive nor entirely reliable.[14] The *Index to Early American Periodicals to 1850* is less ambitious in scope.[15]

Over approximately the past decade a number of very useful aids have become available on the Internet, for example, "The Making of America," sponsored by the University of Michigan, and "The Nineteenth Century in Print," originally part of the "Making of America" series sponsored by Cornell University and now assimilated into "American Memory: Historical Collections for the National Digital Library," a project of the Library of Congress.[16] In addition to these sites, which are open to the general public, there are others that are accessible by either institutional or individual subscription, for example, "Poole's Plus," which embraces *Poole's Index to Periodical Literature* and several other indexes, and sites offered by individual magazines such as the *Nation.* Like *Poole's,* these sites include some of the magazines most relevant for the present study. Thoroughly searchable, they indeed yielded useful material not found in other sources. They nonetheless offer only a minute fraction of the total number of magazines in publication during the some three decades under scrutiny, and experience has proven that pertinent writing is sometimes discovered where one would not expect it.[17] Given the discrepancy between Andersen's early notoriety and the relatively small number of reviews located, it may be that more notices, perhaps many of them, await discovery through enhanced electronic means. All the same, over seventy reviews and articles emerged from the sources available for this study, and they offer considerable insight into the American critical response to Andersen during the time in question.

A substantial number of additional reviews published in American magazines originated in British periodicals. At the time Andersen's works began to cross the Atlantic, and then for years to come, many magazines in the United States continued the practice begun in colonial days of reprinting articles, reviews, and the like that first came out in British publications. Of even greater significance is the fact that throughout the period covered by this study all the major English magazines and reviews were republished in this country.[18] At least between 1850 and 1865, indeed, the *Edinburgh Review* was much more widely read than the *North American Review.*[19] This suggests, of course, that British critics played an important role in shaping Americans' understanding of Andersen, particularly during the early phase of his reception in the 1840s, when, as we shall see, British critical interest in him was most intense. Nevertheless, I have restricted myself to the work of American writers. First of all, the study seeks to determine critical opinion rather than specific influence, whether that of reviewers on readers or that of reviewers on each other, both of which are highly elusive in any event.[20] Given the broad similarities between the two nations' critical responses to Andersen, moreover, it would be of little profit to undertake a thorough investigation of their relationship. Finally, and more practically, Elias Bredsdorff has already presented an extensive examination of Andersen's critical reception in British periodicals.[21] Consequently, I have limited consideration of British reviews to a relatively brief general comparison of Andersen criticism in the two countries, which is found in chapter 7.[22]

At this point I should explain how the term "American writer" is used in this study. The great majority of men and women who wrote the reviews and articles treated in the volume were indeed Americans born and bred. However, a few of them grew up and received their education in one of a number of countries in Europe, coming to the United States as (usually young) adults, and they include some of the most insightful of all of Andersen's commentators in this country. Nonetheless, I have drawn no principle distinction between them and their native-born counterparts, even though the Scandinavians, who form the majority, enjoyed obvious advantages over the Americans. It is fruitless to ponder at what point or to what extent an individual becomes culturally naturalized in an adopted country. If these writers did not scrutinize Andersen through an entirely American cultural lens, whatever that may have meant, they all contributed to knowledge of him within the American context(s), and some of them did so quite self-consciously. One could hardly expect it to have been otherwise in a young immigrant nation such as the United States of the nineteenth century.

Many of the reviews of Andersen's works were anonymous, after the (in later years waning) custom of the time. However, since the majority of the writers, both signed and unsigned, are obscure today to all but specialists, I have provided generally brief biographical sketches of as many as possible in order to create a broad profile of Andersen's critics.[23] Book reviewing in the United States remained anonymous in an important sense even after critics began signing their reviews. That is, their signatures revealed little of them as individuals to their readers, with the exception of a relatively small, if significant, minority of initiates. In order to give American Andersen criticism a truly recognizable face I have therefore devoted a major portion of chapter 6 to the life and work of Horace E. Scudder, who was in many ways a paradigmatic American literary critic and writer, significant yet underappreciated in his own right, as well as Andersen's most faithful American devotee. The magazines and newspapers in which the reviews and articles were published likewise receive attention, for factors such as editors and editorial policy, target readership, and circulation complement the writer profile by suggesting both the nature and reach of Andersen criticism in the United States. Although it is virtually impossible to measure critics' influence on their readers, as intimated above, one may nonetheless reasonably assume that they exerted one of varying kind, breadth, and degree. While the present study therefore admits of nothing more than conjectural generalization, its findings can certainly be considered symptomatic of broader opinion and will surely be of interest to Andersen scholars and other Scandinavianists as well as to students of Danish American literary relations and American literary history.[24]

The three currently existing studies of Andersen's reception abroad approach their material in different ways. The first, a lengthy chapter in Elias Bredsdorff's *H. C. Andersen og England* (Hans Christian Andersen and England), proceeds chronologically.[25] Harald Åström's *H. C. Andersens genombrott i Sverige* (Hans Christian Andersen's Breakthrough in Sweden), on the other hand, is organized by genre.[26] In the most recent study, *Den gyldne trekant: H. C. Andersens gennembrud i Tyskland, 1831–1850* (The Golden Triangle: H. C. Andersen's Breakthrough in Germany, 1831–1850), Ivy Möller-Christensen combines the methods of her predecessors, analyzing cross-sections of reviews at various points along the path of her fundamentally chronological investigation.[27]

The present study, which continues this tradition of straightforward historical-analytical research, also exploits the advantages of the two primary approaches but reverses Möller-Christensen's emphases.[28] American Andersen criticism did not unfold in a more or less coherent manner in response to publication of the various works and reflecting an early breakthrough and later ebb, as was generally the case in England, Sweden, and Germany. On the contrary, it developed in three "waves" of varying dimensions, the final one being the largest and most comprehensive, and certain works and genres received little or no attention at all. Consequently, the study is basically organized according to the genres that garnered the most critical commentary, although due regard is given those that were underrepresented or ignored. Following a statistical overview in chapter 1, chapters 2–4 deal with Andersen's novels and travel books, autobiography, and fairy tales and stories, respectively. Within each of these chapters, however, discussion proceeds chronologically. Moreover, the treatment of statistics in chapter 1 as well as the discussion of general articles in chapter 5 reflect the chronology of Andersen's critical reception and its import. The second part of chapter 6 examines Scudder's writing on Andersen, which itself reveals historical concerns and occupies a key position in the history of American Andersen criticism. The concluding comments in chapter 7, which also casts a comparative glance at Andersen's fortunes in the three countries touched on above, take the chronology of his American reception into account. Additionally, the bibliography of primary sources is arranged chronologically.

The writings chosen for discussion in this study were selected solely on the basis of what they reveal about American critics' perceptions of Andersen and where these notions fit in the contemporary cultural scene in the United States. Length, for example, was no consideration. With numerous notable exceptions, the reviews are generally brief in comparison with their counterparts in England and Germany, a couple amounting to little more than notices of publication. However, one that appeared in the *Southern Literary Messenger*, for instance, suggests so much in its four short sentences that it was deemed worthy of inclusion. Originality was also no criterion. While particularly insightful commentaries are treated as such, the study seeks primarily to describe, rather than to judge, the opinions expressed, and reviews are compared with each other in large measure only to present a complete and balanced picture of Americans' critical response to Andersen. Since the great majority of the writings are not easily accessible to most readers, I have quoted extensively from them, eschewing block quotations in favor of run-in quotations for aesthetic purposes. However, I have not found every review or article to be uniformly revealing and have therefore not considered every aspect of each. For this reason a small number of pieces entered in the bibliography of primary sources as general articles are discussed in chapters dealing with specific genres. Furthermore, I have excluded certain entire writings from examination, either due to a lack of illuminating observations or, in a few instances, simply because I was unable to locate them, though all are listed in the relevant bibliography. One article contains significant commentary on two works, and I have therefore counted it as two pieces, discussed them in the appropriate chapters, and entered them under the corresponding rubrics in the list of primary sources rather than among the general articles. A few writings deal with Andersen in broader contexts and/or together with other figures.

The study addresses two main audiences, Scandinavianists and Americanists, who may or may not have extensive knowledge of each other's fields. For purposes of perspective and clarity I have therefore included a considerable amount of information that will likely be self-evident to one or the other of the groups, for which I ask their forbearance. When listing or referring to Andersen's fairy tales and stories in the collections reviewed, I have retained the often varying titles employed by the contemporary translators. Otherwise, I have relied on the translation by Danish American actor and collector of Anderseniana Jean Hersholt, which is considered one of the best in English.[29] For the Danish titles I have adhered to the spelling found in the critical edition published by the Danske Sprog- og Litteraturselskab (Danish Society for Language and Literature).[30] My general policy has been to use both English and Danish titles in the first reference to a work, the latter in parentheses, and the English title alone in subsequent references. Translations from secondary sources are my own.

Within its general attempt to ascertain and contextualize American critical opinion of Andersen, the study seeks to answer a number of specific questions: Why did Americans comment on Andersen in the first place? Why did they discuss certain works and not others? Why did Andersen's reception in the United States unfold as it did? How does the in part retrospective criticism of the early 1870s compare with that of the later 1840s? That is to say, can one detect an internal development, for example, recognition of the growing realism in the romantic Andersen's later fairy tales and stories? To what extent did Americans view Andersen as a writer for adults as well as for children? Worldwide acknowledgment as the foremost figure in children's literature is a distinction of a kind few mortals can attain. Nevertheless, Danes justifiably lament the fact that exceedingly few foreigners are aware that Andersen wrote novels, plays, poetry, and travel books in addition to his autobiography and fairy tales, and that the latter themselves can be read with pleasure and profit at different levels of sophistication. Answers to these and other questions are proposed in the final chapter.

1

American Andersen Criticism
in Statistical Overview

STATISTICS TELL US NOTHING ABOUT CRITICAL OPINION PER SE. HOW-
ever, they can illustrate the contours of its history and can thus play
a significant ancillary role in its study. The data in the present chapter provide a nuanced overview of the topography of Andersen's critical reception in the United States during the time under scrutiny.
They fall into five groups, each of which is accompanied by a discussion of important aspects of the findings.

The first table lists all the publications of Andersen's works discussed by American critics according to genre and year(s) of appearance and indicates the number of reviews received by each together
with the respective inclusive years. The general articles are treated as
a genre.

The [True] Story of My Life (Mit egen eventyr uden digtning/Mit livs eventyr)	15 reviews, 1847–75
Fairy Tales and Stories[1]	16 reviews, 1848–75
General	3 reviews, 1854–75
A Christmas Greeting (1848)	1 review, 1848
Danish Story Book (1848)	1 review, 1848
Hans Andersen's Story-Book (1849)	2 reviews, 1849, 1852
The Ugly Duck and other Tales (1850)	1 review, 1850
Little Ellie, and other Tales (1850)[2]	
The Story Teller (1850)[2]	
Hans Andersen's Wonderful Tales (1851)	1 review, 1851
The Sand-Hills of Jutland (1860)	2 reviews, 1860
The Ice-Maiden, and Other Tales (1863)	2 reviews, 1863
Wonder Stories Told for Children (1870)	2 reviews, 1870
Fairy Tales and Sketches (1871)	1 review, 1871

Novels	8 reviews, 1845–75
The Improvisatore [*or Life in Italy*]	
[*Improvisatoren*] (1845, 1869)	3 reviews, 1845–69[3]
The Two Baronesses [*De to Baronesser*] (1869)	1 review, 1869
O. T. [*O. T.*] (1870)	1 review, 1870
Only a Fiddler [*Kun en Spillemand*] (1870)	3 reviews, 1870
Travel Books	8 reviews, 1851–72
Pictures of Sweden; In Sweden [*I Sverrig*]	
(1851, 1871)	3 reviews, 1851–63
In Spain [*I Spanien*] (1870)	3 reviews, 1870
A Poet's Bazaar [*En Digters Bazar*] (1871)	2 reviews, 1871–72
Picture Book Without Pictures [*Billedbog*	
uden Billeder] (1847, 1848)	2 reviews, 1847–52
General Articles[4]	23, 1854–95, 9 after 1875

The figures show that Andersen's autobiography received more critical attention than any other single work. The fairy tales and stories garnered a slightly higher number of reviews, but one must bear in mind that they appeared not in one work but rather in eleven different collections, none of which received more than two reviews.[5] The data also reveal that the other genres and individual works each elicited relatively little commentary. Overall, the novels received a comparatively respectable number of reviews. However, *The Improvisatore* and *Only a Fiddler* account for almost all of them, and *Lucky Peer* (*Lykke-Peer*) and *To Be or Not to Be* (*At være eller ikke være*) were ignored altogether. Given the popularity of Andersen's autobiography, in which he related many of his experiences while abroad, it is not surprising that his travel books fared relatively well as a whole, though none achieved a high degree of notice. The one mention of the fairy-tale comedy *Mother Elderberry* (*Hyldemor*) in 1851 attests by virtue of its uniqueness to the silence that prevailed over not only the plays but also the poetry as well as works such as *Journey on Foot to Amager* (*Fodrejse fra Holmens Canal til Østpynten af Amager*), which was Andersen's first major literary success in Denmark.[6] To my knowledge, it is true, the plays and *Journey on Foot to Amager* remain to be translated into English, and no substantial independent English-language edition of the poetry has ever been published.[7] However, numerous individual poems and selections alike appeared in American as well as British magazines, yet exceedingly few writers, even authors of general articles, reflect so much as an awareness that they or the other, untranslated, works exist, let alone familiarity through personal reading of the texts.[8] The general articles bear witness to Andersen's renown and popularity as a personality as well as an author, even many years after his death. More significantly, they suggest that he enjoyed recognition as an artist. In sum, seventy-two writings were devoted to Andersen, forty-nine of them reviews and twenty-three general articles.

As indicated in the introduction, the appearance of these publications did not describe anything remotely resembling a bell curve but rather fell into three distinct clusters. The following table shows in chronological order the number of reviews each work or group of works received during each of these most productive periods, the general articles again forming a group of their own.

	1845–52	1860–63	1869–76
Fairy Tales and Stories	6	4	5
The [True] Story of My Life	5	0	10
The Improvisatore	1	0	2
The Two Baronesses	0	0	1
Only a Fiddler	0	0	3
O. T.	0	0	1
In Sweden	2	1	0
In Spain	0	0	3
A Poet's Bazaar	0	0	2
Picture Book Without Pictures	2	0	0
General Articles	0	4	10
Total	16	9	37

The table confirms the assertion made in the introduction that Andersen received the greatest amount of attention from American critics late in his life, rather than close to the beginning of his career as in England, Sweden, and Germany. The steep increase of writing during the seventies is in large part a reflection of the critical response to the Author's Edition and can surely also otherwise be attributed to the influence of Horace Scudder. The commentaries of these years also covered a much broader spectrum of Andersen's work than those written during the other two phases of his reception in the United States. While notices of the fairy tales and stories dominate the first and second periods, reviews of the autobiography, comparatively numerous early on, outnumber them in the final phase twofold. Curiously, only one of the two volumes of fairy tales and stories published in the Author's Edition seems to have found reviewers. It is during this time that general articles begin to appear with some frequency.

The inaccessibility of individual works or segments of a lifework can obviously have an important bearing on critics' and other readers' understanding of a writer. We shall see evidence that such "nonreception" was a factor in Americans' critical response to Andersen. The table below presents a chronological list of the fairy tales and stories *not* included in any of the editions reviewed in the United States.

"This Fable is Intended for You" (Det er Dig, Fabelen sigter til!) 1836
"God Can Never Die" (Den gamle Gud lever endnu) 1836
"The Talisman" (Talismanen) 1836
"A Rose from Homer's Grave" (En Rose fra Homers Grav) 1842/1862
"A Picture from the Ramparts" (Et Billede fra Castelsvolden) 1846
"The World's Fairest Rose" (Verdens deiligste Rose) 1851
"A Story" (En Historie) 1851/1863
"Everything in its Proper Place" ("Alt paa sin rette Plads!") 1852
"It's Quite True" (Det er ganske vist!) 1852
"The Story of the Year" (Aarets Historie) 1852
"A Good Humor" (Et godt Humeur) 1852
"Heartache" (Hjertesorg) 1852
"Thousands of Years from Now" (Om Aartusinder) 1852
"On Judgment Day" (Paa den yderste Dag) 1852
"The Swan's Nest" (Svanereden) 1852
"Under the Willow Tree" (Under Piletræet) 1852
"Two Brothers" (To Brødre) 1859
"Moving Day" (Flyttedagen) 1860
"The New Century's Goddess" (Det nye Aarhundredes Musa) 1861
"The Teapot" (Theepotten) 1864
"Aunty" (Moster) 1866
"The Rags" (Laserne) 1868
"The Days of the Week" (Ugedagene) 1868
"Chicken Grethe's Family" (Hønse-Grethes Familie) 1869
"What One Can Invent" (Hvad man kan hitte paa) 1869
"What Happened to the Thistle" (Hvad Tidselen oplevede) 1869
"The Most Incredible Thing" (Det Utroligste) 1870
"What the Whole Family Said" (Hvad hele Familien sagde) 1870
"Luck May Lie in a Pin" (Lykken kan ligge i en Pind) 1870
"The Candles" (Lysene) 1870
"Great-Grandfather" (Oldefa'er) 1870
"Dance, Dance, Doll of Mine" ("Dandse, dandse Dukke min!") 1871
"The Great Sea Serpent" (Den store Søslange) 1871
"Ask Mother Amager"[9] ("Spørg Amagermo'er") 1871

"The Gardener and the Noble Family" (Gartneren og Herskabet) 1872
"What Old Johanne Told" (Hvad gamle Johanne fortalte) 1872
"The Cripple" (Krøblingen) 1872
"The Flea and the Professor" (Loppen og Professoren) 1872
"The Gate Key" (Portnøglen) 1872
"The Penman" (Skriveren) 1926

A tally of the list shows that a full forty of Andersen's fairy tales and stories—nearly a quarter of the 156 he wrote—were not contained in any of the editions discussed in American magazines during the time under consideration.[10] Six of them were written after the publication in 1871 of the last volume to receive a review. Depending on Scudder's editorial schedule, another eight could have appeared in one or the other of the two volumes of fairy tales and stories in the Author's Edition, for Andersen placed them as well as a number of others at Scudder's disposal.[11] Scudder may have withheld some of them from the edition because he had recently published or planned to publish them in the *Riverside Magazine* or, later, in *Scribner's Monthly*, though, if the latter was the case, he did not follow through in every instance. Whatever the reasons may have been, he also printed certain pieces in both the Author's Edition and one or the other of the magazines. Why he published the now classic "Auntie Toothache" (*Tante Tandpine*) in the *Fairy Tales and Stories* but not in *Scribner's* is difficult to understand unless he wanted to save something new and special for the Author's Edition. In any event, the works that escaped discussion in American magazines come from every stage of Andersen's productive life, if at the same time over half were written during the middle and especially the late periods of his critical reception in nineteenth-century America.

Of course, the fact that the forty texts were not included in any of the editions reviewed does not necessarily mean that they escaped the commentators' ken and thus did not enter into their thinking on Andersen. These individuals may have read them elsewhere but either had or took no occasion to write about them. Scudder's publication of some of the unreviewed titles in the magazines he edited supports this notion. In a letter to Andersen dated February 25, 1874, moreover, Scudder attributes the limited success of the volumes of fairy tales and stories in the Author's Edition to the existence of "a great many editions, both English and American, sold in this country. Ours is but one of them, and there are many cheaper editions...."[12] Indeed, Bredsdorff lists some fifty that had appeared by the time

Scudder wrote the letter, some of which came out in successive print-ings.[13] On the other hand, it is entirely possible that the reviewers in fact read none, or few, of the pieces that eluded review. This is all the more probable since Andersen was increasingly associated with the nursery, and commentators' knowledge of his work in the genre was likely to stem from their more or less distant childhood reading and/or from perusal of the volume at hand. In any case, this study deals with collections that *were* reviewed, that is, with verifiable read-ings. All the same, the texts not included in these editions must be characterized, in part with a view to those that were, in order to deter-mine which aspects could have informed their writing on him ex neg-ativo. Scudder, one should note, is the only American critic who can reasonably be assumed to have read all of Andersen's fairy tales and stories.

At this point we should pause for a moment to reflect on the ref-erents and usage of certain key terms. The familiar expression "Andersen's fairy tales," stripped of all its pleasant associations and in a formal sense, is little more than a convenience and should not be understood as denoting a distinct genre. In actuality, the texts known as such include a wide variety of narrative kinds, ranging from cre-ative retellings of folktales and "art" folktales, that is, works related to the German *Kunstmärchen* (literally "art fairy tale"),[14] to fables and allegories on to realistic narratives and varied mixtures of the several types. In this study I therefore generally use the expression that Andersen himself eventually settled on to refer to his best-known works, "fairy tales and stories." For present purposes and in strict usage elsewhere, however, I draw a distinction between the "fairy tale" and the "story," the principle difference lying in the presence of the preternatural or the supernatural in the former and their absence in the latter.[15] Thus, "The Flea and the Professor" (Loppen og Profes-soren), like "The Tinder Box" (Fyrtøiet) is a fairy tale, while "The Gardener and the Noble Family" (Gartneren og Herskabet), like "A Story from the Sand Dunes" (Historie fra Klitterne) is a story. This measure is also an expedient, for not all of the pieces fit neatly in these two categories. The role of the wind and the willow as "narra-tors" is a charming aspect of "What Old Johanne Told" (Hvad gamle Johanne fortalte), for instance, but it is incidental to what is funda-mentally a realistic narrative, and I have therefore counted the work as a story. Conversely, much of "Little Ida's Flowers" (Den lille Idas Blomster) is mimetic narrative, but the flowers' and toys' coming to life, even if in a dream, is so central to the text that I have reckoned it as a fairy tale. In literary-historical and even sociocultural terms, however, the distinction between "fairy tale" and "story" offers the advantage of allowing one to differentiate between works that one may deem more or less broadly "romantic" and others which may be judged more or less broadly "realistic." Though one may certainly quibble over the categorization of this text or that, the study proceeds from the assumption that the distinction is broad enough and holds in a sufficient number of cases for the conclusions to be considered generally valid.

The texts not included in the editions reviewed in American magazines break down into fairy tales and stories as follows:

Stories	21
Fairy Tales	15
Mixtures	4

The works are distributed over Andersen's career as follows:

	Stories	Fairy Tales	Mixtures
1870–72	7	4	3
1864–69	2	4	1
1851–61	9	5	0
1836–46	3	2	0

This compares with the following breakdown of the works published in the editions reviewed:

Fairy Tales	90
Stories	26
Mixtures	0

The original versions of these fairy tales appeared between 1835 and 1872. Those of the stories, on the other hand, did not begin to come out until 1855, though they, too, continued to appear until 1872. The stories reached a high point between 1859 and 1863, when sixteen were published, as opposed to twenty-three fairy tales. The year 1863 alone witnessed the issuance of four stories and only one fairy tale. However, a return to the predominance of the latter appears to have occurred in 1868, when nine fairy tales and only one story came out.

The mere numerical relationship between stories and fairy tales reveals factors that may have had a significant impact on the way American reviewers, and thus Americans in general, thought of "Andersen's fairy tales." In terms of percentages, far more stories than fairy tales escaped review in the United States. A little over half of the total number of stories Andersen wrote were not included in the editions reviewed, whereas only somewhat more than 14 percent of the fairy tales suffered this fate. Significantly, eleven of the twenty-one stories, as compared to nine fairy tales, appeared during the 1850s and 1860s, a time when the ratio of stories to fairy tales in general was particularly high. The impression of a return to the fairy tale beginning in 1868 is counterbalanced when one considers the unreviewed stories published during this period, nine vis-à-vis thirteen fairy tales (reviewed and unreviewed). A lack of familiarity with these stories would have drastically reduced awareness of Andersen's trend toward greater realism from the mid-1850s on and reinforced his image as a romantic writer of fairy tales for children.

Several additional factors may have led to the same result. Seven of what one might call Andersen's "classic" works in the genre, which number among the "stories" here, did not appear in any of the editions reviewed: "It's Quite True" (Det er ganske vist!), "A Good Humor" (Et godt Humeur), "The Gardener and the Noble Family" (Gartneren og Herskabet), "Heartache" (Hjertesorg), "What One Can Invent" (Hvad man kan hitte paa), "The Cripple" (Krøblingen), and "Thousands of Years from Now" (Om Aartusinder).[16] The absence of these texts would tend to lower the visibility of the stories as a whole. Moreover, not a single story is among the thirty-six works most frequently reviewed, that is, three or four times. That is to say, the fairy tales enjoyed far greater exposure than the stories, and they did so over a far greater stretch of Andersen's reception in the United States.

The thematic range of Andersen's fairy tales and stories is much broader than his reputation in the United States as a children's writer would suggest. By my reckoning, the category "miscellaneous" alone includes over thirty different themes, from an innocuous but choice criticism of gossip in "It's Quite True" and the value of having a cheerful temperament, as in "A Good Humor," to the superiority of character over birth as a means of determining an individual's worth, which distinguishes "Everything in its Proper Place" ("Alt paa sin rette Plads!"), and the existence of a power that avenges evil, which finds expression in "The Rose Elf" (Rosenalfen). However, Andersen returned again and again to some eighteen core concerns that inform around 70 percent of the texts. These themes, too, range widely, from personal experience such as unrequited love ("The Sweethearts" [Kjærestefolkene], "Ib and Little Christine" [Ib og lille Christine])

and discontent ("The Fir Tree" [Grantræet], "The Flax" [Hørren])
to social issues such as sympathy with the poor ("The Little Match
Girl" [Den lille Pige med Svovlstikkerne], "She Was Good for Nothing" ["Hun duede ikke"]) and human sin and redemption ("The Red
Shoes" [De røde Skoe], "The Girl Who Trod on the Loaf" [Pigen,
som traadte paa Brødet]).

On the whole, the themes of the forty fairy tales and stories not
considered in American commentaries are identical to those of texts
contained in reviewed collections, and in certain instances this lack
of reflection could have had little impact on critics' overall view of
Andersen. The Dane returned most often, for example, to a theme
one might call "the power of art," which frequently means the superiority of a "naive," that is, spontaneous and intuitive, "romantic," art
over the "sentimental," or intellectual and systematic art and poetics,
of a Friedrich Schiller or a Johan Ludvig Heiberg.[17] Some fine works
among the forty unreviewed titles, for instance, "The Cripple" and
"What One Can Invent," enrich this group of texts, but no one familiar with masterpieces such as "The Nightingale" (Nattergalen) or
"The Snow Queen" (Sneedronningen) need read them to be aware
of the prominence of the theme.

In another substantial number of reviewed works, however, Andersen treated the related themes of the critic or criticism and the contemporary cultural scene in Denmark, principally Copenhagen, for
example, "Something" ("Noget") and "The Puppet-Show Man" (Mar-
ionetspilleren). These themes are shared by a relatively significant
number of unreviewed texts, for instance "The Gardener and the
Noble Family," "What Happened to the Thistle" (Hvad Tidselen
oplevede), and "Aunty" (Moster). Even the nine works that praise or
criticize Denmark and its cultural history form a more distinctive category with the addition of the unreviewed "The Rags" (Laserne),
"The Swan's Nest" (Svanereden), and "Two Brothers" (To Brødre).
While only two of the reviewed works reflect Andersen's interest in
technological progress—"Vänö and Glänö" (Vænø og Glænø) and
"The Dryad" (Dryaden)—moreover, four of those not reviewed do
so: "Great-Grandfather" (Oldefa'er), "The Great Sea Serpent" (Den
store Søslange), "Thousands of Years from Now," and "The New Century's Goddess" (Det nye Aarhundredes Musa). In sum, acquaintance
with the unreviewed works would have variously sharpened American
reviewers' awareness of Andersen as a literary and cultural critic or
commentator and especially as an advocate of technological progress.
Such recognition of his concern for real-world, contemporary issues

would have tended to counter the prevalent stereotypical impression of him.

The fourth and final table shows the magazines and newspapers in which the reviews and articles appeared together with the respective inclusive years. They are listed by the number of writings each published.

Southern Literary Messenger	6	1848–62
Harper's New Monthly Magazine	6	1863–84, most 1869–71
Atlantic Monthly	6	1870–75
Appleton's Journal	5	1869–76
Putnam's Magazine	4	1869–70
Ladies' Repository	3	1869–73
Sartain's Union Magazine	3	1848–51
New York Times	3	1871–75
Literary World	2	1847, 1850
International Magazine	2	1851
Continental Monthly	2	1863
Galaxy	2	1870–71
Overland Monthly	2	1871–72
Potter's American Monthly	2	1875, 1878
Harbinger	1	1845
United States Magazine and Democratic Review	1	1847
Christian Examiner and Religious Miscellany	1	1847
Daguerreotype	1	1847
Godey's Magazine and Lady's Book	1	1847
Massachusetts Quarterly Review	1	1847
National Magazine	1	1855
New Englander and Yale Review	1	1860
National Quarterly Review	1	1861
Peterson's Magazine	1	1863
Punchinello	1	1870
Scribner's Monthly	1	1871
What's Next?[18]	1	1874
New York Tribune	1	1875
Scandinavia	1	1885
Century Illustrated Monthly Magazine	1	1892

A sketch of each periodical appears in the appropriate chapter preceding the discussion of the first review or article that was published in it. At this point it is appropriate to observe that the magazines present a spectrum of types, from ones aimed at the general female reader, for example, *Godey's Magazine and Lady's Book,* to the humor weekly *Punchinello* and the Unitarians' *Christian Examiner* on to publications espousing specific philosophical and/or social ideologies such as the *Harbinger.* Despite their wide range most of the publications fall under the category of "quality" magazines, that is to say, ones that featured high literature or otherwise placed substantial to great demands on their readers—characteristics, incidentally, that are not necessarily signaled by the presence of book reviews, as *Godey's* indicates. Indeed, twenty-two of the total sixty-seven reviews and articles that appeared in magazines (ca. 33 percent) were published in four of the most distinguished American periodicals of their time: The *Southern Literary Messenger, Harper's New Monthly Magazine,* the *Atlantic Monthly,* and *Putnam's Magazine.* Together with the less eminent yet still highly respectable *Appleton's Journal* they published twenty-seven writings on Andersen, or around 40 percent of the total. The *Southern Literary Messenger* was active during the early years of Andersen's reception, the others in later stages. The *Messenger* ceased publication in 1864 and thus could not participate in the wave of reviews that began in 1869. *Harper's,* on the other hand, did not begin publication until 1850, when the first wave was already subsiding. *Putnam's* and the *Atlantic* did not appear until 1853 and 1857, respectively. *Appleton's Journal* made its debut in 1869, just in time for the heyday of Andersen criticism in the United States.

2

The Longer Prose

THE NOVELS

ANDERSEN MADE HIS DEBUT IN THE ENGLISH LANGUAGE IN MARY HOWITT'S translation of the novel *Improvisatoren, The Improvisator, or, Life in Italy,* which came out in London in February 1845.[1] The British press responded to the book almost immediately with a review published in the *Literary Gazette* on March 1. Not insignificantly, two American magazines noted the appearance of the novel in relatively short order, the *Living Age* on April 19 and the *Southern Literary Messenger* in the issue for May.[2] While merely announcing its publication, the two periodicals nonetheless offer evidence that Andersen was available to American readers very soon after his entry into the English-speaking world.

It is unclear at what point in the same year Howitt's translation was issued in New York. A reasonable guess would be the summer or early fall, for a review of the novel—apparently the first American commentary on Andersen—came out on October 4. The review was written by Charles A. Dana (1819–97), who later became a national figure as a writer for the *New York Tribune* and then as editor and part-owner of the much admired and imitated *New York Sun,* in which he championed inter alia the antislavery cause.[3] At the time he wrote the review, Dana was associate editor of and contributor to the *Harbinger,* the organ of Brook Farm, an institute of agriculture, industry, and education at West Roxbury, Massachusetts, which is the best known of the many experiments in communal living during the first half of the nineteenth century in the United States.[4] Founded by George Ripley, a leader of the so-called Transcendental Club, Brook Farm is associated through certain members and sympathy or interest with American transcendentalism, a movement that united American Unitarianism and German idealism, especially as interpreted by Samuel Taylor Coleridge and Thomas Carlyle.[5] Transcendentalism

Daguerreotype of Andersen taken by an unknown photographer in 1846 at the age of about forty-one. Reproduced in agreement with Odense City Museums, Denmark.

found adherents in such representatives of the American Renaissance as Ralph Waldo Emerson, Henry David Thoreau, Nathaniel Hawthorne, James Russell Lowell, and James Greenleaf Whittier, some of whom contributed to the *Harbinger*. By 1845, Brook Farm had adopted some of the theories of the French socialist Charles Fourier (1772–1837), who advocated a utopian society based on a mixture of capitalism, cooperativism, and social control realized through an association of units called "phalanxes," among which Brook Farm numbered beginning in 1844.[6] It was within this intellectual frame of reference that Dana, himself an active member of Brook Farm, wrote his review of Andersen's novel.[7]

"In this novel," Dana begins, "we have a charming union of northern sentiment with southern warmth and luxuriance . . . a picture of Italian life by a Dane." While lacking "the physical softness of the south" and though "slightly stiff and angular in its bearing"—the work is after all unmistakably that of a "genuine Teuton"—the novel is "full of the ideal and chivalrous tenderness of the north—a feeling which contains more soul and less sense, more imagination and less grace of movement than the passion of the south."[8] At the core of the work Dana sees "the old tragedy of genius; dependence, misfortune, fruitless aspirations, hopes blossoming fair and soon blighted, wretchedness in full proportion to the capacity for life and joy." He finds it especially significant that souls so highly endowed and sent as "special messengers of heaven" (such as the protagonist, Antonio) should find no place in society. In conclusion he writes, "We can only wonder that a social order in which the poet and the artist are proverbially wretched, has not sooner been called in question. Had men possessed a real, active faith in God, instead of a whining and artificial resignation which is an insult to his mercy, they would have obeyed his commandments by endeavoring to discover a constitution of things in which his choicest gifts would not be worse than wasted."

The *Harbinger* review exhibits several features that came to characterize the general response to Andersen in the United States. First of all, it is quite positive, if not uncritical. It discerns a certain infelicity of form in the novel but affirms its (Northern) idealism and sensitive decorum as well as the predominance of feeling and imagination over thought and plan in it. Of greatest interest, perhaps, Dana appears to have chosen the book for discussion not merely, or solely, because it cropped up on some publisher's list or other but because it appealed to him on both an emotional and an intellectual level. His appreciation of the novel as a *kunstnerroman* (novel about an artist) and high valuation of art and the artist disclose his familiarity and sympathy with romantic ideas commensurate with the work as well as his transcendentalist persuasion. His detection of a call for social action implicit in the novel and his approval of it based on Christian principle reflect both transcendentalist-Fourierist conviction and a willingness to turn Andersen's novel to his own ideological ends.

Charles A. Dana. By permission of the Houghton Library, Harvard University.

A similar, if less obvious willingness manifests itself in a brief review of the Author's Edition of the novel published by Hurd and Houghton in 1869. The notice appeared anonymously the same year in the *Ladies' Repository,* which, as the subtitle indicates, was a monthly *Devoted to Literature, Art, and Religion.*[9] Established nearly three decades earlier, the magazine was edited and largely written by Methodist ministers in conservative Cincinnati in the conservative Midwest.[10] Indeed, it was conceived as a means of providing Christian women with an alternative to more worldly magazines such as *Godey's Lady's Book and Magazine* and the *Lady's Companion* with, in the words of Frank Luther Mott, "their sentimental tales of silly love affairs and their fashions 'direct from Paris.'"[11] The magazine could not boast the likes of many of the contributors to the *Harbinger,* but it published writings by numerous writers, such as the poetess sisters Alice and Phoebe Cary, who were well known during their own time and some of whom enjoyed the esteem of major figures. In its heyday during the 1850s the magazine reached a circulation of some 40,000, but by 1869 it had begun a decline, which led to its demise in 1876.[12]

Only seven lines in length, the notice is less remarkable for what it says about the novel per se than for the overall view of Andersen it suggests. Given the high moral standards of the magazine, which had only lately condescended to publishing fiction, still suspect in some quarters of American society, it is noteworthy that the editor, one Isaac William Wiley, deemed the novel deserving of mention in the first place, that is, in keeping with the magazine's guiding principles. Indeed, the reviewer speaks of the book as the first in a series of the author's "higher works" to be published by the same firm, likely referring to the moral caliber and aesthetic quality of the texts as well, certainly, as to the forthcoming publication of the Author's Edition, which he then announces explicitly.

In a letter to his benefactor Jonas Collin dated July 8, 1846, Andersen relates a conversation he had had with his good friend the Norwegian violinist Ole Bull, who had told him "that the English translations of my novels were pirated in America and winged their way about in cheap editions by the thousands in the New World; that *Only a Fiddler* had been so enormously successful that everywhere in America people had asked him about me!"[13] Even allowing for Andersen's characteristic effusiveness where his fame was concerned, the letter attests to the great resonance his novels experienced early on in the United States. In view of this widespread popularity it is curious that Dana's commentary in the *Harbinger* remained one of only two for-

mal reviews of *The Improvisatore* to be published in American magazines and the only one during the first phase of Andersen's critical
reception in the country.[14] Indeed, it is indicative of the curious
course of Andersen's renown in the United States that some twenty-
five years hence the reviewer in the *Ladies' Repository* felt it necessary
to point out that in the new edition of his works Andersen "appears
as traveler, novelist, and poet," having "already become widely known
through his stories for children."

Nonetheless, the novel received variously revealing, if in part banal,
discussion in other contexts. A review of *In Sweden* that appeared in
the *International Magazine* in July 1851, characterizes *The Improvisatore*
as "one of the most beautiful and intrinsically truthful of the myriad
beautiful books upon Italian life."[15] And another announcement
of the Author's Edition of the novel, published in *Putnam's Magazine*
in November 1869, states that the book "has been read by thousands
since the republication here of the English translation by Mrs.
Howitt."[16] One of these readers was George William Curtis (1824–92),
a New Englander who as a young man was associated with the Transcendental Club and acknowledged Emerson's permanent influence
on his "ideals of character and culture and modes of living."[17] This
experience and the two years he spent at Brook Farm left their
stamp on Curtis's satire of the vapidity of "good" urban society in *The
Potiphar Papers* (1853) and his idealization of the simple life in a series
of fictionalized essays entitled *Prue and I* (1856), his bestknown work.
Gaining early notoriety for humorous travel stories based on his experiences as a correspondent for the *New York Tribune*, Curtis became
an effective publicist and speaker on issues such as civil service reform
and public service in general following the Civil War. However,
he attracted his largest and most faithful audience as the longtime
occupant of the popular "Editor's Easy Chair" in *Harper's New Monthly
Magazine*.[18]

Launched in 1850, *Harper's* quickly won great popularity and a
large readership owing to its serialization of (pirated) novels by popular British authors such as Thackeray and Dickens.[19] Beginning in
1869, it published an increasing amount of writing by American
authors on the order of Melville, Henry James, and William Dean
Howells, rivaling the *Atlantic Monthly* and other literary magazines in
quality and far outstripping them in circulation. Indeed, it was one
of few American magazines to maintain a circulation of over 100,000
between 1850 and 1865, and by 1885 it had doubled that number in
the United States and sold another 35,000 in Great Britain, giving it

the largest readership of any magazine of its kind.[20] Although its pira-
cies and alleged initial exclusion of American writers caused much
resentment on this side of the Atlantic, Curtis and the Easy Chair
apparently remained insulated from the criticism.[21]

In what amounts to a eulogy to Andersen written in October 1875
Curtis recalls reading *The Improvisatore* years earlier upon returning
from a trip to New Hampshire and later being reminded of the novel
during a stay in Rome, where he had seen the triton in the Piazza Bar-
berini, "whose intimate acquaintance [he] had made in the story.
The talent of Andersen is shown in that tale by its sympathetic perception and delicate power of description. It is one of the books
which are full of Italy, so that as you read it in the Valley of the Con-
necticut, or wherever you may be, you are transported to that far
country, and feel and see the very Italy of which in the land itself you
are only sometimes conscious. This is the charm of a few books
only."[22] Perhaps due to his own experience as a writer, Curtis attends
particularly to Andersen's artistry, that is, the vividness of his descriptive passages, which at times appeal to the imagination even more
forcefully than the objects themselves address the senses. Curtis
underscores this power by connecting his trip to New Hampshire
with his reading of the novel, which he undertook following his "pil-
grimage to see the Great Carbuncle of the Crystal Hills, which, as the
Easy Chair is told, still flashes 'far down the valley of the Saco.'"[23]
Through this allusion to and quotation from a story by Nathaniel
Hawthorne, Curtis associates Andersen with another writer noted for
descriptive and imaginative power.[24] He is thus clearly able to discern
the "real quality," that is, the adult sophistication, of Andersen's talent despite being preconditioned to think of the Dane as "always a
child" owing to familiarity with the fairy tales and stories.[25]

One finds similar comments in an article entitled "Reminiscences,"
which appeared in *Appleton's Journal* in October 1876.[26] Though initially edited by an individual who was primarily interested in popu-
larizing science, the magazine soon distributed its typically short articles almost equally among fields that included art, drama, education,
travel, biography, and literature, publishing serialized novels and
some short stories and poems as well as literary criticism by writers
such as Julian Hawthorne, Constance Fenimore Woolson, the Southern poet Paul Hamilton Hayne, and Richard Henry Stoddard.[27]
Founded in 1869, the magazine was not a financial success and
ceased publication in 1881.[28] According to Mott, however, few periodicals better reflected life in the United States from 1869 to 1876.[29]

Distinctly of New York in its accents, *Appleton's* reflected a cosmopolitan interest in foreign literature and travel and generally performed
at a level many found challenging, a fact that may have led to its early
demise. The article was written by James E. Freeman (1808–84), a
genre and portrait painter who moved to Rome in 1836 and spent
the rest of his life there.[30] His recollections of Andersen deal principally with the young writer's stay in Rome in 1833–34, but he also
mentions Andersen's return to the city in 1846, at which time his
works were "known in all countries, and he was very much noticed."[31]

Freeman concludes the section of the article that concerns Andersen by comparing the depiction of Rome in *The Improvisatore* with
other literary and artistic representations of the city: "Andersen's
Rome has another atmosphere from that attributed to it by Madame
de Staël and Hawthorne. In the 'Marble Faun' we breathe a perpetual *sirocco*. Exhalations from gorgeous dying flowers, drowning in
classic, stagnant pools, fill the air. Rome's fountains, ruins, palaces,
appear to smother beneath some unhealthy influence—there is
always lurking about them something uncanny and dangerous.
There are melancholy shadows falling over most things, and hidden
in them are dusty skeletons, scorpions, bats, and mysterious agencies
constantly stimulating unwholesome fancies; and, though his light is
mellow as that in most of the pictures of Claude Lorraine, golden and
soft, yet the air is oppressive to respiration and wanting in vitality."[32]
For Freeman, Hawthorne's Rome exudes the same sense of "Gothic"
mystery and decayed classical beauty and grandeur as the Rome of
Joseph von Eichendorff's *Aus dem Leben eines Taugenichts* (*From the
Life of a Ne'er-Do-Well*) and the Lucca of his *Das Marmorbild* (*The Marble Statue*)—minus the Christian redemption especially prominent in
the latter.

"[T]he pen of Andersen," on the other hand, "paints Rome in its
normal light and shadow. He introduces us to its people; we get a look
into their shops, their houses, *caffes* [*sic*], restaurants. We sing with
them, dance with them, and many of us are ready to kneel with them
at their wayside shrines. His legless Beppo, with a jocund face, offers
us a pinch of snuff, and extends his hand with a merry grin, and we
give him a sou. It is realistic—you and the beggar know each other.
You also make acquaintance with a prince or two, as many priests and
friars as you wish, and numerous artists. It is Roman life as it exists—
Roman life, perhaps, with its most picturesque features presented to
you, but not the Rome of Corinne and Oswald, not the Rome which
Hawthorne in his clever novel has 'transformed' into a theatre, only

fitted for the particular *dramatis personæ* whom he brings upon the stage."[33] Writing in the mid-1870s, Freeman expresses appreciation for the "realism" of Andersen's novel—a valid enough assessment, given the qualification and comparison he offers—very likely an appreciation he would not have shown during the days of the *Dial*. It bears repeating that, whatever the reasons may have been, the familiarity and favor *The Improvisatore* enjoyed early and late did not lead to extensive discussion in American magazines.

Most reviews of Andersen's novels were written in response to their appearance in the Author's Edition. His second effort, *O. T.*, fared even worse than its predecessor insofar as it received only one full review. This critique, however, appeared in the prestigious *Atlantic Monthly* in September 1870.[34] Following its establishment in 1857, the *Atlantic* had risen rapidly to a position of leadership in American letters.[35] At the time the review appeared, the magazine included Emerson, Longfellow, Lowell, Whittier, and other New Englanders in its inner circle of authors, who continued to advocate the idealist and humanist values associated with American romanticism, that "religion of humanity" which was inspired to a significant extent by the German idealism of the later eighteenth and early nineteenth centuries.[36] The *Atlantic*'s circulation was currently in steep decline due to the furor created by an article in which Harriet Beecher Stowe defended her recently deceased friend, Lady Byron, against attacks by the poet's last mistress, but it still retained somewhere between 35,000 and 50,000 subscribers. The laudatory tendency that had characterized its review criticism, which had nonetheless always been strong, had yielded to greater trenchancy in 1866 when William Dean Howells assumed principle responsibility for reviewing and revealed principles of literary realism that were soon to make him a major novelist as well as critic.[37] The *Atlantic* still maintained the policy of anonymity with regard to reviews, but *The Atlantic Index* reveals that Howells in fact wrote the evaluation of *O. T.*[38]

Although the review is substantially longer than that of *The Improvisatore* in the *Harbinger*, much of it deals with matters other than the novel per se, some of which will be considered in the appropriate contexts. Of Andersen as a writer in general, Howells writes, on the one hand, that "[w]hatever else one may say of him, there is no denying that he is a man of delicate and poetical mind, and he has been so long the eminent representative of Scandinavian literature, that his complete works would be expected in any accumulation of classics. But they are not only to be expected; they are to be welcomed,

William Dean Howells. By permission of the Houghton Library, Harvard University.

and very heartily."[39] On the other hand, Howells states that Andersen "is not a writer of strong imagination, and we are tempted to give
his creative faculty no better name than fancy"—this, it soon becomes
clear, despite obvious familiarity with the fairy tales and stories.[40]
Nonetheless, Andersen "has somehow lodged himself securely in the

hearts of old and young, where he holds a place that men of much greater power could not attain."[41] While children know Andersen best perhaps from "The Ugly Duckling," older readers think of him first as the author of *The Improvisatore,* and in this novel, as in others, he restrains an emotional exuberance, which in other genres makes him a superficial observer, to remain "on the whole generally faithful to the spirit of Italian life."[42]

Howells finds *O. T.* inferior to *The Improvisatore* but better than *The Two Baronesses.* Although the conception of the work strikes him as "theatrical," he deems the story to be "wrought out with simplicity and reality."[43] Nonetheless, the novel suffers, like Andersen's other efforts in the genre, from being "burdened . . . with overmuch episode, and the conversation is often trivial, not advancing the narrative, nor developing character."[44] The criticism of formlessness or lack of unity, particularly manifest in poor plot construction, is a recurrent theme in the discussions of Andersen's novels. While the story "struggles over much detail," all the same, Howells writes that "it is all very interesting, and parts of it are absorbing."[45] He is particularly impressed by the "admirable painting of local and individual life," thus, as with Freeman and others, as we shall see, by the realistic element of Andersen's novel writing.[46]

Three responses to *Only a Fiddler* appeared in 1870. One came out in November in the *Galaxy,* which was founded in 1866 as New York's answer to Boston's *Atlantic Monthly.*[47] In this notice, however, which is little more than an announcement of the publication of the Author's Edition, it is not clear that the writer had even read the work: "'Only a Fiddler' . . . is, we believe, one of the Dane's earliest productions. We are quite certain that it is a quaint and charming story." Worse than being uninformative, the notice is valuable only as (one more) implicit indication of the extent to which the—"quaint and charming"—fairy tales and stories dominated Americans' perception of Andersen.

The other two reviews are considerably longer, one covering two columns, the other over five, and both are far more illuminating. The first appeared in the October issue of *Putnam's Magazine.*[48] During the years following its inauguration in 1853 *Putnam's* published many of the same authors as the *Atlantic Monthly* and attained much the same stature as the younger periodical; indeed, it has been favorably compared to English magazines on the order of *Fraser's* and *Blackwood's.*[49] However, its circulation never approached that of the *Atlantic,* varying from 12,000 to 20,000. By 1870, it had lost most of its elite writers and indeed made the November issue its last.[50] At the same time, it had retained and even expanded its cadre of authors who, though presently held to be of a lower order, enjoyed great notoriety during their own time. One of these was Richard Henry Stoddard (1825–1903), who wrote the review in question. A popular poet, Stoddard also became a literary arbiter of the United States through his ten years as a critic for the *New York World* and another two decades as literary editor for the *New York Mail and Express*.[51]

Like Howells vis-à-vis *The Improvisatore*, Stoddard criticizes Andersen's handling of plot in *Only a Fiddler* but adds characterization to the debit side of the author's account: "It is not much of a novel, as novels go now, for neither its plot nor its characters are in any sense remarkable; it is devoid of startling incidents, and it lacks profundity of analysis; it has, in short, so little in common with the novels of Miss Braddon, or Mr. Charles Reade, or Mr. Wilkie Collins, that the merest novice among the story-tellers of the time would hardly put his name to it."[52] Nevertheless, infelicity of form does not determine Stoddard's overall opinion of the novel, for he begins the review as follows: "It is refreshing to turn from the highly-wrought fictions of the day, which deal for the most part with the class of passions and circumstances heretofore confined to the Newgate Calendar, to a natural and simple story like Hans Christian Andersen's *Only a Fiddler*. . . ."[53] Despite the novel's structural flaws, "[I]t is charming . . . as is every thing written by Andersen, who more than makes up for his deficiencies as a story-teller by his inimitable sweetness and freshness, and his perpetual tenderness of spirit."

Here and in the following lines Stoddard renews a motif common among his contemporaries in the United States, that is, the naive character of Scandinavian writers and especially of Andersen—"naive" in the sense of Schiller's notion of naive and sentimental poetry and poets: "There is something child-like in most of the writers of Northern Europe, and Andersen is the most child-like of all of them," the epithet of "immortal boy" being particularly applicable to him. Stoddard contrasts the naïveté of Scandinavian writers with the "sentimental" quality of their American counterparts, who "are what they are by culture, and not by nature; or, more exactly, are writers because they have taught themselves to be such, not because there is that within them which must and will find utterance." While art may reside in the work of authors such as Andersen and (Bjørnstjerne) Bjørnson, it so little resembles the art familiar to Americans that it has the effect of deriving from nature alone. Stoddard concludes the review by asserting, with a certain inconsistency, that *Only a Fiddler* is "characterized by the most loveable qualities of [Andersen's] genius—a genius which knows how to make the simplest incidents interesting, and the simple people dearer to us than all the kings and queens that ever lived."

Beyond what it says about Andersen's novel per se, Stoddard's review is noteworthy as yet another apparent example of reading Andersen's entire oeuvre, indeed of viewing Andersen himself, through the prism of his fairy tales and stories. At the same time, it illuminates the literary and cultural-historical horizon before which Stoddard and many of his American contemporaries saw Andersen as well as other writers. Stoddard's allusions to the British novelists and Bjørnson bear witness to the continuity with European and especially English letters that still prevailed in the United States in 1870 despite, or alongside, self-conscious cultivation of a distinctively American literature.[54] His opposition of nature and culture testifies more broadly to the continuing presence of German idealism and romanticism in the country, albeit as refracted by American transcendentalists and their successors in the genteel tradition with their peculiarly American accents.[55]

The second of the two longer reviews of *Only a Fiddler* appeared in the *Atlantic Monthly* in November 1870, and, like that of *O. T.*, was written by William Dean Howells.[56] Howells sees the novel in a more uniformly positive light than Stoddard: "It seems to us that this romance is not only much better than that of Herr Andersen, which we noticed two months ago, but an improvement even upon 'The Improvisatore,' which we were then inclined to think the best of the author's works."[57] Howells considers the present novel almost as good as *The Improvisatore* with regard to the charm of its characters and the setting of its story. However, he adjudges the plot to be superior to that of both earlier novels: "[It] is far more connected and interesting than that of 'O. T.'. . . . There is more vitality of general purpose, more certainty of design, in the details of this than in either of the other romances."[58] Howells affirms the episodic nature of the plot: "As is usual with Andersen's romances, this is told in what affects one as a series of episodes, though every chapter as a whole contributes to the progress of the story."[59] In a discussion of the novel's characters, indeed, he presents the irregular course of the novel as a virtue: "It is, in fact, an air of freedom in the movements of the persons which is one of the greatest charms of the book: they come and go; perhaps we see them but once; they are never strictly

accounted for; the changes wrought in them by time are only incidentally noted."[60]

Howells discerns no great novelty in Andersen's characters themselves, but he qualifies his criticism by stating that only the rarest of
great poets are capable of creating more than a couple of distinctive
figures in a single work. Moreover, he "does not know that any personage of the story is infirmly done, and the persons are of sufficient
number to have excused some inefficiency of characterization."[61] His
attentiveness to the type of protagonist and central concern common
to all three of Andersen's early novels is patent: "Herr Andersen's
hero, as far as we have made his acquaintance, is likely in each of the
author's works to be an unworldly-minded, innocent-hearted youth,
placed at odds with mankind by a blot upon his birth, or by the pos-
session of genius—which is, perhaps, the worst sort of illegitimacy."[62]

Howells underscores Andersen's ability to evoke mood and to elicit
emotion, opining that *Only a Fiddler* is "full of the most charming
lights, the most melancholy shadows, the most pathetic blending of
both."[63] He assumes that his readers, by dint of familiarity with
Andersen's writing, will readily believe that the work is "full of Denmark as well as humanity; a book by Andersen could not be otherwise."[64] His only unmitigated criticism of the novel "is that it is too
sad for so gloomy a world as we are obliged actually to live in"—
perhaps a concession to current *Atlantic* publisher and editor James
T. Fields, who disliked literature he found depressing.[65]

It is perhaps most characteristic and insightful of Howells that he
detects and appreciates realism in the novel where it was lost on most
others, including Andersen himself: "The author speaks scornfully of
realism in fiction, but he is a pre-Raphaelite in some things; and he
is apt to spend so much time upon the beautiful rendering of particulars in his pictures, as to lose his control over the whole effect; but
here everything promotes this."[66] In the midst of quotations from the
text Howells pauses to comment revealingly on one of his favorite
passages: "The whole study of this amusingly slipshod household is in
the best vein of the author, whose humor certainly gains from the
despised spirit of realism in which he paints the Knepuses."[67]

Andersen's later novels received little or no attention. In his review
of *O. T.* Howells writes that *The Two Baronesses*, "though the plot is vio-
lent and extravagant to the point of offence, has many characters and
pictures of Danish life which convey their own assurance of truth"—
an acknowledgment of the novel's realism.[68] The December 1869
issue of *Harper's New Monthly Magazine* notes that the novel is "rich in

quaintly beautiful conceits, and far more interesting than 'The Improvisatore,'" conceding, however, that "neither volume possesses the charm of the smaller stories [i.e., the fairy tales and stories] which have made Andersen such a favorite in American households."[69] The *Ladies' Repository* for January 1870 merely announces the novel's publication.[70] In September 1857, *Putnam's Monthly Magazine* proclaimed that "Hans Christian Andersen's new book (*To Be, or Not To Be*) is not a success. The fairy story-teller makes a poor theologian," only then to cite excerpts from two British reviews.[71] Horace Scudder's translation of Andersen's last novel, *Lucky Peer,* appeared in *Scribner's Monthly* from January through April 1871 but apparently elicited no critical discussion.[72]

THE PICTURE BOOK AND THE TRAVEL BOOKS

Some of the early American reviews devoted to Andersen were garnered by *Picture Book Without Pictures* and *In Sweden.* An anonymous two-and-a-half column announcement of *Picture Book,* in Meta Taylor's translation of Friedrich de la Motte Fouqué's German version, appeared in the *Daguerreotype* on September 4, 1847.[73] This magazine compiled its highly eclectic content primarily from European sources, reprinting, for example, a lengthy review of Andersen's first three novels, *Picture Book, A Poet's Bazaar,* and two collections of fairy tales and stories that originated in the British *Blackwood's Magazine.*[74] The present, independent review introduces *Picture Book* principally through excerpts from the preface and certain of the *aftener* (evenings), or sections, restricting its commentary to brief expressions of approval such as "these charming little sketches," which are "full of truth and feeling."[75] At the same time, it bears witness to the repute of the texts by stating that "in Mrs. Taylor's elegant version they must attain still greater popularity" than in Mary Howitt's earlier translation.[76]

The review of *In Sweden* mentioned in connection with *The Improvisatore* appeared in two issues of the *International Magazine* in 1851.[77] The *International* was a short-lived literary magazine (1850–52) that nonetheless published works by then-prominent writers such as Bayard Taylor and Horace Greeley as well as serials by major British writers and translations from the French and the German.[78] Owing to a bent of its editor, Rufus Wilmot Griswold, it specialized in book reviewing, offering much solid literary criticism.[79] While often attributed to Griswold, however, this criticism was actually written by his assistant, Charles Godfrey Leland (1824–1903).[80]

Born in Philadelphia, Leland studied at what is now Princeton University and then, already infected by the contemporary enthusiasm for German culture, at the Universities of Heidelberg and Munich. Subsequently entering the Sorbonne, he participated in the republican uprisings of 1848. His interest in German literature resulted in extensive translations from the work of Heinrich Heine as well as his own Heine-esque and Irvingesque *Meister Karl's Sketch Book* (1855) and *Hans Breitmann's Ballads* (1914), a collection of burlesque German American dialect poems that relate the adventures of a survivor of the March revolutions. Leland edited a number of magazines before devoting most of his energies to the study of folklore and spending much of his later life in Europe.

In the first installment of the review Leland characterizes Andersen's work as "very genial summer reading, consisting of detached sketches of Swedish life and scenery, with interludes of poetic reverie."[81] He then defends the volume from English critics, who "complain that it is not sufficiently well translated," for he senses in it "the same weird child-likeness of feeling which his [Andersen's] readers will recall" and that is expressed in the "peculiar, subdued strain of northern sentimentalism, which is more the complexion, than the substance of his style."[82] Distancing himself from his British counterparts and thereby representing a growing trend among his American colleagues, Leland appears to affirm the same "Teutonic" sensibility as Dana in the *Harbinger* review and, moreover, to suggest that Andersen's childlikeness is not to be confused with puerility, that is, that it represents style rather than substance. The remainder of this part of the review consists mainly of excerpts from the text.

The second part begins with a reference to the earlier discussion of Andersen's "latest and most delightful book, the *Pictures of Sweden*," continuing, "but the inspiration of nature is more powerful with him than that of history, and he is never so felicitous as when painting the scenery of his native country [!], though he has certainly indulged, to a greater extent than a sober taste can approve, in that passion for the fantastic and visionary, which has been but too visibly manifested in some of his later and slighter works."[83] Leland's fondness for the book is manifest. He, like Howells and many others, responds particularly to Andersen's depiction of place. However, he is disturbed by what he regards as the work's lack of contextualization in sociopolitical reality and even more so by a related extravagance of imagina-

Yours truly
Charles G. Leland.

Charles Godfrey Leland. By permission of the Houghton Library, Harvard University.

tion that he apparently also finds in certain works other than the novels, most likely some of the fairy tales and stories. Here, Leland sounds a note that is not uncommon in American Andersen criticism, even that written before the advent of realism, when one might more reasonably expect to encounter it. American romanticism, at least in its New England expression, was indeed generally more "sober" than its counterparts in Germany and Scandinavia, and one frequently finds censure of the fantastic as well as of sentimentality in the review criticism of the time.[84]

For Leland, as for almost all American commentators, however, Andersen's virtues more than compensate for his shortcomings. Following additional excerpts from the text, Leland writes, "The book, to those who are not repelled by a certain quaintness of manner from the enjoyment of a work of true genius, will form a permanent and delightful addition to those pictures of many lands which the enterprise and accomplishment of modern travellers is creating for the delight of those whose range of locomotion is bounded by the limits of their own country, or by the four walls of a sick chamber."[85] Ignorance of Andersen's age as well as his nationality does not prevent Leland from concluding with a quite positive and characteristic flourish: "Andersen has grown old in years, and with age he has increase of art, but he was never younger in spirit, and his genius never blossomed with more freshness and beauty."[86]

Another review of *In Sweden* came out under the heading "Pictures from the North" in the *Continental Monthly* for April 1863.[87] The *Continental* originated in Boston in 1862 as a means of furthering the development of an American national character and championing the causes of union and emancipation.[88] Accordingly, it published numerous political articles in support of these issues and commented on the progress of the Civil War, to the great disadvantage of the South. While it had a distinguished list of contributors that included Horace Greeley, it not only came with the war but went with it as well, ceasing publication in 1864. The review of *In Sweden* was most likely written by Charles Godfrey Leland, who, since working for Griswold, had become the first editor of the *Continental*.[89]

In contrast to his earlier review Leland initially seems to approve of the historical decontextualization of Andersen's work. He begins by musing over the virtue of contrast: "It is worth while to live in the city, that we may learn to love the country; and it is not bad for many, that artificial life binds them with bonds of silk or lace or rags or cobwebs, since, when they are rent away, the Real gleams out in a beauty and with a zest which had not been save for contrast."[90] After further random thoughts on the subject, he continues: "Mostly do I feel its charm when there come before me pictures true to life of far lands and lives, of valley and river, sea and shore. Then I forget the narrow office and the shop-lined street, the rattling cars and hurried hotel-lodgment, and think what it would be if nature, in all her freshness and never-ending contrasts, could be my ever-present."[91] Leland then relates that these reflections were elicited by the sketches of Sweden from the pen of the "fairy-story teller" Andersen and wonders whether they may strike the reader as pleasantly as they did him: "They have at least the full flavor of the North, of the healthy land of frost and pines, of fragrant birch and sweeter meadow-grass, and simplier [sic], holier flowers than the rich South ever showed, even in her simplest moods."[92] A translation of the first section of the work, "We Journey" (Vi reise), follows.

At this point in the review Leland's intent is not entirely transparent. The segment that ensues thus comes as something of a surprise: "There is true fatherland's love there. I doubt if there was ever yet *real* patriotism in a hot climate—the North is the only home of unselfish and great union. Italy owes it to the cool breezes of her Apennines that she cherished unity; had it not been for her northern mountains in a southern clime, she would have long ago forgotten to think of *one* country. But while the Alps are her backbone, she will always be at least a vertebrate among nations, and one of the higher order. Without the Alps she would soon be eaten up by the cancer of states' rights. It is the North, too, which will supply the great uniting power of America, and keep alive a love for the great national name."[93] Whatever may be said about Leland's interpretation of history and the cultural impact of climate, it becomes evident that he is more concerned with the pines and cool of New England and the heat and humidity of the American South than with northern and southern Europe. That is to say, the former Sorbonne student of 1848 contrasts Sweden with Italy, alluding to Garibaldi's Piedmont and the unification of the peninsula two years earlier, in order to assert his own republican and unionist sentiments in the ongoing American Civil War.

After additional reflections that redound to the great discredit of the South, Leland reprints three more sections from the text of the work: "The Grandmother" (*Bedstemoderen*), "The Cell Prison" (*Cellfængselet*), and "Sala." Absorbed by the mood of the latter, he writes: "Silence, stillness, solitude, loneliness, faraway-ness; hushed, calm, remote, out of the world, un-newspapered, operaless, un-gossipped—was there ever a sketch which carried one so far from the world as this of 'Sala'? That *one* shopboy—those going or coming cows—the tombs, with wornout dates, every point of time vanishing—a living grave!"[94] But now it is time to return to the present: "Contrast again, dear reader. Verily she is a goddess—and I adore her. Lo! She brings me back again in Sala to the busy streets of this city, and the office, and the 'exchanges,' and the rustling, bustling world, and the hotel dinner— to be in time for which I am even now writing against time—and I am thankful for it all. Sala has cured me. That picture drives away longings."[95] Near the end of the review Leland summarizes: "Verily, he who lives in America, and in its great roaring current of events, needs by a glance at Sala to feel that *here* he is on a darting stream ever hurrying more gloriously into the world and away from the dull inanity—which the merest sibilant of aggravation will change to insanity"—until, the review as a whole suggests, the next time a need for another contrast is felt.[96]

As with *The Improvisatore* and Dana, *In Sweden* had a generative effect on Leland. Andersen's name is mentioned only twice in the six pages of the review, and the appraisal of the work encompasses only two short sentences: "Reader, our Andersen is an artist—as most children know. But I am glad that he seldom gives us anything which is so *very* much of a monochrome as Sala."[97] Indeed, the second of these sentences is less a judgment of Andersen's work than a reflection of Leland's more immediate purpose in writing the review. Beyond providing an occasion for political statement, or in the process of doing so, *In Sweden* inspires Leland to elevate the North–South divide in the American conflict to near mythical proportions and, from this high vantage point, to offer his reader and himself both respite from the challenges of the epic events and resolve to persevere to glory.

The Author's Edition of *In Spain* (*I Spanien*) and *A Visit to Portugal* (*Et Besøg i Portugal*), which appeared together in one volume in 1870, received three reviews. The first was a brief, anonymous notice that came out in *Punchinello* on May 14 of the same year.[98] This New York illustrated weekly, which had published its first issue only a month and a half earlier, sought to become the American counterpart of London's humorous and satirical *Punch*.[99] It is interesting today perhaps chiefly for having been financed by the corrupt heads of the Erie Railway and Tammany Hall, including, of course, the infamous William M. "Boss" Tweed, whom the publication preceded into oblivion later in the year.[100] The critic expresses one insight, with a certain accent, that should be of interest in a country that thinks of Andersen virtually exclusively as a writer for children: "As usual, ANDERSEN is not abstruse in his way of putting things. His narrative is adapted alike for the juvenile mind and for the adult. There is no periphrasis in it." However, the remainder of the review was not necessarily designed to flatter the Dane: "[T]herefore the book should be a very popular one when summer time sets in, and people look for some quiet *délassement* which will not compel them to think."

Harper's review of August 1870, treats the volume at somewhat greater length and generally more kindly: "There is just that flavor of romance and chivalry in Spanish history and Spanish character to awaken the quiet enthusiasm of this kindliest of writers, just that poetic element in his character which seizes and portrays the bright side of that land of chivalry and dreams."[101] Therefore, the work can be characterized as a "thoroughly genial, kindly, pleasant, readable book." Try as he may, however, the reviewer cannot suppress the judgment of superficiality that emerges more unequivocally from the earlier review: "That he [Andersen] hardly sees its [Spain's] darker side, or, seeing, passes it by in silence, is little ground of criticism. One would hardly go to Hans Christian Andersen to get a complete analysis of the most contradictory character in history, as the character of the Spaniard is." It is rare that a critic openly discloses the tacit assumptions upon which his views rest. Much like R. H. Stoddard in his discussion of *Only a Fiddler,* however, the present reviewer does so when he writes, "And one could, perhaps, find nowhere in literature so appreciatingly portrayed that side of it [the Spanish national character] which we practical Americans rarely perceive, which, indeed, we are hardly capable of appreciating, except as it is interpreted to us." The idea that Americans were constitutionally incapable of appreciating "romance and chivalry," or "chivalry and dreams," is belied by the great popularity of Sir Walter Scott earlier in the century and the current vogue of romance, especially of the melodramatic variety, against which Howells rebelled.[102] As intimated earlier, however, there was truth to the notion that the compound which formed the American national character contained a healthy dose of pragmatism—a fact that in 1870 was becoming ever more apparent precisely in the criticism of Howells and others.[103]

The third review, which was written by Howells and appeared in the *Atlantic Monthly* in September 1870, continues in the vein of ambivalence colored more by mild condescension than approval.[104]

Howells begins with the words, "Pretty nearly what sort of book Herr Andersen would write about Spain any one could tell from a general knowledge of his other books; and no one having this acquaintance need be surprised to find the present volume entertainingly sentimental and quaint, with a current of real or well-affected simplicity, and touches of delicate poetry—in the prose parts."[105] At the end, Howells writes that the work is "agreeable" on balance.[106] However, he adds that it should not be read at one sitting, but should rather be "resorted to again and again, as the impression of each successive picture and sentimentalization fades away."[107] For the volume "is really a series of sketches of the surface of life" in the countries visited: "Generally, a photograph goes as deep as these; the study of the people, when there is any, is entirely subjective, and whatever is below the surface is Andersenish rather than Spanish."[108] In the middle part of the review, amid a number of passages drawn from the text, Howells addresses another, related issue, and with similarly mixed feelings: "Our poet (for such he is when he writes prose) travels partly by railway through Spain, yet he finds it full of romance and quite the Spain of most people's castles. In fact, it would probably be hard to destroy the world of fantasy in which he lives by any excess of modern conveniences. . . ."[109]

Danish Andersen scholars have long expressed dismay over the linguistic garb in which Andersen has appeared to English readers, especially during the early years of his presence in the English-speaking world.[110] Few American critics have addressed the question of translation, but Howells does so here. He is at pains to make clear that Andersen's poetic touches are found in the prose, rather than the verse, portions of the book: "We wish to be careful in regard to the locality, for Herr Andersen has seen fit to intersperse the account of his travels in the Peninsula with many copies of verses, which we suspect not to have been poetry in the original Danish, and which in the translation are made out very melancholy doggerel."[111] He then cites a passage from the section entitled "Malaga" as far as the verses beginning with the line "Ja Guult og Rødt er Spaniens Farver"[112]— in the translation, "Yes, yellow and red are the colors of Spain"—in order to "illustrate what we have been saying in praise and blame of the author. . . . An awkwardness in the versification of these undesirable lyrical bursts, and more than occasionally in the prose expression, forbids us to believe the translator's work quite well done, though we think he renders the author's spirit well. . . ."[113]

Of course, Howells was wrong about the original form of the poems (as well as about the incompatibility of imagination and technical progress in Andersen's mind), and one may find that the verses, at least those cited in the review, do not read as poorly on their own as he allows, if at the same time they are not entirely faithful to Andersen's Danish. What is clear is that Howells was unaware, or nursed a dislike, of the practice of interspersing prose with poetry that was common in German and Scandinavian romanticism.[114] Howells's criticism of the poetic interludes, which is of one cloth with his rejection of Andersen's sentimentalism and "fantasy," stems ultimately from his own realist convictions, which are so strong that they lead him to end the review with the admonition, "of course, the verses are not to be read at all, under any circumstances."[115]

The *Atlantic Monthly* also reviewed the Author's Edition of *A Poet's Bazaar* in October 1871.[116] In substance, the review is not unlike the earlier ones that appeared in the *Atlantic,* but its tone is quite different. This is likely due to the fact that Howells turned over primary responsibility for book reviewing to others the same year.[117] The lion's share of the duty went to Thomas Sergeant Perry, who was at that time a tutor in French and German at Harvard.[118] However, *The Atlantic Index* reveals that the reviewer of Andersen's book was in fact Norwegian American novelist, university instructor, and, later, professor Hjalmar Hjorth Boyesen.[119]

Recalling Andersen's journey through Germany, Austria, Italy, Greece, and Turkey, which inspired the book, Boyesen writes that the author's "'Bazaar' is stocked with his reminiscences of those lands and their people, and the graceful fancies which travel must suggest to a spirit so peculiarly open and sympathetic. It is in these, of course, rather than in the facts narrated or the information given, that the value of the book lies; it is because the 'Bazaar' is full of Andersen, that it is so charming." Even at this early stage of the review it is evident that Boyesen responds positively to a narrative whose character is determined by impressions and mood rather than by social reality. Far from creating a hindrance, such a subjective manner of seeing enhances observation, for, contrary to Howells's assertion in his review of *In Spain,* it enables Andersen to penetrate the surface of things and to reach their essence—subject engaging subject and coaxing it to awareness: "[Andersen's work] abounds in his characteristic descriptions of persons and places, in which the finest effect is attained without elaboration or detail. His impressible mind is immediately attuned, and, entering with his whole soul into the situation, he never fails to bring it vividly before the reader's eye. He never omits anything essential to the *ensemble,* yet he never disturbs the artistic result by overloading his picture."

Interestingly, Boyesen writes, "If there were any special school of colorists in literature, as there is in painting, Andersen would be in the foremost ranks of such a school. The color, or what artists call the tone, seems to be the prevailing element in every picture from his pen; and the drawing exists, only so far as it is necessary to bring the colors out in the strongest relief." Of course, such a "school" was currently forming in the writing of New Englanders such as Rose Terry Cooke, Mary Wilkins Freeman, Sarah Orne Jewett, and Celia Thaxter as well as Southerner Joel Chandler Harris and "Westerner" Bret Harte.[120] Romantic and realist impulses may have dominated the thought and work of American local colorists and Andersen in inverse degrees. However, despite apparent unawareness of the regionalism gaining momentum in various parts of the country, and quite in accord with Howells, Boyesen draws attention by implication to the fact that Andersen's novels, travel books, and even some of the later fairy tales and stories show a romantic on the way to realism, if more of a poetic and psychological than a social kind, although a social element is certainly present.

Boyesen then moves momentarily beyond Andersen's *Bazaar* per se to view it in comparative terms, operating with some already clearly established stereotypes: "Andersen has the happy faculty, in common as we believe with the more prominent writers of Denmark generally, of being able to strike the medium between that aerial lightness of the French, which almost seems too slight to give expression to deeper sentiment or passion, and the massive heaviness, which in German literature so often hides the beautiful under the rubbish of ponderous words and clumsy phrases." He then highlights the lyricism of Andersen's text: "There are passages in 'A Poet's Bazaar' which, as they read in the Danish, are both in rhythm and sentiment musical enough to make you question whether there is anything but the rhyme lacking to make them poetry; and in some instances you half unconsciously stop to examine whether they are not actually written in metre." Boyesen feels that this musical rhythm suffers, but does not entirely disappear, in translation and offers a passage from the text as evidence. In conclusion, he writes again more broadly, "Independent of its own literary value, 'The Poet's Bazaar' [sic] is a work of more than ordinary interest as affording a key to all the other writ-

ings of the same author. On every other page we find sketches of
scenes, objects, and persons which we immediately recognize as having furnished the material for the plot, descriptions, and characters
in the author's later works. 'A Poet's Bazaar' is thus, perhaps, an
autobiography in a truer sense than 'The Story of My Life.'"

Another review of *A Poet's Bazaar* came out in the *Overland Monthly*
in January 1872.[121] Founded in San Francisco in 1868, the *Overland*
was first edited by Bret Harte, who published some of his early work
there as well as pieces by Mark Twain and other noted writers, thereby
helping to make it, in Mott's words, "a western *Atlantic Monthly*."[122]
By the year of the anonymous Andersen review, however, Harte had
gone East. Although the magazine reached a circulation of 10,000
during its first year of existence, it had by now begun a decline that
led to cessation of publication after a seven-year run.[123]

The accents of the *Overland* review so closely resemble those of its
predecessor in the *Atlantic* as to lead one to believe, at the very least,
that the two authors were kindred spirits, if not equals in talent. The
writer begins by stressing the autobiographical nature of the *Bazaar:*
"We do not at present recall a writer who confides in the public to so
great an extent as Andersen. *The Story of His Life* [*sic*] is a heart-con-
fession that keeps no secret from the world. *A Poet's Bazaar* is a supplement to that confession, as if the poet had not been explicit
enough in the story, and hastened, therefore, to elaborate detail. We
confess the charm of this ingenuous trust in humanity."[124] The
reviewer also underscores Andersen's power of empathetic observation as well as the poetic quality of his prose: "The sincerity of the
author is stamped upon every page, and few men are so keenly observant and so sympathetic. These pictures of travel in Germany, Italy,
Greece, and the Orient are highly colored, and exquisitely finished.
Many of his descriptive passages are extremely poetical. . . ."[125] Following an example drawn from the text, he adds that Andersen "is
not long in giving words to the song [mentioned in the passage
cited], almost as musical as the waters of the lovely bay that surrounded him."[126] He closes by devoting a couple of paragraphs to
Andersen's remarkable life, something that was not at all uncommon
even in reviews of the Dane's creative work.

∽

Taken as a whole, the reviews of Andersen's longer prose reveal that
English-language translations of the works were available in the
United States almost as soon as in England. Together with other kinds

of evidence they also indicate that the novels in particular attracted a large readership and attained great popularity. At least in Dana, Stoddard, Curtis, and Boyesen they found critics who played a significant role in American letters and/or criticism during their own lifetime. Howells, of course, is remembered today less for his editorial work and review criticism than as a novelist who long ago entered the canon of American literature. Even as a reviewer, however, he possessed perhaps the highest profile of all those who wrote on Andersen, and his several critiques were published in the leading literary magazine of the time. Indeed, a substantial number of the reviews appeared in *Harper's* and *Putnam's* in addition to Howells's *Atlantic,* thereby addressing an elite and, collectively, large readership.

A number of Andersen's critics, early and late, make a point of emphasizing that he was a writer for adults as well as for children. For those writing during the 1870s this was very likely due to the appearance of the Author's Edition, eight of whose ten volumes were devoted to works other than the fairy tales and stories and that made Andersen's range unmistakable, at least in theory, and, surely, in reality for some readers. Insight into this breadth was especially propitious since certain reviewers more or less manifestly read the other works with an eye to the fairy tales and stories. Generally speaking, the reviewers responded favorably to the travel books but, for reasons reiterated below, preferred the novels. To the extent that comparisons were made, either explicitly or implicitly, *The Improvisatore* and *Only a Fiddler* vied for first place, followed in order by *O. T., The Two Baronesses,* and *To Be or Not to Be. Lucky Peer,* we recall, was not discussed.

In the early *Harbinger* review Dana concentrates on the thematic dimension of *The Improvisatore,* the problematic relationship between the artist and society, without neglecting questions of form. Howells and other later critics, on the other hand, are preoccupied with description, mood, and other formal matters, though certainly mindful of theme. One may be tempted to attribute this in part to the transition from romanticism to realism that occurred between 1845 and 1870 and is reflected here in a discrepancy between, on the one hand, an implicit sense of the self-evident nature of one's tacit assumptions about art and, on the other, a more apparent sense of the need to establish a new aesthetic program. However, one should bear in mind that in his two-part review of *In Sweden* Leland praises Andersen's descriptive power while criticizing his lack of consideration for sociopolitical reality and extravagance of imagination—concerns one associates with realism—as early as 1851. Indeed, his appre-

ciation of the work in his review of 1863 derives in part from the fact
that the book variously calls to mind the concrete rush of current
events—nine years before the appearance of Howells's first novel.
The distinctions of literary history are rarely, if ever, as clearly defined
as they often appear in literary historiography. We will have further
occasion to observe that in American literature, perhaps because of
its late blossoming, the chronological boundaries between romanticism and realism are less regular than, for example, in Danish or German letters.[127]

Andersen's reviewers use the word "imagination" in two different
senses: as the ability to create images of real things in the reader's
mind and as the power to bring to the mind's eye things that do not
exist in reality. Those who comment on Andersen's imagination in
the first sense judge it positively, though in one review Howells does
not find it to be strong. Those who remark on his "fantasy," on the
other hand, view it negatively. Several critics also fault Andersen for
superficiality in his treatment of character and culture, primarily with
regard to the travel books but also in connection with one of the novels. On the positive side, they appreciate the poetic, or musical, quality of his prose and deem his simplicity and naturalness charming and
refreshing.

It is interesting, though perhaps ultimately futile, to contemplate
the origin of the widespread perception of Andersen's "charm" and
"freshness." Certainly, the writings themselves have something to do
with it, but there is much about *O. T., Only a Fiddler,* and other works
that is anything but charming and refreshing. One suspects that this
understanding of Andersen owes a great deal not only to the fairy
tales and stories, despite their many gray and dark tones, but also, as
we shall see in the next chapter, to Andersen's own idealized autobiography as well as to preconceived notions about "Northern" literature. Andrew Hilen, for example, writes that the exceptionally popular Longfellow gave many Americans, including his New England
brethren, their earliest impressions of the Scandinavian world, presenting them with a romanticized image of the North as a kind of
"Baltic Spain," that is, a land of "legend and romance," that reflected
his reading of Scott and his own predilections far more than historical or contemporary reality.[128] In any case, this view of Andersen as
well as other aspects of the reviews disclose a self-conscious sense of
continuity with European literature and culture among the American literati that coexisted on the whole peacefully with their fervent
desire to foster the development of a specifically American literature.

Several reviewers exhibit this sense of cultural commonality and/or (largely) restrained cultural patriotism through the contexts in which they consider Andersen and the uses to which they put him. Dana places Andersen in the service of his own romantic-socialist ideals, which themselves align him with European traditions or currents. Stoddard views Andersen through a Schillerian lens, which the Dane himself would have recognized as being relevant to his experience vis-à-vis the critical—and "sentimental"—Heiberg and as determining the values of tales such as "The Nightingale" and "The Snow Queen." Curtis uses Hawthorne as a point of reference for characterizing Andersen's imagination and skillful verbal brushwork, while Howells proceeds from the perspective of a realist. Leland at once elevates Andersen onto a virtually timeless mythical plane and positions him squarely within the framework of the Civil War. In this sense, some of Andersen's reviewers clearly mirror developments in the literary-cultural and political history of the United States.

3

The Autobiography

It would not have been entirely inappropriate to discuss Andersen's autobiography in the preceding chapter together with the longer fiction—one is tempted to say, the *other* longer fiction. We have seen that several critics comment on the autobiographical nature of both the novels and the travel books, and the earliest review of the autobiography itself likens it to the most extravagant of romances. Certainly, the German title of one version, which in English reads *The Fairy Tale of My Life without Poetry,* an allusion to Goethe's autobiography, *Poetry and Truth,* was misleading, for in the book Andersen presents anything but a (provisionally) complete portrayal of his life, instead dwelling on the high points and avoiding the low, except for the ill treatment he felt he received at the hands of Danish critics.[1]

In any case, Andersen surely devoted more time to the depiction of his life than to any other single work, a period that extended over almost forty years and, in a sense, began in Germany and ended in the United States. His first autobiographical attempt, written in 1832, was intended for publication only if he died prematurely. Lost for many years, it was rediscovered and then published only in 1926.[2] He wrote his first sustained autobiography at the suggestion of his German publisher to accompany an edition of collected works that was issued early in 1847.[3] Eight years later there appeared what is considered to be his definitive autobiography, *The Fairy Tale of My Life* (*Mit Livs Eventyr*), which was based in part on the Danish manuscript used for the German edition. He later wrote additional chapters covering the period from 1855 to 1867, which were then published together with the earlier version in New York in 1871, six years before becoming available in Denmark.[4]

1847

Mary Howitt's translation of the German version of the autobiography came out in both British and American editions in 1847. They must have appeared in rapid succession, for the first British review, which was published on July 17, predated its American counterpart by little over a month.[5] This review, which was followed by four others over the final months of the year, appeared in the August 21 issue of the *Literary World*. Mott characterizes the magazine as the "first important American weekly to be devoted chiefly to the discussion of current books."[6] As such, it provides significant insight into literary life in the United States during the late forties and early fifties despite its demise due to a fire after only some seven years of existence. Initially, it had a distinct bias toward New York, where it was published and which was currently engaged in defending its status as the literary center of the country against Boston and the transcendentalists.[7] However, it adopted a fundamentally conciliatory review policy upon the accession of Charles Fenno Hoffman to the editorship in May 1847.[8]

Hoffman (1806–84) is associated with the so-called Knickerbocker School, a loose fraternity of New York writers that arose in the wake of *Diedrich Knickerbocker's History of New York* by Washington Irving (1809) and cultivated a correspondingly witty, satiric style, dominating the literary scene in the city until around 1837.[9] Although popular during his time for both his poetry and prose, particularly books of travel and nature sketches and a novel, Hoffman devoted much of his energy to editorial work and review criticism for several magazines.[10] Like many contemporary New Yorkers, he proceeded in his thinking about literature from a neoclassical point of view, putting a premium on the moral utility of a work and the moral character of the writer, as revealed in emotional warmth, while not neglecting questions of artistry. Owing in part to his desire to support writers in the creation of a national literature, he also took an Addisonian approach to book reviewing, writing in a later issue of the *Literary World* that "that criticism is most true which rather *seeks* the good than the evil, albeit not to shun our defects or to deny them where they exist."[11] Although the review of Andersen's autobiography is anonymous, the nature of the discussion coupled with the identity of editor and reviewer in many smaller contemporary American magazines suggest Hoffman as the most likely author.

Hoffman must have read the same works by or about Scandinavian writers as Stoddard, and he must have read them with the same eyes, for his "Teutons" have a distinctly naive, or primitive, air about them. In a lengthy introductory paragraph he declares that the heathens' and barbarians' southward descent upon the civilized world of yore continues to date, but with a difference: "It is thought now that leads the van. The descendants of Odin still press to the south: not with spear and buckler, but with minstrel song, legendary tale, and the statuary of demi-gods. Tegnér, Bremer, Andersen, Ole Bull, and Thorwaldsen, have ceased to be national and become universal property."[12] Following this expression of general familiarity with the contemporary culture of the North, Hoffman writes, characteristically, "Without depth of imagination, with little of passion, but great singleness, truthfulness, and freshness of portraiture, for they are not creative (we speak of literature), they are infusing the elements so much needed—the primitive, the savage—into minds hackneyed by civilization and pressed by conventionalism."[13]

The reviewer then turns to Andersen, immediately revealing the most compelling evidence for identifying him as Hoffman: "Of the book before us . . . one has no heart to speak severely. The very man, Hans Christian Andersen, is in it with all his generosity, piety, childlike simplicity, freshness, and we know not what that is lovable, so that when we would smile at puerility, or weary at limitedness, we suppress both as wrong to one of the purest and most sensitive natures which God ever suffered to be wounded by a hard world. Our critical pen slips aside, and we take the book [,] into heart and favor, as cordially as we would the true-hearted writer himself, were he at our elbow."[14] Hoffman is impressed that Andersen's " 'Story' has so little pretension, is interspersed with so much of anecdote, and frank confession, exposing a heart so full of goodness and purity, that we read on as if it were indeed a story, not the experience of a life. There is no romance of high-wrought sentiment, no great events,—and yet, the results [of Andersen's rise from poverty to fame] is [sic] almost equal to the tales of the wildest romance."[15]

After citing several passages from the text, Hoffman reflects further on the (stereo)typical Northern poet and on Andersen as a representative, apparently forgetting some of his earlier musings: "These northern regions are peculiarly the nurseries of the imagination[;] with little of action, little to dissipate the intensities of fancy, the inhabitants[,] living secluded, thus denied the lively play of mind upon mind, either sink into an indolent and gloomy superstition, or indulge in solitary musings in the highest degree favorable to poetic production. Andersen seems from the first to have been singularly sensitive, too keenly alive to the opinions of others, dreamy, affectionate, and slow in the development of thought and character, as is to be expected from the latitude in which he was reared."[16] For Hoffman, Andersen provides a strong contrast to the egotism of Schelling and Goethe: "We deal gently with what the world called his 'vanity,' and would substitute the word 'appealingness.' Surely, a quality so amiable, which caused him so much to distrust himself, and so confidingly to appeal to others, is entitled to a less severe appellative, most especially when combined with the highest moral endowments."[17] Hoffman goes on to say that Andersen *was* what he wrote and thus could not be certain how his writing would be received. Greater self-confidence might have made him better able to apply "the rules of Art," but he was who he was, and one must take a writer as he presents himself.[18] Hoffman concludes his discussion of this "chatty and most pleasing work" by terming it "a record of impulse, of feeling, rather than thought," from which "few extracts of mere sentiment, or gems of thought, can be made."[19]

Owing in significant part to his primitivist understanding of Scandinavian culture and Andersen, Hoffman articulates impressions that are also enunciated within other frames of reference, as we saw in chapter 2, for example, the author's deficits in creativity and artistry and the prevalence of feeling over reflection and a concomitant lack of profundity in his work. Perhaps in keeping with the nature of autobiography as well as his own predilections, however, he stresses features of Andersen's personality which he finds appealing as well as the Dane's highly moral character. Andersen's morality and especially the "romance" of his life became leitmotifs in reviews of his autobiography.

The review in the *Literary World* was followed in October by another in *Godey's Magazine and Lady's Book*.[20] *Godey's* was the most widely read general magazine for women of its day, attaining by 1849 the then unheard of number of 40,000 subscribers and by 1860 150,000.[21] In its pages one can trace the history of Victorian manners, taste, and dress in the United States and also find something of art, music, and education, if no politics. While publisher and first editor Louis A. Godey had little literary sense himself, he was wise enough to persuade Sarah Josepha Hale to become coeditor in 1837. Hale (1788–1879) already enjoyed considerable esteem as an editor, the author of, inter alia, novels, sketches, and poetry, and particularly as a champion of women's education and other women's issues.[22] Under her editorship *Godey's* published works by the most popular writers of the time, including several associated with the New England Renaissance (the magazine was based in Philadelphia). However, it never became a literary magazine of high caliber, typically offering moral-sentimental tales that were, according to Mott, "pure as the driven snow" and which were filled with characters who are "often so pious and good that we hate them heartily."[23] Appearing under the rubric "Editors' Book Table," the review of Andersen's autobiography would appear to have been written by Hale.[24]

The review represents at base a variation on one of the leitmotifs mentioned above, beginning with the words, "A beautifully-told and true story—one almost of romance." Hale could not have substantiated her assertion of the book's truth unless she meant that it was "true" in the sense of "compelling." However, she may well have used the word in the sense of "historically accurate," or in both senses, for due perhaps to Andersen's apparent disarming candidness, or "naturalness," she, like many other reviewers, seems to take him at face value. After relating a number of events in Andersen's improbable rise to fame, Hale writes, "It is a book of vicissitudes, and shows the efforts of a mind conscious of its own abilities to overcome obstacles almost insuperable, and at last to meet with the reward which such great talents were entitled to." No less than certain reviews of the novels, and long before most of them, Hale's brief critique evoked the notion of genius to characterize Andersen and to explain his success. Whether attributable to Andersen's self-promotion or not, this notion became firmly linked to his "life."

In November of the year a review of the autobiography appeared in the *Christian Examiner and Religious Miscellany*.[25] Founded in Boston by the influential clergyman and intellectual William Ellery Channing, among others, and associated through its editors and contributors with Harvard University, the magazine was one of the most important American religious periodicals of the nineteenth century, espousing the Unitarian point of view for over fifty years and, for a time, that of transcendentalism.[26] The *Examiner* published articles on philosophy, history, education, and sociopolitical issues as well as theology. While belles lettres occupied little space, the magazine gained a reputation for distinguished reviewing.[27] The editors during the mid to late forties, Alvan Lamson and Ezra Stiles Gannett, were both Unitarian ministers who played notable roles in the controversies in which their church was engulfed during the first half of the century.[28] Although they reportedly did much to improve the magazine's reputation for erudition and skill, they were not literary men per se and apparently left reviewing to others. The notice of Andersen's autobiography is one of very few early reviews that bear a signature of sorts. Reading "B———t," however, it sheds uncertain light on the writer's identity for the modern reader.[29]

The reviewer for the *Examiner* also attends to Andersen's self-portrayal in the autobiography, taking him at his word: "This very interesting book is so written, that the reader feels, while turning over its pages, that it is as trustworthy in its details as it is simple and natural and beautiful in its style; and also—what cannot be said of every autobiography—that he is gaining an insight into the author's real character, as well as a knowledge of his various fortunes." This reviewer, too, is taken with the "fairy tale" of the life of an author "who struggled for a long time with extreme poverty and its attendant difficulties, without allowing his temper to be soured or his faith either in God or in man to be weakened, and finally, by his writings alone, which are distinguished not less by moral purity than by intellectual power, secured for himself a European reputation, such as but few, in the most favorable circumstances, have been able to acquire." Consistent with his Unitarian, that is, Christian humanist, background, the reviewer notes Andersen's continuing faith in both man and God as well as his moral purity.[30] He is one of few who read Andersen's life as an expression of intellectual vigor. For those unfamiliar with the author, whose number he must have assumed to be large, he includes a thumbnail sketch of Andersen's biography.

Two reviews of the autobiography appeared in December, one of them in the first issue of the *Massachusetts Quarterly Review*.[31] The magazine was ostensibly edited by Ralph Waldo Emerson, his friend and protegé James Elliot Cabot, and Theodore Parker, but in actuality Parker was forced by his cohorts' lack of commitment to the project to assume total editorial responsibility, which, however, he did willingly enough.[32] For Parker (1810–60), a restless philosopher, theologian, and writer, had been the moving force behind the establishment of the periodical in the first place, seeking to fill the void created by the demise of the transcendentalists' organ, the *Dial*, three years earlier. However, this quarterly was to be more vigorous than its esoteric and ethereal predecessor, the *Dial* with a beard, as Parker put it. Its contributors and contents indeed proved to be more heterogeneous, though social issues occupied the center of attention, which led one contemporary to call the publication a beard without the *Dial*.[33] Bearded or not, the magazine apparently failed to attract a sufficient number of subscribers to survive beyond its third year, one less than the *Dial*. In addition to articles on social questions its pages contained literary criticism, some poetry, and reviews. Parker himself wrote most of the latter and thus in all likelihood that of Andersen's autobiography.[34]

It is perhaps indicative of Parker's subjective approach to criticism that about half of the short—two-hundred-word—review is devoted to one particular incident related in the book:[35] "Andersen was once troubled by a swarm of critics, and thus writes of them. 'The newspaper criticism in Copenhagen was infinitely stupid. It was set down as an exaggeration, that I could have seen the whole round blue globe of the moon in Smyrna, at the time of the new moon. That was called fancy and extravagance, which there any one sees who can open his eyes'. . . . He was not wholly above such criticism, but 'felt a desire to flagellate such wet dogs, who come into our rooms and lay themselves down in the best place in them.'" One can easily imagine the appeal such a passage must have had for an individual who suffered as long and as severely as Parker did from criticism of his allegedly extravagant ideas.[36]

In any case, the reviewer finds the book to be "a simple and unaffected little autobiography" that is "full of delicate little touches of nature" and, significantly, is "not without a good-humored satire." In contrast to some other commentators this reader opines that the "occasional notices of the distinguished men of the time" do not constitute name-dropping, but rather "enhance the variety and liveliness of the story." He concludes his discussion by asserting that Andersen "everywhere gives indications of a warm, humane, generous, heart— though possessed of no very lofty imagination." Like so many of his contemporaries, Parker exhibits concern for the character revealed by the author of the book. Less common and therefore especially noteworthy is his appreciation for Andersen's wit and flair for satire.

The second of the reviews published in December 1847, appeared in the *United States Magazine and Democratic Review*.[37] The periodical had been created ten years earlier with the aim of making it a first-rate literary magazine, and it has indeed been called perhaps the most brilliant of its time, at least up to the departure of its founder and first editor, John L. O'Sullivan (1813–95), in 1846.[38] The friend of Hawthorne, Bancroft, and other influential figures, O'Sullivan obtained contributions from the best writers of the day, from Bryant

on to the young Walt Whitman.[39] Although his politics eventually led
him down some dead-end paths, he shared the ideal of America's manifest destiny and a distinct cultural patriotism with many coevals.[40]

An optimistic view of America's prospects survived O'Sullivan's
departure from the magazine, if one can judge by the focus and tone
of Andersen's reviewer, who begins as follows: "The autobiography of
a man whose 'life is a lovely story—happy and full of incident,' is
surely worthy of attention. Men are rather prone to exaggerate their
sufferings than their enjoyments; hence one half of the world is con-
tinually complaining to the other, without ever seeming to think that
each one already has sorrows enough of his own. A few cheerful spirits, who never cease to work with heart, head, and hand really have
the burdens of society to bear. An author, who comes complaining of
'man's heartlessness,' of the 'world's selfishness,' and of a thousand
other things, with the whole catalogue of which the brood of whin-
ers is familiar, we always approach with much distrust, for such usually have an inclination to inflict upon others what they most fear
themselves. When, on the other hand, one comes, and with due modesty and simplicity, tells the story of his life, at some moments of which
he has felt a gratitude so strong that he wishes to 'press God to his
heart,' we are at once inclined to give him our hand and embrace
him as a real benefactor."[41] The reviewer admires Andersen's positive approach to life so much that he is willing to overlook the shortcomings of its portrayal: "If Andersen has not best performed the
most difficult task, he has certainly done it with the most cheerfulness. If his 'sketch' is less interesting as a study than the autobiography of Goethe, still we meet with none of those formidable
hypochondriacal 'crotchets' which darkened some portion of the
great poet's life, and at the close of a long life of uniform prosperity
and success, wrung from him the sad confession that he had seen but
very few days of real happiness."[42]

From the perspective of this reviewer the increasingly common
admiration of Andersen's victory over circumstance appears in an
uncommon light: "He has passed through trials that would have dis-
couraged a less hopeful spirit—that would have crushed a less cheerful one; hence, we do not fear that it is a smiling prosperity, instead
of the *real working, struggling man,* that speaks to us. From the depths
of poverty and obscurity, *with his own hands,* he has worked his way
through every obstacle, until he has become, not only one of the first
literary men of the age, but also the admired guest of the kings and
queens of Europe."[43] In the context of the times, and as described

here, the course of Andersen's life assumes distinctly Jacksonian, if not (pre)socialist, overtones. This gives unwonted meaning to the customary emphasis placed on Andersen's youth and early manhood in the choice of passages and events for citation or recounting.[44] Far from being a hindrance, poverty proved to be a gift: "Poverty, after all, has been to him as to others, the greatest blessing. No other master is sufficiently relentless for the school of genius."[45]

At the end of his review the author returns to his point of departure: "Andersen's habitual cheerfulness, even amid his sorest misfortunes and saddest wants, seems to us a peculiar and lovely trait of character. In these days of complaining we like to hear a man say, 'How bright and beautiful is the world! How good are human beings! That it is a pleasure to live becomes ever more and more clear to me.' How much better it is to endure the storms of life with fortitude and cheerfulness—like Milton, to 'bear up and steer right onward,' than to give up in despair and die, like poor sensitive Keats at the first attack."[46] The reviewer then turns his attention more pointedly to the American present: "We wish our country might have many such men, devoted to nothing but literature,—wedded to it 'for better or for worse.' We of course speak not now of the peculiarity of Andersen's genius, it must be left for another time. Such as he must stop the noisy mouths of those who are booing up and down the land, like Carlyle's Moon Calves, in regard to our national literature. If some calculating utilitarian should inquire the per cent. profit on the productions of such men, our answer must be, though to him very likely unintelligible, 'Philosophy can bake no bread, but she can procure for us God, Freedom, Immortality.'"[47]

Despite quoting extensively from the text, the present reviewer shows little interest in the particulars of Andersen's life or artistry, postponing scrutiny of his genius to another occasion, which apparently never came, and reflecting only once, negatively, on the book as autobiography. His considerable concern centers not so much on Andersen's character as on his *naturel*, or disposition, which he indeed finds exemplary, especially insofar as it bespeaks a working-class background. The reasons for "those days of complaining" are unclear. On the political front the Mexican War was currently being brought to an end, successfully in the view of expansionists, but related tensions surrounding the question of slavery in the new territories and states remained and may have been the object of the reviewer's allusion.[48] Certainly, he uses Andersen's perceived constitutional optimism as a rhetorical weapon in the struggle to establish a national literature.

1871–75

Between 1871 and 1875 nearly a dozen reviews of Andersen's autobiography came out, clustered almost evenly around the appearance
of the book in the Author's Edition and Andersen's death. The first
was published in the *Galaxy* in May 1871.[49] This monthly originated
in 1866 in New York, the product of local patriotism and competition
with Boston and an attempt to fill a perceived need for a national
magazine that would represent the whole country as well as the
Atlantic Monthly represented New England.[50] Mott writes, "Contemporary judgment was in general agreement that the *Galaxy* articles
were, in the first place, fresh, various, and original; and in the second
place, bold, vigorous, and direct."[51] The magazine printed considerable quantities of mediocre verse and sentimental prose, but it could
also boast, for a time, the editorship of Mark Twain and published
works by him as well as Henry James, Walt Whitman, Sidney Lanier,
and many lesser notables. According to Mott, the literary criticism
was, and continues to be, important.[52] Nonetheless, circulation never
rose above 23,000, which it reached in the year of our review, and the
magazine was absorbed by its chief competitor, the *Atlantic Monthly*,
in 1878.

Precise attribution of the *Galaxy* review is impossible, but one may
reasonably assume that it was written by either Edmund Clarence
Stedman or James F. Meline. A renowned poet and critic in the genteel tradition, Stedman (1833–1908) worked as a coeditor for *Putnam's Magazine*, whose review of *Only a Fiddler* appeared during his
tenure, before moving to the *Galaxy* after *Putnam's* was absorbed by
Scribner's Monthly in 1870.[53] Meline (1811–73), having practiced law
and worked as a banker for most of his life, spent his later years contributing criticism to newspapers and magazines such as the *Galaxy*,
for which he wrote mainly on French and German literature.[54]

The review opens with a lengthy paragraph on its governing
theme, namely the idea that the "Germans and Scandinavians appear
to have more talent than taste for autobiographies," for "[l]ate and
few as are their works in that branch of literature, they sparkle with
spirit and freshness." In contrast to the self-centeredness of the
French and the provincialism of the English, "[t]he Northern nations
are more cosmopolitan; and self, as they record it, absorbs more color
from outward things than it reflects upon them. There are few writers who might not make a more interesting story of the world as it has
affected them than as they have influenced it." Compared with the

reviews of the forties, the Scandinavians retain their naturalness yet gain in sophistication.

Not surprisingly, then, the *Galaxy* critic finds Andersen's autobiography fresh and original: "His record of life expresses the very spirit of his books, described in the words of a critical countryman, meaning to be unkind, as 'charged with sensibility and childishness.' They have in spite of these qualities, or rather because of them, won a distinct and high place in the world's regard, which this unaffected story of his life will confirm." No less than the "sensibility and romance born with him, that make his books so bright and rare" and "have never passed out of his growing life," this reviewer, much like certain ones considered in chapter 2, appreciates Andersen's ability to commune with places and people and to extract their essence: "These pages are full of little vivid touches of scenes, little kindly epigrams on character, noted at the instant they glanced upon him during his frequent journeys over Europe. Venice is 'the wreck of a spectral gigantic ship,' 'a dead swan on the muddy water.' England is 'a land of freedom, where one almost dies by etiquette. . . . Rachel looks like an image of mourning'. . . . Andersen scarcely needs to tell us that travelling is like a Medea draught which always makes one young again; and its effect on his impressionable spirit is nowhere better expressed than in the attempt to describe a landscape, which he gives up because he had forgotten all impressions except the smiles of a child."

What other commentators deem weakness and vanity, this critic considers simply an extension of the emotional responsiveness that allowed Andersen to forget everything but the child's smiles: "The same sensitiveness appears in his complaints of harsh criticism, and of the coldness which in early days treated him as a prophet without honor at home, as well as in his naive way of expanding under the warmth of praise." The reviewer's admiration of Andersen's character is understated but nonetheless manifest: "And his frank confession of the influence of others upon his tastes and character, show how steady and generous have been his admiration for strength and goodness. . . . [I]t is long since we have enjoyed an autobiography in which so much candor inspires so much respect for its subject."

During the period in question newspapers devoted a substantial amount of space to book reviews, and the *New York Times* was no exception. Founded in 1851, the paper had numerous established competitors, chief among them the *New York Sun*, the *New York Herald*, and the *New York Tribune*. However, it achieved almost immediate success, attaining a daily circulation of around 36,000 by 1871, which placed it in a respectable position behind its major rivals.[55] When the anonymous notice of Andersen's autobiography came out on May 17 of that year, the paper was engaged in its long and ultimately successful campaign against the Tweed ring and the corruption of Tammany Hall, for which it gained great respect. Indeed, its editors seemed much more interested in politics than in culture.[56] From its inception, however, its second and third pages were devoted to reviews and general articles, and the discussion of Andersen's autobiography appeared appropriately on page 2.[57]

The review begins with a half-truth: "This autobiography is now for the first time translated into English, and contains chapters additional to those published in the Danish edition [of 1855], bringing it down to the Odense festival of 1867, which the author looks upon as the crowning honor of his life." The confusion is easily enough explained, for the title page of the volume itself bears the words, *"NOW FIRST TRANSLATED INTO ENGLISH."*[58] However, in the "Advertisement," which serves as a preface, Horace Scudder faithfully traces the genesis of the autobiography and its history in English, beginning with Mary Howitt's earlier rendering of the German version and acknowledging his usage of it.[59] One suspects that the publishers sought to capitalize on the "novelty" of the translation and Andersen's great popularity by stretching the truth on the title page.

In any case, the critic's obvious ignorance of the 1847 British edition clearly betrays something only implicit in certain other reviews, namely, that over the intervening twenty-four years the "English" Andersen had not survived intact in America's cultural memory. To be sure, the reviewer writes, "Andersen's works are so well known that they make the events which suggested and gave rise to them . . . full of interest" and though "[d]read of the sea has . . . prevented him from visiting America . . . nowhere has he warmer friends, and they will eagerly embrace this means of becoming better acquainted with the man who has so long been held in high esteem as a writer." However, the critic's lack of familiarity with a work that was so popular and often reviewed during the late 1840s suggests that he had only some of the fairy tales and stories and perhaps *The Improvisatore* in mind. What did survive the nearly two and a half decades unchanged are responses to the work that escape the stereotypical only to the extent that they reflect fresh reading. Following a glance at Andersen's rise to fame, the reviewer states, "The author has written no more charming a wonder-story than that of his own life." This, he continues, "is told with delightful simplicity and frankness"; all is "confided to the reader with the most pleasing *naïveté,*" and the familiar people and places seen along his life's journey "receive a new charm, seen through the medium of his fresh poetic spirit."

Scribner's Monthly published a review of Andersen's autobiography in June 1871, only some six months after it came into existence.[60] The magazine was successful from the very outset, printing 40,000 copies of the first issue and never any fewer.[61] Bearing the name *The Century* beginning in 1881, it enjoyed a run of sixty years and was, in Mott's words, "characterized by the highest aesthetic and moral ideals and was often an effective force in political and social reform."[62] Its early success was due largely to the decade-long editorship of Josiah Gilbert Holland, who, according to Mott, should be on any list of the five or six best magazine editors in the United States.[63] As the *Century,* the magazine eventually published writers on the order of Jack London, William Dean Howells, and Mark Twain and cultivated a tradition of Southern writing that included Joel Chandler Harris's Uncle Remus stories. Early on, however, Holland also printed works by the likes of Frank Stockton, Bret Harte, Henry James, and—Hans Christian Andersen. With its second issue, in December 1870, *Scribner's* absorbed *Putnam's Monthly* and Horace Scudder's *Riverside Magazine for Young People,* in which sixteen of Andersen's fairy tales and stories had appeared.[64] Scudder had obtained seven additional ones, and three of these then came out in *Scribner's.*[65] Especially given the tenor of the anonymous review, one might well surmise that Scudder wrote it himself, were it not for a telling matter of chronology that Scudder would have been the least likely person to confuse.

The review begins, "There is something wonderfully fit in Hans Christian Andersen's writing his own life . . . for who else will ever have the opportunity? Is not Andersen the very genius of Fairy Tale consigned to perpetual youth? It seems to us that our grandfather must have read 'The Ugly Duckling' in his childhood [!], just as our grandchildren are now reading it [!]."[66] The erroneous perception that Andersen had been around for five generations indicates more than a lack of information on the part of the critic. If suggesting a breach in the continuity of his reception in the United States, much like the *Times* review, it also reflects the high degree to which Andersen had become a "timeless" fixture in Americans' awareness.

The reviewer chooses the word "homely," rather than "homey" or "natural," to capture Andersen's essence, but he means the same thing: "[A]nd if ever there was a life which was homely in the best sense of that word, a word that will keep its color however often washed, it is Andersen. From his childhood in the little house in Odense, through all the queer experiences of his boyhood to the present time, when he is perpetually flitting from one household to another, royal, ducal, or plain citizen, he keeps that homely soul of his which treats all the world as sitting at his fireside."[67] Like his colleague at the *Galaxy,* the writer assesses Andersen's sense of self in a positive, if not necessarily flattering, manner: "That Andersen is egotistic is plain enough, but it is not the egotism that is born of selfish conceit, but the egotism of a child that has never learned to say *I* but keeps on saying *me,* or speaking of himself in the third person, as somebody whom he is earnestly interested in."[68]

Typical of his guild, the present critic takes Andersen literally: "The autobiography shows Andersen so frankly that there is really little left to find out about him, one would think, for we not only know what Andersen thinks of himself but what others think of him, and what he thinks of what others think of him!"[69] The reviewer believes that the reader will respond to Andersen's life much as Andersen's countrymen did: "We are struck with this fact, that in his immediate surroundings Andersen, in the course of his life, has passed through one period when he was petted as an amusing original; through another when he was disliked by many who had at least amused themselves with him, and that now, where he is known most intimately he is esteemed most highly. We think this will be found to be the effect upon the reader of this singular autobiography. He will begin by sympathizing with the struggling lad; he will become impatient of his excessive unbosoming of himself; but at last will lay down the book with a hearty respect for him, and a conviction that there is sterling worth in the man, and that he is worthy of the love which has been given him."[70]

The anonymous notice that appeared in *Harper's New Monthly Magazine* in July 1871, manages to do the nearly impossible: to traverse the forty-eight years separating Andersen's departure from and triumphal return to Odense in thirteen lines introduced by the first sentence of the autobiography's opening paragraph and concluded by the final one.[71] Though hackneyed on the whole, it is quite positive in tone, showing especial appreciation of "the delightful faith" that pervades the author's life and "makes it always and every where life in the sunshine."

The *Atlantic Monthly*'s response to the book two months later treats Andersen's biography in a similarly cursory fashion at the beginning.[72] However, it subsequently offers one of the most penetrating discussions of the author's self-portrayal ever written in the United States, shedding light both on Andersen himself and the reviewer and his cultural horizon as well. That the appraisal displays a certain ambivalence is not surprising when one learns that the writer was William Dean Howells.[73]

As he had done in his review of *In Spain* a year earlier, Howells questions the quality of the translation: "It might be better translated, for it has the faults which mar nearly all the versions of Andersen's books since the Howitts ceased to make them; it seems to be done by one not native to English, and it not only abounds in Danish idioms, but has here and there grotesque infelicities of expression that seem due to the translator's ignorance of English. Much of the flavor of the original must be lost in this awkward process, and we suspect that the author's meaning suffers at times."[74] To my knowledge no commentary on Scudder's rendering of the autobiography exists. However, Erik Dal rates him as a "fair" translator of the fairy tales and stories and thus better than the majority of his British predecessors, who were "mostly . . . people with neither talent, linguistic knowledge, literary sense, nor simple tact," a number that apparently includes Mary Howitt, whose translations of various works Dal calls "bad."[75] While one would therefore assume that Scudder's handling of the autobiography should at least be no worse than his success with the fairy tales and stories, perusal of the text in the Author's Edition in fact tends to support Howells's judgment of its English style, though one may not wish to render as harsh a verdict as he. Now, accomplishment in original composition is no guarantee of achievement in translation. In view of Scudder's already respectable record as a writer in various forms as well as Dal's comments, however, one may be inclined to assume that many or most of the lapses in style occur in that substantial portion of the autobiography, which Scudder, perhaps injudiciously or unavoidably, retained from Mary Howitt's work.[76]

Howells has words of appreciation for the autobiography as such: "The book is exceedingly entertaining, as autobiography always is, and the author makes us thoroughly acquainted with his character as well as his fortunes."[77] Toward Andersen the man, however, he has reservations: "We do not think that for the sake of the tender regard we all have for him, we could have desired to know him quite so well, and yet the truth about men of genius is no doubt the best after all, as it is about everything else. Andersen's character, tried by our Anglo-Saxon standard, is not what we should call a manly one; though here there may be some fault in our standard, which we ought not to apply too freely to the emotional people of Continental Europe. An American or an Englishman of Andersen's character we should have no scruple in describing as a sentimental snob. He is everywhere bursting into tears of grief or joy. . . ."[78]

Howells has especially mixed feelings about Andersen as a social creature: "[H]e regards himself with wonder and awe on account of the personal friendship borne him by the great; he basks in the condescension of nobles, and hugs himself upon the favor of kings. He is not altogether to blame for this, for royalty and aristocracy stood by him when the reviews and the theatres would none of him. But he must always have been difficult to manage by those who could not patronize him, and the reader feels that for much of his suffering at the hands of critics and people he had himself to thank."[79] Howells is not blind or indifferent to Andersen's solidarity with the poor, however: "When we have said all this . . . we feel that we have done him a tacit injustice, and we must acknowledge that, in spite of his obsequiousness, there is a sturdy sympathy with the people of his own origin, and a hatred of aristocratic pretension, of which there can be no more doubt than of his genius or his vanity."[80] At the same time, Howells believes that Andersen has gone beyond his origin without owning up to it: "He affects you very often as a man grown conscious of his own simplicity of nature, and resolved to make the most of it; his *naïveté* appears studied, his emotions premeditated, only his humor and his ideality seem at all times unrestrained. You weary of his meek diligence in recording the honors and the compliments paid him, and wish that he had either more modesty or not so much."[81]

Few reviewers comment on Andersen's sense of humor, much less the satire found in much of his work, so it is noteworthy that Howells acknowledges the genuineness of Andersen's humor and gives examples both witty and moving: "The earlier and the latter parts of his book are the most entertaining, especially the former; and the first pages are exquisitely humorous and tender in their description of his child-life before the death of his romantic, ambitious father. . . . Nothing can be more amusing or more touching than the description of the bed in which the poet was born, and which his father had ingeniously fashioned out of the catafalque of a deceased nobleman, leaving the funereal trappings of black velvet still on it."[82]

Howells finds Andersen's autobiography valuable as an introduction to the literary scene in Denmark but expresses dissatisfaction in this regard as in others: "The book is useful in making known the literary world of Denmark, with its surprising treasures of poetry and drama, and its not at all surprising jealousies and enmities. This is done in a more fragmentary way, of course, than could have been wished, but Andersen is essentially sketchy, and what he cannot indicate by a few touches must remain obscure."[83] Howells concludes the review by returning to an earlier point: "It is right to say, however, that upon his own griefs from the Copenhagen literati he dwells very fully, and presents a very finished picture of the sufferings a tender-hearted, vain, weak man of genius endures at the hands of a sarcastic and critical public. Andersen's lamentations are not very respectable, but on the other hand it is not creditable to the Danes that his recognition was in a manner forced upon them by outside pressure."[84]

The January issue of the *Ladies' Repository* for 1873 contained a review of the autobiography written by Emily F. Wheeler, an author and journalist who contributed numerous stories and general interest articles to this magazine and other periodicals of the time.[85] Clearly, she responded to Andersen's personality in much the same way as Howells: "There is a perpetual charm in *naïveté*. Girlhood—all ignorance and innocence, all frankness and folly—is a type of its fascination. In a man, one who has the fame of genius, it allies itself sometimes a little too closely with sentimentalism. The hero of his own story plays upon ingenuousness, child-like frankness and faith, as charmed strings to the public ear. The 'dear child of nature' sometimes unpleasantly reminds us of his second cousin, the natural."[86]

Wheeler's reaction to the "Wonder Story" of Andersen's life and his relation of it is equally ambivalent. Having cited the first paragraph of the book, she writes: "One feels the charm of the first sentences, and does not, till deeper in the book, weary of its perpetual repetition; especially as, in some respects, it is literal truth. The child of fortune, the charity scholar, become a world-renowned author, a friend and companion of kings, may well claim for his life a measure of the marvelous. And the mixture of simplicity and worldliness that makes the charm of Andersen's stories, seems, judged by his autobiography, a reflex of his own character. He is always his own hero; dreamy, sensitive, ambitious, and with a large spicing of vanity. The child-like heart demands admiration for its *naïveté*. In his Life, he at once charms and annoys us with his frankness. The poet is too much of an egotist. But that is one of the privileges of genius."[87]

Wheeler renders an extensive account of Andersen's life in a mixture of narrative and quotations from the text. Unlike many reviewers, she gives every period its due, if pausing at parts she knows will appeal most to readers, for example, those dealing with Andersen's visit to London in 1847, his "love of children," and Jenny Lind.[88] She also makes observations about Andersen's works along the way, especially the fairy tales and stories, which will receive attention in the next chapter. Of the poems, for example, she writes that they "were popular, but the critics declared him no poet. Judged by the bits scattered through his Life, the critics were right. Possibly, however, the translation does not do them justice. He at least writes poetry in prose"[89]—notions familiar from Howells's review of *In Spain*. Befitting a religious periodical, even one grown more liberal with age, Wheeler closes with an approving glance at Andersen's faith: "In the greatest honors that came to him, the God who had guided him was remembered. His religion seemed to be of the most child-like type; and the stray sentences that reveal his belief, have an odd charm in the mosaic of worldly incident that surrounds them. Going down into a happy old age, he closes most appropriately his autobiography with a prayer: 'Leave me not when the days of trial come.' "[90]

Numerous tributes appeared in the American press on the occasion of Andersen's death on August 5, 1875. A few of them warrant comment in the present chapter if only for the odd observation confirming or nuancing already established facts or impressions. Three were published in New York newspapers the day after Andersen's death, one of them in the *New York Tribune*. Beginning publication in 1841, the *Tribune* had risen to a position of preeminence among American newspapers. By 1865 it had reached an exceptional total circulation of almost 300,000 and was for perhaps a century to come the only paper in the country that enjoyed truly national distribution.[91] Readers of the midseventies knew it perhaps best for its crusade against slavery, its wayward course through Reconstruction, and its support of founder and longtime editor Horace Greeley's ill-fated campaign against Grant in the presidential election of 1869.[92] From the outset, however, the *Tribune* had been strong in review criticism, which at that time was largely the purview of the monthly and quarterly magazines, and at varying points could boast the opinions of notable figures such as Margaret Fuller, George Ripley, and Bayard Taylor.[93]

This strength only grew greater under Whitelaw Reid, who served as Greeley's first assistant, or managing editor, and later succeeded him on his death in 1872. Unlike most newspapermen of his time, Reid had a college education, having taken a degree in science and the classics at Miami University of Ohio, and at one point considered a career in education and letters.[94] His personal culture and intellectual pursuits had a salutary effect on his staff, most of which he retained from the previous dynasty.[95] Under Ripley's leadership, for example, the literary department experienced what has been called a "golden age of criticism," which was "probably the finest of any newspaper in the country."[96] Considering the *Tribune*'s commitment to the arts and its ultimate source, it comes as no surprise that Reid himself wrote, and signed, the tribute to Andersen.

The article is most remarkable simply for having appeared in a publication of the highest quality such as the *Tribune* and over the signature of its editor-in-chief—lucid indications of the high regard in which Andersen was held in the United States at the time of his death. Indeed, Reid writes, "While thus traveling from place to place he was producing the books which have rendered him so popular everywhere, and gained him especially the affection of the young."[97] Despite the last phrase, Reid cites as the "principal of these works" not only the fairy tales and stories but also several of the travel books, though, surprisingly, none of the novels. He then continues: "All of these have been translated into nearly every European language, and have found their way to the peasant's hut as well as to the royal palace." The repute of Mary Howitt's translations obviously survived the intervening some thirty years—and Scudder's work—unblemished: "The English translations have been mostly from the pen of Mary Howitt, who succeeded admirably in retaining the charm of the author's style." Reid devotes most of the article to a retelling of Andersen's "wonderful" life, about which Americans apparently never tired of reading. He concludes by quoting a letter written by Andersen a few months before his death to express thanks for a sum of money and a book presented him by an organization called the American Children's Present in gratitude for his writings and in the false belief that he was poor.[98]

The day following Andersen's death also saw the publication of two anonymous articles only a few columns apart in the *New York Times*.[99] The first and far shorter of them, which is untitled, succinctly rehearses the "fairy tale" of Andersen's life: "HANS CHRISTIAN ANDERSEN, most poetic of novelists and most childlike of men, is dead. The story of his life is as charming as any of his novels, and his own character possessed a certain elevated purity and high-strung sensitiveness which suggest an ideal creation of fiction. It reads like a romance to follow the steps of the boy of fourteen who would learn neither tailoring nor shoe-making, but clung fast to the belief that he would live to be a poet, and who, without either education or decent clothes, went up from his native village to the capital to 'try his fortune.' Yet the raw, ungainly lad who, when he went on the stage as a 'super,' was afraid to stand upright because his waistcoat was too short to meet his trousers, lived to fascinate the world fifteen years later with the *Improvisatore,* and to follow up that wonderful book with a series of stories which are the delight of young and old in every clime. There is hardly a great statesman, and hardly a ruler of men who has passed 'behind the veil' attended by any such universal tribute of emotion as will be elicited by the tidings of the death of the Danish novelist, who ranks less among the illustrious than among the well-beloved names of literature."[100]

A number of words appearing in the article reflect commonplaces of the American reception of Andersen: "childlike," "charming," "character," "purity," "sensitiveness," and "romance." Also characteristic is the notion that Andersen inspires less awe than familiarity, in the original sense of "close relationship," a notion illustrated by the comically endearing reference to his ill-fitting clothing. Not so typical, if hardly unique, however, is the acknowledgment that his fairy tales and stories appeal to adults as well as to the young. A couple of reviewers observe the poetic quality of Andersen's longer prose, as we have seen, but the author of the present article is one of the noteworthy few who apparently think of the Dane principally as a novelist rather than as an author of fairy tales.

Despite its greater length the second of the two articles is less interesting than the first, offering in essence only a more detailed sketch of Andersen's life. However, the writer repeats a significant point made by the realist Howells and a few others, namely, that *The Improvisatore* contains "unrivalled descriptions of the scenery and manners of Southern Europe."[101] He adds, more broadly, that "[i]n many respects as a descriptive writer, in depicting scenes, men, manners, and customs, he is unsurpassed if not unrivaled." Much as in the shorter article, significantly, the author introduces Andersen as "the celebrated Danish poet and novelist." In his concluding remarks, to be sure, he makes the by now familiar assertion that "[a]s a writer of fairy tales Andersen stands in the very foremost rank." However, he continues, "As an author—poet, playwright, novelist, and wit—he has shed considerable lustre over the literary annals of little Denmark, and will ever occupy a page of honor in her history."

The last of the writings to be discussed here appeared in *Potter's American Monthly* in November 1875.[102] Debuting in 1872 under the name *American Historical Record*, the magazine was originally devoted to the history of the United States and American biography.[103] In January 1875, however, John E. Potter assumed ownership and made it more general in character, as reflected in its new subtitle, *An Illustrated Magazine of History, Literature, Science and Art*. While attractively illustrated, featuring the work of the then famous historical painter and popular historian Benson J. Lossing, who also first edited it, the magazine nonetheless never acquired a cadre of contributors equal to those of more successful periodicals.[104] In 1882, a couple of years after exchanging history for travel as an area of emphasis, it ceased publication.[105]

While certainly in keeping with the magazine's interest in biography and literature, the anonymous piece on Andersen is more a tribute in the manner of those published in the New York newspapers than a general article. It, too, consists primarily of a biographical sketch, stressing like many others before it the events leading up to Andersen's first literary successes and briefly summarizing his subsequent life. Like the writer for the *Times*, the author has especially kind words for the "fairy tales for children," which he calls "the most charming things of the kind conceivable."[106] However, he also introduces Andersen as "the well-known poet and novelist," foregrounding *The Improvisatore*, which "stands unrivaled as a picture of scenery and manners in Southern Europe."[107] He shares the opinion of commentators who regard the works as mirrors of personality: "His works reflect his own kindly and open disposition, and are marked by humor, invention, and a poet's enthusiasm."[108] The writer concludes with words that would surely have pleased Andersen: "Possessing a delicate irony, joined to the thoughtful habit of the far North, and a richness of imagination truly oriental, the combination resulted in making of him one of the most thoroughly original writers the nineteenth century has produced."[109] Among other flattering observations, the author's final comments acknowledge Andersen's often overlooked sense of irony and show appreciation for the turn and degree of his imagination, something not to be taken for granted in an era of realism.

~

As with his novels and travel books, Andersen's autobiography elicited discussion by contemporary noteworthies such as Hale, Hoffman, Parker, and Reid, also receiving the scrutiny of Howells, who was in the midst of his tenure as editor of the *Atlantic Monthly* and was already a major force as a critic. Their opinions appeared in an array of magazines ranging from the popular *Godey's* to the highbrow *Harper's* and also found an outlet in two of the leading newspapers of the time, which means that some of their thoughts reached literally hundreds of thousands of readers. Many of the magazines as well as the two papers either had long runs or are still in publication, and most belong to the "quality" type. Even short-lived periodicals such as the *Massachusetts Quarterly Review* warrant attention because of their distinction and/or ideological orientation.

Reflecting a tradition going back to the seventeenth century, Hoffman and the anonymous reviewer of the *Christian Examiner,* among others, display primary interest in the moral fabric of the life portrayed in the book and, ultimately, its potential to improve the reader. Indeed, character or personality figure at least to some extent in all of the reviews, as one would expect in discussions of an autobiography. These reviewers, like those of Andersen's novels and travel books, are struck by attributes such as naturalness and childlikeness, occasionally viewed as sentimentality or puerility. Not surprisingly, the author's vanity comes to the fore in these reviews, though not all the writers condemn him for it. Certain commentators, for example Parker and the *Galaxy* reviewer, exhibit a more subjective, romantic orientation in their explicit or implicit concern for the experiential dimension of reading the book. Especially in such responses questions of genius, imagination, and artistry arise. Several reviewers categorically affirm Andersen's genius. In spite of some unequivocally positive opinions, however, the majority pass an at best lukewarm verdict on his imaginative faculty and his execution of the autobiography. All the same, a number recognize his humor, irony, and satire. Howells represents the realist camp in his view of the book's style and depiction of social reality, as does O'Sullivan's successor in a more restricted sense.

During the major phases of Andersen's critical reception in the United States, as in general, his autobiography received more reviews than any other single work he wrote, which is in itself a sign of the renown, if not necessarily the understanding, he attained early on.

Despite indications of a cultural memory lapse between 1847 and 1870, including a tacit assertion of his "timelessness," numerous notices disclose an already high level of familiarity with his work now deepened by acquaintance with his life. And regardless of the substantial ambivalence or indifference expressed toward him as an artist and an individual, the reviewers treat him as a figure of self-evident stature in the republic of letters. In at least one respect, moreover, they consider him to be unique. Virtually all of them reflect to one degree or another on the "romance" of Andersen's ascent from poverty to acclaim, that is, to that (intentional) mythic quality of his self-portrayal which W. Glyn Jones and Ivy York Möller-Christensen have remarked upon recently.[110] Now, the idea of pulling oneself up by one's own bootstraps, especially against seemingly overwhelming odds, has universal appeal; the great international success of Andersen's life story bears ample witness to this fact. However, the idea had peculiar resonance in mid- and later nineteenth-century America, where, as in Andersen's life, it represented both myth and reality. Soon to be associated popularly with the name Horatio Alger, Jr., and titles such as *Bound to Rise* and *Struggling Upward*, indeed, the notion was one of those closest to the heart of the young nation.[111] A sense of shared aspiration and experience in this regard may well be one of the chief reasons why, as the tribute in the *New York Times* states, Andersen enjoyed such "well-belovedness" among Americans.[112]

4

The Fairy Tales and Stories

AFTER THE MID-NINETEENTH CENTURY A CONSIDERABLE NUMBER OF American critics and their readers were clearly aware that Hans Christian Andersen was the author of novels and travel books as well as his autobiography. Nevertheless, it is safe to say that at least by the 1870s most Americans thought of him first and foremost as a writer of fairy tales. Several reviewers clearly read the longer fiction through the lens of the fairy tales and stories, and in his eulogy on Andersen's death George William Curtis asserts outright, "But whatever his larger works, the delightful fairy tales, so familiar in every land . . . are the true flowers of his genius."[1] Mindful of the qualification stated in chapter 1, it bears repeating that the fairy tales and stories received roughly the same number of reviews as the autobiography, the single most often discussed of Andersen's works. While most were clustered in the late 1840s and around 1870, like those of the other works, a significant percentage of them appeared in the intervening period as well.

Given the status of the fairy tales and stories in the American mind, it may come as a surprise that their renown did not lead to a substantially greater number of reviews. No less surprising is the fact that those written were, on average, far shorter than the critiques of Andersen's other works. None appeared in *Harper's* or the *Atlantic Monthly*, which reviewed several volumes of the Author's Edition, and few were published in other top-flight magazines. *Wonder Stories Told for Children* received two reviews—no loud echo in itself—and complete silence reigned over *Stories and Tales*, which perhaps partly explains the general lack of awareness of the later Andersen's growing realism. When pondering this state of affairs, one should take into account the fact that juveniles were regularly reviewed in American magazines of the time.[2] Horace Scudder's own *Seven Little People and their Friends* of 1867 received two columns in the *Atlantic*, and his *Dream Children* of the following year was afforded a page in the hoary

North American Review.[3] In both reviews Andersen serves as a touchstone for practitioners of the fairy tale! Whatever the reasons for critics' neglect of his fairy tales and stories may have been—a topic that will be addressed in chapter 7—this disregard is itself an important aspect of Andersen's reception in the United States. On the credit side of the ledger one should mention that the reviews of the tales are often illuminating despite their small number and brevity and that relevant comments appear in reviews of other works as well as in the eulogies written on Andersen's death. Moreover, the tales are the focus of some of the longer articles and essays discussed in chapter 5 as well as of Scudder's studies, which are treated in chapter 6.

1848–54

American reviewers did not respond as rapidly to Andersen's fairy tales and stories as to his other works—another sin of omission, as it were. In 1846 five British collections came out to an immediate critical reception in England; in less than two years, indeed, nine different editions elicited seven separate reviews in British periodicals.[4] One of the first volumes to appear, Mary Howitt's *Wonderful Stories for Children*, was also issued in New York in 1846, however to deaf critical ears in the United States.[5] Among the collections published in 1847 was Charles Beckwith-Lohmeyer's *A Christmas Greeting to My English Friends.*[6] It was apparently an expanded version of this book, issued in 1847 by C. S. Francis of New York, that attracted the first review of the tales in this country.[7]

The review appeared in New York's *Union Magazine* in April 1848.[8] The name of this monthly reflected the founder's attempt to capitalize on the influence of the American Art Union, an organization that boasted some ten thousand members.[9] A well-illustrated magazine "of Literature and Art," the *Union* sought to compete with *Godey's* and other periodicals addressed primarily to women.[10] Indeed, it was edited or coedited from its origin in 1847 to 1851 by Caroline M. Kirkland, who published a large contingent of women writers including Lydia H. Sigourney, Lydia M. Child, Catherine Sedgwick, and the internationally popular Swede Frederika Bremer. She also attracted contributions from authors such as Charles Fenno Hoffman, Rufus Wilmot Griswold, and Richard Henry Stoddard as well as figures on the order of Longfellow, Lowell, and Poe, whose "The Bells" and "The Poetic Principle" first appeared in the *Union*. At the end of 1848 the magazine was bought by John Sartain, then probably the best-known copper engraver in the country, and was henceforth called *Sartain's Union Magazine*. However, it did not prosper and left its owner a debtor in 1852.[11]

Caroline Kirkland (1801–64) came to the editorship of the magazine already well known for three realistic, satirical books in which she drew on her eight years of life in the rude Michigan Territory.[12] These volumes provided a corrective for the romanticized portrayals of the wilderness proffered by James Fenimore Cooper and others, reaping praise from critics such as Poe, who called the author one of the country's best writers.[13] On returning to New York, Kirkland wrote numerous essays and short stories for the *Union Magazine* and other periodicals, but her increasingly moralistic and sentimental tone did not earn her the same accolades as her books on the West, and she is remembered today chiefly as a pioneer of realism and in connection with women's studies. In addition to her original contributions to the *Union* Kirkland wrote the typically short book reviews that appeared in the magazine.[14]

Kirkland's notice of *A Christmas Greeting* begins as follows: "One of the most charming autobiographies of the day is 'The True Story of My Life' by the Danish poet, Andersen: and among the striking facts there narrated with so much feeling and simplicity, is the extraordinary popularity of his stories for children. Indeed, although his literary fame ostensibly rests upon his romance, 'The Improvisatore,' he seems to have become known in the north of Europe chiefly through his felicitous invention as a story-teller." After relating Andersen's fondness for reciting his stories at table, Kirkland continues: "Undoubtedly they owed not a little of their charm, on such occasions, to the manner and voice of the speaker; yet the fine observing faculties and eminent truthfulness and love which distinguish Andersen's character, admirably fit him to write for the young. The volumes of his tales heretofore published, have been very popular; and we doubt not such will be the case with the little book before us, which is issued in a very neat style, as one of Francis & Co's [*sic*] Little Library."

Kirkland offers little of the description and analysis one expects from a review, but her words are nonetheless illuminating in several respects. First of all, they reveal that she was quite conversant with Andersen's autobiography, perhaps even more so than with the fairy tales and stories themselves. They also confirm the fact that Andersen's early reputation in the United States rested on *The Improvisatore*.

Respecting the contents of the volume at hand, it is clear that Kirkland understands the notion "stories for children" literally, that is, without regard to the sophisticated *Kunstmärchen*. Accordingly, the inclusion of the "little book" in Francis's Little Library requires no comment. She discloses moreover that Americans knew and had warmly welcomed the volumes of tales already published, however their intended audience was perceived, and reviews or no. Like many critics of her generation, Kirkland reflects the neoclassical concern for the author's moral character, and Andersen clearly passes muster.[15] Considering her own early writing, it is not surprising that of all the salient aspects of the tales and Andersen's artistry she chooses to emphasize his "fine observing faculties," on which Howells and others remark, for the most part much later, in connection with the novels and travel books. One can only surmise her exact meaning, but in view of the fact that she is dealing with fairy tales, including the elusive "The Shadow," rather than stories, it would appear that she is foregrounding Andersen's ability to express experience or to delineate character as well as to render a faithful depiction of the surface of life. In attributing the charm of the tales, when told at table, to the manner and voice of the speaker, she approaches, perhaps unwittingly, a profound truth about Andersen's style, namely, that it is "orally inspired" rather than literary in character, which represents a significant source of difficulty in translating the works adequately.[16]

The *Living Age* noted the appearance of *A Christmas Greeting* in the May 1848 issue, and the *Southern Literary Messenger* announced the American edition of Charles Boner's *A Danish Story-Book* in July of the same year, echoing one of Kirkland's sentiments by characterizing the book briefly as "[o]ne of the most graceful *juveniles* we have seen for a long time."[17] However, the next more concerted effort to assess the tales came with a review of Mary Howitt's *Hans Andersen's Story-Book* that appeared in *Sartain's Union Magazine* in February 1849.[18] By this time Caroline Kirkland shared the editorship and, apparently, the book reviewing of the magazine with John S. Hart (1810–77), who later, as a professor at Princeton University, taught what is said to have been the first college course on American literature and wrote a textbook on the subject for schools and colleges.[19] Currently a teacher in Philadelphia, whither Sartain moved the editorial offices upon purchasing the magazine, Hart indeed appears to have been the sole editor for all practical purposes.[20] It is impossible to determine the author of the review beyond doubt, but the comments themselves suggest either a more observant and insightful Kirkland or, more likely, her colleague.[21]

In any event, the review is quite positive in tone: "There has been nothing in the way of children's literature more charming than the quaint and delicate fancies of this author. A vein of quizzical mysticism runs through them, heightened by pathetic touches, and preserved from frivolity by a fine moral tone—suggestive rather than monitory. Their quiet humor makes them as fascinating to mothers as to children; and an infusion of Mary Howitt leaves nothing to desire. The edition just published by Messrs. Francis is in the neatest form, with beautiful illustrations; and the Memoir by Mary Howitt, is in her own sweet manner. We recommend this book with confidence."[22]

In all its brevity the review at least touches on several prominent features of Andersen's fairy tales and stories that are all too often overlooked even in more extensive discussions. Though the ubiquitous label "charming" introduces the review, the writer's central concern is clearly the moral nature of the works. Significantly, he gives to understand that their morality is implicit rather than explicit, that is, that it emanates from the texts as wholes rather than residing, for example, in an appended lesson. He categorizes them as children's literature, to be sure, pointing to the fine illustrations in the volume, but is quite aware of their maturity. Moreover, he locates the source of their maturity in their humor, a core element of the works too often neglected but apparent enough in "The Emperor's New Clothes," "The Princess on the Pea," "The Galoshes of Fortune," and others among the twenty-two pieces that comprise the volume. Why the humor of the tales makes them fascinating to mothers, rather than to fathers, or to both, is not clear. Perhaps the restriction to women speaks for Kirkland's authorship or for what at this time in history was a virtually universal association of women with the nursery. The "quizzical mysticism" surely refers to the supernatural element of the works, particularly the opaqueness of texts such as "The Shadow" and "The Snow Queen," which elicit discussion among Andersen scholars to this day.[23] Although Caroline Kirkland is considered an early realist—assuming for a moment, counterintuitively, that she wrote the review—it is worth noting in passing that she, in contrast to William Dean Howells in the early seventies, spoke most favorably of Mary Howitt's English style.

A notice of three newly published collections of fairy tales and stories came out in the *Literary World* on November 16, 1850.[24] By this point in time Charles Fenno Hoffman had relinquished the editor-

ship of the magazine, which was now owned and edited by the brothers Evert Augustus Duyckinck (1816–78) and George Long Duyckinck (1823–63).[25] The elder brother had earlier coedited the short-
lived but reputedly brilliant magazine *Arcturus,* and the two later
collaborated on the *Cyclopaedia of American Literature* (1855), the most
comprehensive work of its kind around midcentury.[26] Both were
prominent members of New York literary society and enabled many
writers to make their first appearance in print.

The authorship of the notice remains obscure—was the writer one
of the Duyckinck brothers or even Caroline Kirkland, who was reviewing for the *Literary World* as well as for *Sartain's* about this time?[27]
Whatever the case may be, one can state with absolute certainty that
the individual was not as familiar with Andersen as Hoffman: "Three
of the delightful little volumes of the Swedish [!] story-teller: simple
and fanciful, and in their pure style and clear morality, among the
pleasantest educational books of the age. Hans Andersen is a capital
teacher for the young, and carries them away in moonlight fancies
and fairy adventures, which do not destroy their liking for every-day
objects. We imagine a worthy boy, after reading one of Hans Andersen's stories, would eat his supper with a superior relish." "Delightful," "simple," "fanciful," "clear morality"—such adjectives and the
concern for morals recur frequently in critical reactions to the fairy
tales and stories. Despite the alleged clearness of their morality and
"educational" value, the emphasis placed on their imaginative and
supernatural elements suggests that this reviewer, like his colleague
at *Sartain's,* considers the "lesson" to be tacit. Moreover, he sees no
danger of the tales creating conflict between the worlds of fancy and
reality in (young) readers. On the contrary, banally or involuntarily
humorous though it may be, his example of the works' possible
impact on the reader implies that they exert a positive influence precisely in real-world matters and that they do so by addressing the character of the individual as a whole rather than one particular moral
issue or another via the intellect, as in the fable, especially in its eighteenth-century instantiation.

Another review of the three collections discussed in the *Literary
World* appeared in *Sartain's Union Magazine* in February 1851.[28] This
critic's identity is also elusive, but at least one expression speaks for
the individual who reviewed *Hans Andersen's Story-Book* for *Sartain's* in
1849, most likely future Princeton professor John S. Hart: "The Scandinavians in these latter days seem destined to carry off the palm
against the world. They can boast the most distinguished singer

[Jenny Lind], the first of living female novelists [Frederika Bremer], the greatest of recent dramatists [Bjørnstjerne Bjørnson], and the only successful writer of fairy tales. Just as fairyland seemed vanishing before the clear sunlight of utilitarianism, Hans Andersen, with the magic of his peculiar genius, drew once more the mystic spell over the scene, and peopled the earth anew with these elfin tribes. As a story-teller for children, he stands at this time unrivalled. Many a young eye throughout England and America will beam with pleasure, at the announcement of another volume of his Tales, translated into the mother tongue."

The reviewer devotes half of his notice to an expression of respect for the culture of Scandinavia, which, as we saw earlier, was presently experiencing great popularity in the United States. However, he does so less for the sake of Northern culture per se than to stress and contextualize Andersen's success as a writer of fairy tales—here, to be sure, without acknowledging their appeal to adults, mothers or otherwise. Reminiscent of the formulation "quizzical mysticism" used in the earlier *Sartain* review, the "mystic spell" cast over the "scene" again highlights the magical, or supernatural, element of the tales, which, in a volume containing "The Tinder Box," "Thumbelina," "The Wild Swans," and "Little Ida's Flowers," is possibly more pronounced, if less enigmatic, than in *Hans Andersen's Story-Book*.[29] The reviewer makes what is perhaps his most interesting observation in the key third sentence, where he counterposes "fairyland," read the romantic, idealist imagination, and "utilitarianism," that is, that amalgam of Benthamite, rationalist-materialist, and industrialist ideas which grew increasingly more firmly alloyed over the course of the nineteenth century. The reviewer gives both their due: formerly on the verge of vanishing, "fairyland" persists thanks to Andersen—a good thing, the phrasing indicates; utilitarianism possesses the metaphorical character of "pure sunlight," also a good thing, if not quite as much so. In this not quite perfect state of equipoise the reviewer resembles the Andersen of "Vänö and Glänö," in which modern technology supplants legend and the balance tips to the side of modernist sobriety, not, however, without a concomitant sense of impoverishment.[30] Indeed, the reviewer's relative optimism cannot conceal the fact that the imagination's once powerful hold on life is weakening—and already at midcentury. Some twenty-five years later Horace Scudder would draw a similar comparison, but before a fait almost accompli.

In December of 1852 the *Southern Literary Messenger* published a review of *Hans Andersen's Story-Book*, which Francis reissued the same year.[31] The *Messenger* was founded in 1834 in Richmond, Virginia, as a means of encouraging Southern writers to assert their cultural independence from the North, and the magazine indeed became the leading voice of the region.[32] However, it spent most of its thirty years of existence on precarious financial footing, never rising above four thousand subscribers, which led one editor to complain in 1861 that Southern patriotism, that "funniest of things," "enables a man to abuse the Yankees, to curse the Yankees, to fight the Yankees, to do everything but quit taking the Yankee papers."[33] Despite its regionalist rhetoric, the magazine in fact published Northern writers from its inception, including many of those mentioned in these pages. One editor, himself an ardent Southerner, went so far as to express pride in his Northern contributors, albeit during the 1840s. The most prominent figure in the history of the *Messenger* was Edgar Allan Poe, who edited the magazine in 1836 and wrote for it again in 1848–49. With the exception of its stance on slavery and its concern for Southern history, the periodical was much like its Northern competitors, down to its moral-sentimental stories. Following Poe's early criticism, which made the magazine a name, book reviewing became irregular, but it enjoyed a resurgence in the 1850s, during which the comment on *Hans Andersen's Story-Book* appeared.

The review was one of several published under the title "A Handful of Autumn Leaves" by John Esten Cooke. Cooke (1830–86) was soon to become popular in North and South alike, particularly as a writer of novels and romances indebted to Irving, Cooper, and Alexandre Dumas (père), that is, prose that was idealized and sentimental, like most fiction of the age, but also highly entertaining.[34] At the time in question he was a friend of John Reuben Thompson, editor of the *Messenger* from 1847 to 1860, who called on him both to contribute to the magazine and to coedit it in his absence in 1850 and 1854.[35] Cooke presents Andersen's volume as a "collection of the Danish novelists [*sic*] juvenile tales, which Francis has just published for children; and for me. Who does not love Andersen: that bright hearted, bright-souled, bright-eyed Dane? Who has not been delighted with the simple and grand pathos of 'The Little Match Girl,' 'The Snow Queen,' and 'The Picture Book Without Pictures?' [*sic*].[36] For my part, I have almost a personal affection for the honest heart, which conceived these pure and touching thoughts: as I have an admiration perfectly genuine, for the hand which placed those thoughts in such bright and moving words."

Cooke is especially taken with the *Picture Book Without Pictures*. The work, he writes, "proves to me that a poet of the first rank was spoiled, when Andersen became a novelist; though certainly he ranks high as a poet also, in his native land. Here and in England he is known scarcely atall [*sic*], but as the author of the 'Improvisatore.' Andersen has a peculiar child-like tenderness, which bears a striking resemblance to the same quality in Jean Paul Richter. The two men are alike in many other points. There is much quaintness about Andersen, and a power of assimilating his own thoughts to a child's which is very striking. . . . Some of the 'Pictures' in this little book, are perfect paintings; and it is quite evident that the artist has been to Italy, and acquired the artist-eye. He can thus at any time, group the suggestive points in a picture or thought, and convey a perfectly distinct idea to the reader. The soul of the poet, the eye of the painter! all honor to the child poet." Following a couple of passages from the text, Cooke concludes, "A painter would certainly find no difficulty in painting these scenes, and so with all of Andersen's works. There is, above and beyond all, about this man and his writings, a cheerful, hopeful, loving atmosphere, which will make him and his books favorites with all readers."

Cooke makes a number of points worth noting. One need not be acquainted with his own work to recognize him as a romantic, for he speaks in the very first sentence, and then elsewhere, of the tales' impact on him, or his personal experience of them. They were published "for him"; he has an almost personal affection for their creator. This experience is emotional and imaginative in nature, for it is the simple yet grand pathos of the tales that delights him and the artist's eye apparent in them that impresses him. The word "moral" never occurs, the single word "pure" merely alluding to the notion. Cooke expresses marked appreciation for the individual revealed in the texts—whom he apparently knows from his autobiography and first novel—especially for his optimistic outlook on life and cheerful, tender disposition. The comparison to Jean Paul with regard to tenderness, quaintness, and the ability to see the world through a child's eyes is high praise, for the German novelist ranked among the most popular writers of his nation in the United States during the 1830s and 1840s, partly due to the influence of Carlyle and Madame de Staël, and remained popular well into the second half of the century.[37] Like Howells and other reviewers of the novels and travel books Cooke respects Andersen's artistry, specifically his poetic prose and his ability to extract the essential features of a scene—or an idea—and to transform them into an appropriate verbal image. Despite Gotthold Ephraim Lessing's *Laokoon,* the Horatian concept of ut pictura poesis—or, in this case, ut pictura fabula—regained ascendancy during the nineteenth century, even before the advent of realism.[38] More than once Cooke speaks of the volume of tales and its author in connection with children's literature. Nonetheless, and perhaps as overtly as any other reviewer, he writes of both as an adult for adults.

In the April issue of the *Messenger* in 1854 we read the following lines: "Hans Andersen, that noble poet whose bright pen seems illuminated always by the internal light of noble thought, is no longer at liberty to compose brilliant 'Improvisatores,' but must expend his thoughts and time and toil upon fairy tales; upon 'Wonder Books' and 'Picture Books,' and countless histories of Kay's and Gerdas, little match girls, and all the personages who people the bright realm of Faëry."[39] Even as reproduced here, the passage is informative. While the piece in which it appears is unsigned, the light metaphor, which occurs five times in less than ten lines, the reference to the *Picture Book,* and the allusions to the two tales all recall the preceding review and speak eloquently for Cooke as the author.[40] Moreover, the passage demonstrates that eight years after the first edition of Andersen's fairy tales and stories appeared in London and New York at least some Americans thought of the Dane primarily as a novelist, though *The Improvisatore* preceded the tales into the English-speaking world by only one year. The rhetorical stance of the passage, finally, implies a negative verdict on Andersen's shift from long to short prose.

However, a different picture emerges when one considers the environment in which the passage is situated. It appears in an article entitled "The New Literature," which is in almost equal parts a review of two children's books and a short informal essay on a related phenomenon of current interest. In what he calls a "prolonged introduction" to the review proper Cooke observes that "[n]o trait in the literary development of the age is more striking than the importance which seems suddenly to have attached to what we call juveniles— books for children, that is to say."[41] He then points to the appearance the preceding year of several children's books written by authors such as Stoddard and Hawthorne, whose *A Wonder Book* and *Tanglewood Tales* were published in 1852 and 1853, respectively. Subsequently, he asks in mock concern, "Where will it end?" and then, extending the ploy, writes of several major British and French figures in the same tongue-in-cheek manner as in the passage on Andersen. Finally revealing his true opinion, Cooke avers that he rejoices in the development, for "[i]t will improve letters. Intellect is above all too self-reliant, and is apt to exalt the brain above the heart—a great mistake, a fatal error. The pure intellect divorced from the heart, by which we mean the sympathies, impulses, feelings of every description, which characterize our moral nature, is a machine without a regulating wheel—a ship without a compass."[42]

Here, Cooke delivers himself of what amounts to a romantic manifesto writ small, revolving around sensibility as a bellwether in life and art and as an expression of man's moral character—somewhat belated even in the American context, to be sure, but illuminating for present purposes all the same. Cooke feels that the new literary movement has "the desired tendency" and thus, by inference, the potential to counter the ongoing "march of intellect" initiated by British Member of Parliament, Lord Chancellor, and cofounder of the distinguished *Edinburgh Review,* Henry Peter Lord Brougham (1778–1868), in an attempt to promote practical knowledge.[43] Clearly, Cooke ranks Andersen among the leaders of this movement, considering the fairy tales and stories to be important manifestations of sensibility and, thus, morality. While others shared his perception of the works' moral spirit, he would appear to have had little company in his view that writing for children is a highly desirable pursuit for major authors. And though American critics reckoned Andersen matter-of-factly among contemporary authors of stature, Cooke probably had even fewer colleagues who could have written, with Andersen, among others, in mind, "There is no room for doubt—the child rules and leads in contented vassalage the best minds of the Old and the New World—Europe and America."[44]

1860–63

In the summer of 1860 a collection of eighteen fairy tales and stories entitled *The Sand-Hills of Jutland* (*En historie fra klitterne*) appeared in London and Boston, eliciting a brief comment in the August issue of the *Southern Literary Messenger.*[45] With the May number of that year John Reuben Thompson had turned over the editorship of the magazine to George William Bagby, a longtime contributor and friend. In contrast to Thompson and John Esten Cooke, who tended toward earnestness and even exaltation in their writing, Bagby (1828–83) was a humorist known for witty stories, satiric sketches, and especially realistic but favorable portrayals of life among the common folk of antebellum Virginia.[46] Indeed, humor and satire characterize the editorials and reviews he wrote for the *Messenger.*[47]

The title story of the collection suggests what perusal of the contents confirms: that the volume does not contain Andersen's lightest fare. Indeed, disappointment, pain, a sense of the transience of life, and the Christian promise of compensation often more implicit than explicit dominate a significant number of these works, some of which display a realistic style. Bagby's comments are therefore only partly understandable: "Hans wields a dark, grey goose quill, very sharply pointed. His stories are wild, weird, satirical. It is a fine thing to make a female stork act out the follies of the gentler sex. Nobody blames you for it." Bagby's overall characterization applies to so few works in this collection—"The Bottle Neck" for example—that one suspects he allowed a preconception to influence his reading or, worse, did not read them all. The intent of his comment on "The Marsh King's Daughter" is unclear: Does he approve of the satirist's self-exculpatory sleight of hand, or is he criticizing the veiled nature of the satire, feeling that a less circuitous approach would have been more responsible and thus more honorable? Unlike most of his peers, and whether based on the works in the present volume or not, in any event, he clearly perceives the satirist in Andersen—perhaps it sometimes takes one to know one—as well as the darker side and the imaginative dimension of his work.

Before leaving Bagby and the *Southern Literary Messenger,* which did not survive the Civil War, mention should be made of a more sober article he published in the issue for July–August 1862.[48] Entitled "A Witch in the Nursery," the piece presents a critique of international writing for children past and present. Toward the end, Bagby opines, "In educational books—education of children by means of books of a direct and personal kind—we are supplied to overflowing. More than enough have we of little primers of all the arts and sciences, and geographies and histories, and the useful knowledges; but, of books well suited to the earliest and best feelings, and the purest principles, as indirectly, but no less profoundly, instilled through the heart and the imagination, oh! how few, in comparison with the masses of trash, or of sanguinary and otherwise unwholesome excitement! At the top of the best of this class of books we should place the children's stories of Hans Christian Andersen. . . ."[49] Bagby appears to ensconce

Andersen in the nursery as firmly as any of the Dane's American reviewers, though one should consider the fact that many of them—including Bagby himself, judging from his earlier appreciation of Andersen's satire—momentarily suspend their awareness of Andersen as a writer for adults when engaged in the seemingly self-evident and less demanding business of discussing him as a children's author. Even if Andersen had never written for anyone beyond school age, however, he would have earned a unique and permanent place in the hearts of men like Bagby, who respected what they saw as his ability to mold the souls and minds of the young through the power of fantasy and emotion. In this regard, indeed, Bagby foreshadows the greatest of Andersen's disciples in the United States, Horace E. Scudder.

Another notice of *The Sand-Hills of Jutland* came out in the *New Englander* in November of 1860.[50] Published in New Haven for most of its run, from 1843 to 1892, the magazine was associated with Yale University and was thus a leading voice of Congregationalism and orthodox morality in its time.[51] Though never an exclusively theological review, it gave considerable space to religious matters, criticizing Catholicism and transcendentalism, among other things, and based its choice of articles, fiction, and poetry largely on religious considerations. Despite its provenance the magazine never exceeded 1,000 subscribers. While presently reckoned among the best of contemporary religious quarterlies on the whole, its literary criticism was not distinguished. The identity of Andersen's reviewer is unknown, but it may well have been William L. Kingsley, a Yale man, Congregational minister, and the editor of the magazine at the time the review appeared, certainly someone of a similar turn of mind.[52]

The review describes the collection as a "new volume of stories by that prince of modern story tellers, HANS CHRISTIAN ANDERSEN. We found them capital reading in the warm days of summer, and, we doubt not, others will find them equally good in the long evenings of winter that are so soon to come. Seated on the rocks, with the cool sea-breezes blowing full upon us, we yielded ourselves to their fascination, and cared not to ask whether these new stories were better or poorer than those which gained a world-wide reputation for their author. It was enough that they bore unmistakable evidence of the source from which they came. Of course they are extravagant as any tale of the Arabian Nights. Of course they are simple as a nursery rhyme. But they bear the marks of the inspiration of genius, though they set at defiance every rule of criticism. Then the spirit they breathe is so tender, so gentle, so kind, at times so joyous; they manifest such a sympathy for the poor, for the down-trodden and all who are in distress; the lessons they teach, without being too obtrusive, are so pure, and so elevated, that we cannot but wish the widest circulation throughout the whole land."

Following his introductory remarks, the reviewer expresses, in a manner consistent with his respect and fondness for Andersen, a reservation that has not been lost on later critics, namely, that the fairy tales and stories written after 1850 do not uniformly reach the level attained by those published earlier.[53] Moreover, the "mysticism" and simplicity they retain weigh against them for him, in contrast to many other writers. On the other hand, he appreciates the (flawed) genius of the tales, which he virtually identifies with their originality, as well as the tacit quality of their "lessons." In spite of these more romantic considerations, one suspects that his ultimate approval of the volume rests on a neoclassical respect for the character revealed in it, especially as expressed in concern for moral integrity and the poor in spirit and pocket.

In the spring of 1863 a new volume of stories appeared under the title *The Ice-Maiden, and Other Tales.*[54] The collection has the distinction of being the first by an American translator, one Fanny Fuller of Philadelphia, who adhered to the then not unusual practice of working from a German version of the original.[55] The volume elicited two reviews in April of the year. One came out in *Peterson's Magazine,* a monthly modeled after *Godey's* that became the leading periodical of its kind in the nation, boasting 140,000 subscribers in 1869.[56] Little more than an announcement of publication, the notice describes the collection merely as "a very credible performance" by the translator. The second review appeared in the *Continental Monthly,* which was discussed in chapter 2.[57] Indeed, it came out in the same issue as the notice of *In Sweden* treated in that chapter, the last edited by Charles Godfrey Leland, and was thus most likely written by him as well.[58]

The review begins with what can only be considered the highest praise: "Probably no writer of stories for the young ever equaled Hans Christian Andersen; certainly none ever succeeded as he has done in reproducing the nameless charm of the real fairy tale which springs up without an author among the people—the best specimens of which are the stories collected by the Brothers Grimm in Germany." Later scholarship would reveal that the Grimms' adaptations of what were in fact folktales were often so extensive that they can virtually be considered original works, much as in the case of several stories by

Andersen that are based on Danish folktales.[59] If the people never spoke directly through either the Germans or the Dane, however, at least Andersen independently captured an element of the "primitive," which the romantics cherished and associated with childhood in both the individual and the human race, an element which he put to a use dear to the nineteenth century: "But this exquisite fascination of an inner life in animals and in inanimate objects, which every child's mind produces from dolls and other puppets, and which makes fairies of flowers, is by Andersen adroitly turned to good moral and instructive purpose, without losing the original sweet and simple charm which blends the real and the imaginary. Here he surpasses all other tale writers, nearly all of whom, in their efforts at simplicity in such narratives, generally become supremely silly."

Leland appreciates the subtle sophistication of the fairy tales and stories: "Perhaps the highest compliment which can be paid them is the truthful assertion that any person can read them with keen interest, and never reflect that they were written for young people." In contrast to the reviewer in the *New Englander,* he finds no decline in the quality of the later works, which are "all in Andersen's usual happy and successful vein; for he is preëminently an *equal* writer, and never falls behind himself." Moreover, he recognizes and welcomes the realism of the title work and the faculty for observation apparent in the others as well, though he obviously values their more fanciful features: "Poetry and prose meet in them on equal grounds, and any of them in verse would be charming. The main reason for this is that such stories[,] to charm[,] must set forth natural objects with Irving-like fidelity; nay, the writer must, with a few words, bring before us scènes and things as in a mirror. In this 'The Ice Maiden' excels; Swiss life is depicted as though we were listening to *yodle* songs on the mountains, and felt the superstitions of the icy winter nights taking hold of our souls." Indeed, Leland writes of the other three stories— he can devote some detail to them because there are only four in all— more as they appeal to him as an adult than as they might be read by a child: "'The Psyche' is an art-story. Most writers would have made it a legend of 'high' art, but it is far sweeter and more impressive from the sad simplicity and gentleness with which it is here told. 'The Butterfly,' on the contrary, is a delightful little burlesque on flirtations and fops; and 'The Snail and the Rose Tree' is much like it. Both are really fables of the highest order, or shrewd prose epigrams."

Like Howells in a couple of his *Atlantic* reviews, Leland includes thoughts on the quality of the translation, deeming it "well translated;

very well, notwithstanding one or two trifling inadvertencies. . . . A *Skytte,* for instance, in Danish, or *Schutz* [*sic*], in German, is generally termed among the fraternity of sportsmen a 'shot,' and not a 'shooter'. . . ." The passage is significant because it suggests that Leland had a command of Danish sufficient to enable him to read Andersen's fairy tales and stories in the original, which would lend his comments on the works and the translation a distinction and authoritativeness lacking in most.[60] This seems all the more probable since he then writes, "But the spirit of the original is charmingly preserved, and Miss Fuller has the rare gift of using short and simple words, which are the best in the world when one knows how to use them as she does"—the best, certainly, in the sense of the most appropriate, since, according to Anker Jensen and others after him, it is precisely the repeated use of a large number of simple words that characterizes Andersen's unique style.[61]

1870–75

An inexact but nonetheless instructive measure of Andersen's stature in the United States of the nineteenth century is the frequency with which his name appeared randomly in American magazines and newspapers of the time, that is, in addition to reviews and articles devoted specifically to his works. A search of even the relatively few magazines accessible on the Internet yields dozens of hits related to him.[62] As mentioned earlier, he figures in reviews of several of Horace Scudder's collections of stories.[63] In one published in the *Atlantic Monthly* in 1863, for example, Henry Mills Alden writes that Scudder's stories are more consciously works of art than Andersen's "in an intellectual sense," by which he means that Scudder's tales are more literary in style, those by Andersen having been "written, we imagine, very much as they were told."[64] The column "Table Talk" in an issue of *Appleton's Journal* published in 1869 contains anonymous words of praise for Andersen as an artist and an individual, calling him "not only the most brilliant and gifted, but also the most modest and kind-hearted of story-tellers. Here is what he wrote recently about the fairy tales of his Norwegian rival Bjornson [*sic*]: 'These fairy-tales, I honestly believe, are the best which have appeared in Europe for many years past.'"[65] Such random occurrences would likely reward an independent study. The one demonstrates an awareness of the orality of Andersen's narrative style in the tales; the other exhibits the high regard in which his artistry and character were held. Both disclose that by the 1860s Andersen and his fairy tales and stories were very much abroad in the—lettered as well as general—American public, notwithstanding the fact that the later editions received so few formal reviews.

The initial critical response to Andersen's *Wonder Stories Told for Children,* the first of the two volumes of tales contained in the Author's Edition, appeared in the April issue of *Putnam's Magazine* in 1870.[66] We recall from chapter 3 that *Putnam's* had by now descended from the high point it reached during the 1850s. However, older figures such as William Cullen Bryant still contributed occasionally, and the postwar generation that now dominated the magazine's pages included Howells.[67] According to Mott, the writing in the departments at this time was better than that in the articles.[68] Among the former was "Literature—At Home," for which Edmund Clarence Stedman was responsible until the issue in question. It is not certain whether Stedman wrote the comments on Andersen's tales or whether the author was his successor, Parke Godwin (1816–1904), a journalist and reformer who supported Brook Farm, writing for and then coediting the *Harbinger,* and who was later associated with New York's *Evening Post* for forty-five years, the last four as editor.[69] However, internal evidence provided below points to Stedman.

The marvelous nature of the works governs this reader's impressions: "They [the "wonder stories"] are happily named, for among the various elements which enter into their composition the element of wonder is most prominent, holding the same place in them that it does in the romantic epics of Tasso, Ariosto, and Spenser, and that its more vigorous development, Imagination, does in 'The Midsummer Night's Dream' [*sic*], and 'The Tempest.' What Shakespeare is in the drama, that Andersen is in fairy-lore, of which he is the greatest master that ever lived. The fairy-story tellers of France, Charles Perrault, Madame D'Aulnoy, and their followers, occupy but a scanty plot of ground in Fairy Land beside his possessions,—a mere strip of barren, workaday soil on the hither edge of his fruitful, enchanted kingdom. They who most resemble him are the nameless tellers of German *Märchen,* and to him the best of these 'Are as moonlight unto sunlight, or as water unto wine.' It was observed of Swift by Stella [the Dean's intimate, Esther Johnson] that he could write beautifully about a broom-stick, but Andersen exceeds Swift, in that he can write beautifully about many a smaller thing than a broom-stick,—a pack of cards, a pen and an inkstand, a tinder-box, a tin soldier, a slate-pencil,—in short, about any thing that we can name. His invention is inexhaustible."

In a general announcement of the Author's Edition that appeared in the same department in the November issue of *Putnam's* for 1869, Stedman writes that Andersen's "wonderful children's stories . . . are in the world of fairy-lore what the plays of Shakespeare are in the larger world of the drama."[70] The phraseology and location of the passage alone offer convincing evidence that Stedman wrote the review in the later issue of the magazine, but that is not all. To be sure, the comments represent more a panegyric to Andersen than an analysis of his stories, and, as one of the leading American critics of his time, Stedman could certainly have delivered a rigorous commentary.[71] However, Stedman was also something of an aesthete, a romantic writing in a dawning age of realism. In his circle of friends, which included the poets Richard Henry Stoddard, Bayard Taylor, Thomas Bailey Aldrich, and others, Stoddard's *Songs of Summer* (1855) had inspired a movement of poetry for poetry's sake. In his own later *Poets of America* (1885), the first serious survey of American poetry, he rejected the ethical and polemical zeal of the preceding generation in favor of the meditations arising from "simple love of beauty and song" of his own.[72] It is above all the premium put on invention and imagination in the review, not to mention the poetic quality of its diction, that betray Stedman as the author.[73]

Not all of Andersen's reviewers were as favorably impressed by the imagination displayed in his fairy tales and stories as Stedman. In her treatment of the autobiography in the *Ladies' Repository* Emily F. Wheeler concedes that the texts show Andersen's poetic powers to best advantage and are the most likely of all his works to secure him enduring fame.[74] Even in the midst of generally positive comments, however, her reservations shine through: "His other writings become insignificant beside these [the tales]. For them his genius seems perfectly fitted. . . . Tiny but daintily perfect are these tales; and how hard it is to write such little things well, only those who have tried can understand.[75] They are not less artistic because small; and for quaint humor and tender purity they are unique. It is a fairy world to which he transports us; and his frost-work is none the less beautiful that it withers in the warm light of reality. One of the most popular ["The Fir Tree" (Grantræet)] tells of the fortunes of a fir-tree, that in its native wood sighed for greater splendors, that became a Christmas-tree, and, after a night of glory, was left to die; and its pathetic perfection makes it uselessly affecting to imaginative readers."[76]

Another reviewer for the *Ladies' Repository,* or Wheeler in a more censorious mood, criticizes the disparity between faerie and reality in the fairy tales and stories more pointedly: "Hans Christian Andersen is sufficiently well known as a writer both for adults and children. With many he is a great favorite. We admire him as a writer for his style, his imagination, his easy and simple power of expression, and a certain *naive* grace in telling a story. We do not admire as a general thing his stories for children. They deal so largely in the element of wonder, in those unreal and impossible spheres of supernatural and superhuman events, which, while they may be well enough for children to dream about once in awhile, are not wholesome to dwell in."[77]

The review is interesting both for its acknowledgment of Andersen's poetic range and appeal, as late as 1870, and for its criticism of the fairy tales and stories. The latter appears to spring from a realist sensibility, according to which the things of this world best occupy the mind, as well as from a psychological fastidiousness which, later in the nineteenth century, would lead in the United States to the bowdlerization of the Grimms and Andersen and then, in the twentieth, to their banalization by Hollywood. The present reviewer was not alone in these sentiments. In his review of *O. T.* in the *Atlantic Monthly* Howells asserts that Andersen's "fancy is apt to run wild, and his emotionality is so abundant that he too often indulges himself in the luxury of wringing his little readers' hearts upon no just occasion whatever."[78] Thereupon, he cites the example of "The Fir Tree" (to which Wheeler may be indebted), a tale he regards as "so pathetically and carefully told, that it is wickedly and uselessly affecting in a world where there is possible and actual human sorrow enough to make children wretched with, if they must be tormented before their time. . . ."[79]

The collection of fairy tales and stories in the Author's Edition was not the only one to appear in 1870. That year, an even larger volume containing the work of several translators came out in London under the title *Fairy Tales and Sketches.*[80] In June 1871 it was reviewed in the *Overland Monthly,* probably by W. C. Bartlett, the editor of San Francisco's *Evening Bulletin,* who had replaced Bret Harte as editor of the magazine earlier in the year.[81] Given the nature of Harte's work, it is safe to say that Andersen would not have fared as well at the hands of the departed editor as he in fact did: "We can not be displeased with the good man's gentle egotism; his lovely life has bloomed out in the loveliest stories ever written for the delight of little folks and children of larger growth. No such beautiful fairy tales and sketches as these brightened the childhood of the mature men and women of this English-speaking generation. It was not until 1836 [!] that any of Andersen's novels were translated into English, and the first of his wonderful stories for children, so far as we know of them, did not appear until long afterward. These fairy tales are characterized by delicacy of imagination, ingenuity, and an artful artlessness which are most charming. Yet, under all the playful improbability of the fairy tale is a vein of gentle satire which commends the tale to wiser heads than those of the children. The author does not bore the little folks with the hidden moral of 'The Ugly Duckling,' nor with the mild sarcasm which is embedded in the story of the Princess, whose claim to royal birth was established by her having slept uncomfortably with the pea concealed under her pile of swan's-down mattresses. And one may search all through Andersen's stories for one which has no purpose."

The most compelling of the reviewer's observations are his repeated indications that the fairy tales and stories can be read with profit by young and old alike. They are written for the "delight of little folks and children of larger growth"; they are characterized by "artful artlessness"; they reveal an element of satire that appeals to "wiser heads than those of the children"; and none of them lacks a "hidden," or implicit, moral purpose, which in its contexts and ramifications in life is certainly more apparent to adults than to children. Unlike the individual who discussed Andersen's autobiography the same month in *Scribner's Monthly*, this reviewer has a sufficient grasp of literary history to know that the Dane did not write for his grandparents. However, his inaccuracy or uncertainty regarding when *The Improvisatore* and the fairy tales and stories first appeared in English nonetheless reflects an aura of timelessness about Andersen and his work. This nimbus is only heightened when one realizes that the review is generic, that is, that it could apply to any collection of Andersen's tales. The two texts mentioned specifically are not even included in the volume ostensibly under review. One therefore need not be inclined to cynicism to consider the possibility that the reviewer did not bother to read the pieces in this collection.

The final writings to be discussed in this chapter were all published on the occasion of Andersen's death, the first of them appearing in the New York weekly *Appleton's Journal* on August 21, 1875.[82] At this point in time the department "Editor's Table," in which the comments appeared, was the bailiwick of Oliver Bell Bunce, who was best known for his early plays, though he later wrote novels and popular history.[83] Written only a couple of weeks after Andersen's death, the piece is more a eulogy than a review in the strict sense, but it is clear that the fairy tales and stories were uppermost in the author's mind: "The singular sweetness, simplicity, and purity of all Hans Christian Andersen's writings reflect the quality and give the keynote of the man himself. Of few authors can it be so emphatically said, as he himself used to say, that his works were himself. They are serene like himself, and exhibit all his delicate shades of feeling. They are ever instinct with a love of mankind, a bright way of looking upon the world (which he often called 'the good world'), and, above all, a very sincere and childlike love of children."[84] Bunce underscores both the extent and uniqueness of Andersen's appeal: "He was one of the cosmopolitan writers, like Dickens, like Victor Hugo, like Turgeneff, like Longfellow. It is very rarely that even the greatest literary genius can impose his works upon foreign minds; it is still more rarely that a man can write as Andersen did, so as to please at once Danish and English, German and Russian children."[85] The fact that Andersen "was as welcome at the firesides of St. Petersburg and San Francisco as at those of Copenhagen" demonstrates that "without a very wonderful imagination, and even without the highest faculty of dramatic power, he was a master of the chord of nature which touches the universal human heart."[86]

Bunce continues with a litany of Andersen's personality and character traits, as they impressed themselves upon his work: "He was kind, unselfish, cheerful, fresh, clear, and simple, a gentlest teacher of the virtues, with a light, pure, graceful, fancy, which lent poetry and imparted pleasure to his thoughts, and made the few simple principles he wished to inculcate easy to receive; and the emotions he thus touched are those which civilized humanity partakes in common. . . . Those who knew him speak of him as a sort of typified innocence. . . ."[87] For Bunce, the most gratifying deduction to be drawn from Andersen's influence, "personally and in a literary sense, is that *goodness* of intellect is able to exercise a power often denied to intellectual *greatness*," whereupon he compares Andersen favorably to Jonathan Swift.[88] In conclusion, he writes, "It is an honor that Hans Andersen would have been happiest to cherish that his loss will chiefly be felt by the little children of the nations."[89]

To one willing to disregard its superlative and virtually hagiographic tone, the review discloses an awareness that Andersen's poetic world knows no boundaries of nation or age. The "chord of nature" he strikes so masterfully resonates in the "universal human heart" at firesides the world over, an image that suggests an international community and communion of reader and listener, young and old, in the—oral—narrative situation evoked. Andersen is a teacher of virtues and principles that are shared by "*civilized* humanity" (my emphasis). However, his attractiveness for the mature is obscured here by his dominant portrayal as a "man-child" in the literal sense of the word, one who is inseparable from an oeuvre allegedly imbued with a "very sincere and childlike love of children" and whose loss will be felt primarily by children. It is part and parcel of the primitivist view of the author that he is said to hold sway over his readers without "dramatic power" and through intellectual goodness rather than intellectual greatness; though possessed of imagination, he must be content with a "light . . . fancy." In addition to some valid insights and felicitous formulations, Bunce's remarks nonetheless exhibit essential features of the Andersen myth that soon arose in the United States and still prevails today.

The same can be said of the other two pieces written on Andersen's death, both of which came out in September 1875. Eulogistic comments appeared anonymously that month in the *Penn Monthly,* which was then nearing the middle of its run, from 1870–82.[90] Associated with the University of Pennsylvania through one of its founders and editors, Professor Robert Ellis Thompson, the magazine was the organ of the Philadelphia Social Science Association and focused on sociology, politics, and art, offering some poetry but no fiction. Nonetheless, the writer declares that "[t]he whole world laments Hans Christian Andersen. Always a poet, whether he wrote in prose or verse, his exquisite writings have passed into the literature of every European tongue. He dwelt on the borders of Elfland, in close communion with the world of legends. To him its spirits were visible; for his ear, at least, they had a tongue, and he delighted to be their chosen interpreter, and paint, with his powerful pencil, their shadowy portraits. He seemed to combine the Northern with the Southern mind. No imagination ever painted the beauties of Fairy-land more charmingly than his, and no one wrote more sweetly of sunny Italy than did this man, born and brought up beneath the cloudy Danish sky. His heart was cheerful and his writings healthful and harmonious. There was nothing morbid about him, and even his melancholy was of the cheerful autumnal kind. He was a warm-hearted, genial man, as his books reveal,—one who loved his fellows; and his name, among those of the story tellers who have blessed the earth and won the affection of mankind, leads all the rest."[91]

The writer is patently familiar with *The Improvisatore*. His encomium to Andersen's supposed combination of the Northern and Southern minds recalls both a dichotomy experienced as problematic in the North from the Renaissance on to the twentieth century and Goethe's polemical distinction between the "healthy" spirit of (German) classicism and the "unhealthy" spirit of romanticism, here revaluated, to be sure. However, he saves his loftiest comments, which, even in an age still hospitable to sentiment, approach preciosity at points, for Andersen's handling of fairies, for which he is the "chosen interpreter."

George William Curtis makes remarks of similar substance and form in the eulogy he published from "The Editor's Easy Chair" in *Harper's New Monthly Magazine*, part of which was cited in chapter 2:[92] "It would have pleased Hans Christian Andersen to know how sincerely he was loved by the children of many lands. He was himself always a child, and the peculiar charm of his writings is a kind of artless consciousness—a consciousness that is saved from being unpleasant by its genuine childlikeness. His extreme simplicity of character, his evident and absorbing delight in himself, sometimes conceal the real quality of his talent."[93] Beyond the by now familiar characterization of Andersen's own authentic "childhood" and relationship to children Curtis speaks of the fairy tales and stories proper: "But whatever his larger works, the delightful fairy tales, so familiar in every land, constantly appeared, like violets on a sunny bank in springtime. These are the true flowers of his genius. He was always a child fed on fairy lore, and such tales were his natural expressions. . . . They are not disguised sermons, and do not leave a moral, like a pretty flower which a child gathers, and in the act out flies a busy bee and stings. They are in themselves moral, of course, as every good thing is; and Andersen's humor and perception were too true and fine not to see and to enjoy the kind of moral which there is in his story of the 'Ugly Duckling'. . . ."[94] Curtis's acknowledgment of the implicit morality of the fairy tales and stories as well as of Andersen's humor and perceptiveness (not to mention his comments on *The Improvisatore* discussed in chapter 2) suggest a recognition that the Dane was more than a grown child and that the tales are more than child's play. However, his conclusion serves only to emphasize the prevailing drift of the article: "To be loved by children, to be a classic of the nursery, to do to all tender-souled and fairy-minded younglings all the world over what his father did to him—to make them happy after their own kind—this is the rare fortune of Andersen, his pure fame. . . . When he came back, famous, to Odense, his old native town was illuminated. And for how many a year will countless homes and hearths be lit up with joy at his coming in the eyes of children brighter than the windows of Odense!"[95]

~

Most of the reviews of Andersen's fairy tales and stories appeared in respectable magazines. The *Southern Literary Messenger,* which published more of them than any other periodical, was topflight, and *Putnam's* as well as *Appleton's* were very nearly so at the times the writings appeared. With the exception of *Peterson's,* however, their circulation ranged from small to middling, and several had runs of only a few years. Moreover, the question remains: Why did not more quality magazines, especially *Harper's* and the *Atlantic*—whose critics were obviously familiar with the works—issue more reviews of precisely those writings for which the well-known and admired Andersen was eventually best known and generally most admired? All the critics who discussed them were competent, and a couple, like Cooke and Stedman, had true critical acumen. However, the group as a whole was the least accomplished of those considered heretofore. Clearly, the fairy tales and stories did not receive the best the American periodical press had to offer.

Of course, this does not mean that what the magazines offered is of negligible interest. The brevity as well as the anonymity of certain reviews make it difficult to determine the author's critical frame of reference, to be sure. Those in which it is discernible, however, yield an insight that is not altogether predictable: While the writings of the earlier and middle years are neoclassical or romantic in orientation, as one would expect, those that appeared during the later period are predominantly romantic as well. That means that Andersen's fairy tales and stories received little scrutiny, even of a censorious kind, from exponents of realism. During these years the realist conviction itself may have dissuaded potential reviewers from discussing them. This neglect, coupled with the composition of the volumes characterized in chapter 1, may then in turn have impeded recognition of the realistic tendency present in Andersen's later fairy tales, or, more properly, stories.

To reviewers of the longer prose and the autobiography it was an inescapable fact—and at least for a year the primary fact—that

Andersen wrote explicitly for adults, even if some of the writers, either wittingly or unwittingly, read the works with the fairy tales and stories in the back of their mind. This was not necessarily the case with critics who wrote on the tales themselves, especially around 1870. Yet, from the beginning a substantial number of them—close to half—perceived in varying degrees that the works have dimensions that are accessible, or fully accessible, only to the experience, intelligence, and insight of an adult. Evidence of this apprehension is found inter alia in the numerous references to the implicit morality and humor or satire of the tales as well as in the comparisons of Andersen to an international array of major authors of past and present. As in connection with the autobiography one notes signs of ahistoricity in the writers' view of the Dane, and particularly the pieces published on his death show that the Andersen myth was certainly in the making. On the whole, however, the reviews of the fairy tales and stories demonstrate that this myth was not yet full-blown. In the American mind of the 1870s Andersen may have stood in the doorway to the nursery, but he had not yet had the door closed behind him.

5

The General Interest Articles

As STATED IN THE PRECEDING CHAPTER, RANDOM REFERENCES TO authors in periodicals bear witness to their presence in the collective consciousness of a nation. How much more eloquent, then, is the testimony provided by general interest articles, which by their very nature presuppose widespread familiarity and/or appeal. A substantial number of such pieces began to appear in the United States within a decade of Andersen's debut in the country. Some go beyond the bounds of the reviews in various ways. While the majority were published in magazines, several came out as chapters of books. Most of the authors were literati, but the group also contains an artist, a diplomat, and a few who were accomplished in more than one field. Though some of the pieces are principally critical in nature, others are based on personal reminiscences, and still others are both at once. The lion's share were written during Andersen's lifetime, but a few appeared up to two decades after his death. Despite, or in certain instances precisely because of, these departures the general interest articles variously complement or supplement the insights offered by the writings considered heretofore.

Even before the Civil War, biography and writing about travel had become exceedingly popular. A magazine article published in 1857, for example, bears the title "The Biographical Mania."[1] Four years earlier a contemporary had written, exaggerating for effect, that everyone traveled abroad at the time, to which Mott adds that nearly everyone wrote about it as well.[2] It was a book that combined both autobiography and travel in which the first general interest piece on Andersen appeared. Entitled *You Have Heard of Them*, the volume came out in 1854 under the signature "Q," a pseudonym used by Charles G. Rosenberg, an Englishman who came to the United States in 1849 or 1850.[3] By the time the book was published, Rosenberg (1818–79) had written two novels as well as a life of Jenny Lind and a chronicle of her tour of the United States in 1850. He was also known as a music, drama, and literary critic and, more notably, as an artist

Photograph of Andersen at the age of fifty-five taken on July 10, 1860 by Franz Hanf-staengl. Reproduced in agreement with Odense City Museums, Denmark.

and illustrator. Cultivating various genres, he exhibited his work in several galleries and academies in London, Philadelphia, and New York. Rosenberg traveled widely in Europe, and *You Have Heard of Them* contains his reminiscences of meetings with numerous representatives of the arts then prominent in Europe, from painters and composers to singers, dancers, actors, and, of course, writers such as Andersen.[4]

In chapter 11 of his autobiography Andersen weaves a visit with Major Friedrich Anton Serre and his wife at their estate near Dresden into the description of his trip to Germany in 1844.[5] Some fifteen years later that long-standing friendship, which was punctuated by such visits, would inspire the tale *The Old Church Bell* (*Den gamle Kirkeklokke*), in which Andersen pays tribute to the much revered Friedrich Schiller.[6] Andersen's diary contains a record of his second visit to the Serres, which took place in February 1846, indicating that he read aloud before a large circle on February 24, though not what, that he was awfully tired (gruelig træt), and little else.[7] Nonetheless, the only evidence available suggests that it was on this occasion that Rosenberg called on the Serres and met Andersen.[8]

Most of the nine-page chapter on Andersen—one of the longest in the book—foregrounds not the ostensible subject but rather the author himself, who is clearly at pains to entertain his reader and to cut a dashing figure in the process. First weighing the virtues of Dresden as a cultural center and recounting the circumstances that brought him to "Madame du Serré . . . the Countess Merlin, or Lady Blessington of Dresden," he proceeds to the luminaries present during his visit, who included Berthold Auerbach, a prominent exponent of German local color fiction, and then dwells for two pages, and with obvious relish, on a pretty "Fraulein" with light hair and dark eyes whom he "would have kissed . . . had the room been empty."[9] Despite such flippant gallantry, Rosenberg's comments on Andersen, who must wait a full six pages for the author to get to him, are instructive in their way.

Only nine years after Andersen's works began to appear in the United States there may still have been news value for some readers in Rosenberg's description of the Dane, who was "assuredly no beauty" and whose "weak" mouth he characterizes as "asinine": "In a word, his case was anything but correspondent to its reputed contents."[10] If possible, Rosenberg was even less impressed by Andersen's manner, which was "simple and *naif* in the extreme. Nay! it was more, for it was stupid."[11] On hearing that Andersen had come to the Serres' to read a story—he calls it a "*novellette*"[12]—he had wished that he had stayed in his room. The solemnity with which a table is placed in the center of one side of the drawing room and two candles are set upon it remind him of evening prayers during his boyhood, and he shudders at the look of length about the manuscript Andersen draws deliberately from his pocket. However, the experience that follows brings a pleasant surprise.

When Andersen read, "[h]is pronunciation was clear, and intelligible in the extreme. A Dane by birth, although he generally—Nay! almost invariably wrote in the German language—it was like that of all foreigners who have completely acquired a tongue differing from their own, singularly distinct. His reading was good, pure and unaffected. As he warmed into the interest of his tale, his eye lost its stolid and glassy character of expression. It began to glisten with something like fire and energy. He used no action to accompany his elocution, if indeed I may apply such a term to mere reading. He read like a gentleman, and not like a professional man. I was able to follow him with the greatest ease. Where anything trenching on humor occurred in his story, he was peculiarly happy in giving it effect. Suffice it, that I enjoyed the sitting much."[13] After commenting on the visible effect of the tale's humor and sentiment on Andersen's listeners, Rosenberg permits himself a digression on reading aloud: "Believe me, reading oneself into popularity—especially when you are, as Andersen was in the present case, sure of your audience—must be a very agreeable method of achieving a reputation. The writer does not know, whether tears are shed, or smiles wreathed over his melancholy thoughts, or his tersest and most brilliant modes of expression. But he who reads his own writings, in some respects like the *Improvisatore*, gathers the laurels of the moment, with his own fingers. He notes the impressions which he has awakened, and revels in the emotions to which he has given birth. So at least did Andersen; for I have never seen any man look happier than he did, when after an hour and a half, he closed the manuscript, and retired from the table."[14]

In the course of the evening Rosenberg was presented to the "lion," with whom he had a "very agreeable conversation," agreeable to him "from the opportunity of hearing a man speak in familiar intercourse, whose name and writings I had so long known. As an acquaintance, Andersen was very agreeable, though in some things, curiously soft-natured, for a man who has risen from the humblest life, by the sheer force of his talents. As a conversationalist he is far from brilliant, although he has great readiness of language, and has a pleasant voice. But he has very essentially a kind and benevolent heart. This, necessarily, I did not discover. It was in my subsequent knowledge of the writer, that I found out how much good was locked up in his singularly ungainly exterior."[15] However favorable an impression Andersen made on Rosenberg, it did not prevent the former illustrator for a humor magazine from studying his famous fellow guest for a caricature, which he later drew on the flyleaf of his journal.[16]

Indeed, his final thoughts relate to Andersen's awkwardness: "As a man he is *gauche* in the extreme—and that *gaucherie* I have contrived to confer upon the pen-and-ink sketch of him."[17] At the end of the chapter he turns his attention from Andersen back to the pretty Saxon "Fraulein."

Rosenberg obviously fell victim to a not uncommon misconception about the language in which Andersen wrote, one stemming from the fact mentioned earlier that some of the early English translations of his works were based on German renderings. And his admiration for Andersen's pronunciation of German, which was far from native, may lead one to question his own proficiency. However, his command of the language was entirely sufficient for him to appreciate the reciprocal relationship between Andersen and his listeners in what is the prototypical narrative situation. He says nothing about the style of the fairy tales and stories per se, but his comments on Andersen's "elocution" while reading *ad alta voce* indicate an intimate relationship between oral and verbal style, hinting at its impromptu nature. Like many another commentator, Rosenberg voices appreciation for Andersen's rise from obscurity, finding his mild manner at variance with the qualities apparently prerequisite for such a feat. In general, he appears to presuppose no great familiarity with Andersen among his readers, whether right or wrong, and to feel that someone who is a literary and social lion in Europe is worth knowing, or knowing better, in the United States.

Credit for inaugurating American Andersen scholarship usually goes to Horace Scudder for the article on the fairy tales and stories he published in the *National Quarterly Review* in 1861, and the piece is doubtless the first extensive scholarly study of Andersen in the country.[18] In view of the uncertain boundary between scholarship and general interest writing in contemporary magazines, however, one might consider giving the honor to Richard Henry Stoddard for a hybrid article he published in the *National Magazine* in November 1855.[19] Entitled simply "Hans Christian Andersen," the article could be taken as a review of the autobiography, for the greatest part of it represents an account of Andersen's life and contains liberal quotations from the text. However, Stoddard does not refer to any specific edition of the work. Indeed, the most recent English-language versions had appeared three years earlier, covering Andersen's life only until 1846, and Stoddard refers to events that had occurred since then; there is no evidence to suggest that he was able to read the new Danish version that came out earlier in the year. Moreover, para-

Engd. by Capewell & Kimmel N.Y.

R. H. Stoddard.

Printed by J.Kelly

Richard Henry Stoddard. By permission of the Houghton Library, Harvard University.

graphs at the beginning and end as well as comments in between reflect an independent, if not sustained, attempt to determine the nature and significance of Andersen's life *and* work up to the time of writing.

Launched three years earlier in New York, the *National Magazine* was a venture of the Methodist Church designed to offer "the attractions of *Harper's* without those 'morbid appeals to the passions' to be found in fiction."[20] Though the editors included the capable Abel Stevens (1815–97), who was known as editor of several Methodist periodicals as well as for historical and biographical works related to his church, the magazine did not thrive, perhaps precisely because of its policy toward fiction, and ceased publication after only six years.[21]

During the second half of the nineteenth century Richard Henry Stoddard (1825–1903) ranked among the major poets of the United States, below Brahmins such as Longfellow, Emerson, and Lowell, but in the upper echelon nevertheless.[22] In the introduction to his memoirs, which were published in the year of his death, his friend Edmund Clarence Stedman writes that Stoddard lived through the burgeoning of letters in New York, "to the evolution of which he contributed his full share."[23] In another passage Stedman states, more broadly, "[h]e . . . steadily contributed a vital portion to the current and to the enduring literature of his land and language."[24] This he did principally through some dozen volumes of poetry, much of which was first published in magazines. Stoddard also expanded Americans' literary horizons through, among many other things, biographies of figures such as Irving and Bryant and editions of writers on the order of Longfellow and Poe.[25] Stedman writes further that "in his [Stoddard's] prime there were few important literary names and enterprises, North or South, but he was 'of the company,'" and in his memoirs Stoddard includes chapters on his relations with Lowell, Hawthorne, Poe, Longfellow, and Whittier as well as Thackeray and a number of his closer literary friends.[26] As literary editor of the *New York World* from 1860 to 1870 and of the *New York Mail and Express* from 1880 to his death, he played an important role in determining the shape of American literature and critical opinion about it. For over thirty years his home was a center of New York literary life.

Given the company he kept in books and in society, it comes as no surprise that Stoddard was a romantic.[27] In his *Recollections* he defines poetry as "the revelation of ideal truth and beauty," adding that "[w]e must not pull the ideal down to us, but rise to the ideal."[28] Poethood was a high calling for him, "for the artist is the man with a single aim and ambition, a single passion and determination, a single life, which must be lived out in its own way, and at any cost."[29] With Lowell—and himself—in mind, he wrote that the true poet accepted and exercised his calling, not "for his bread . . . nor to increase his income, but because it pleased him to do so. He chose his own subjects"[30]—which in Stoddard's case did not include sociopolitical issues such as abolition, states' rights, or the Civil War. His friend Stedman, himself an aesthete, writes, "Stoddard and his group were the first to make poetry—whatever else it might be—the rhythmical creation of beauty."[31] Later critics have questioned Stoddard's success in this endeavor. However, it is a truism that writers write both from within and for their own time willy-nilly, most certainly if they want to be read by their contemporaries. Consequently, the judgment of their coevals should not be summarily dismissed in favor of those ever-shifting historical currents of opinion within the stream of "eternity." Rather, it should be given the same due regard that Stoddard himself gave the "Knickerbocker" Fitz-Greene Halleck and Longfellow, both of whom had already fallen on hard times among critics by the later nineteenth century.[32]

The article on Andersen may be one in a series of biographical and critical papers that Stoddard agreed to write for "a magazine in New York" soon after paying a visit to Hawthorne's "Wayside" in 1852.[33] He begins with an insight already apparent at this early stage of Andersen's presence in the United States, surely not only on the basis of the poet's own words: "The biography [sic] of Hans Christian Andersen is as much like a story as any of his novels or fairy tales—it runs through many of both under various disguises, and lends to them a peculiar charm."[34] Stoddard then makes observations that have a virtually programmatic character: "As related by himself in 'The Story of My Life,' it [Andersen's autobiography] is exceedingly agreeable and interesting, not so much from the amount of incident which it contains, as from his fresh and pleasant manner of telling it, and the representative character it assumes: for Andersen seems the representative, the *beau ideal* of the common life of genius, typifying its struggles, its sufferings, and its triumphs. All that we have ever read of clever boys, and talented men going out into the world to win fame, recalls itself back to memory as we pore over his simple and earnest pages."[35] It is clearly Andersen's youth and early manhood that most impressed themselves upon Stoddard's mind, for he dwells on them at length, giving comparatively short shrift to the artist's years of triumph.

Through the force of his rhetoric, his growing reputation, and a magazine article of a comparatively lengthy six two-column pages, Stoddard contributes to the development of a fundamental aspect of the Andersen myth. Indeed, he was the first American writer who directed his countrymen's attention to the "representative" character of Andersen's life as an artist and a social being. His interest in Andersen's ascent was not fortuitous. Stedman writes that the "story of Dickens's boyhood, as told by himself, is not more pathetic, nor is its outcome more beautiful, than the story of Richard Henry Stoddard's experience. . . ."[36] Stoddard's youth in Massachusetts and New York was itself one of privation in which he received even less schooling than Andersen, and only as he neared his thirties was he able to exchange his blue collar for a white one and the beginning of a financially secure existence with leisure for writing. He experienced his lack of formal education and polite upbringing as distinct liabilities, which partly explains why he treated members of his circle with deference and expressed gratitude that Hawthorne and other noteworthies did not look down on him.[37] His background prepared him well to recognize Bryant for his "laborious life" and the "determination which kept him a poet through it all" and may well have inspired him to write the article on Andersen.[38]

Bringing the reader from the point where the autobiography ends up to the present, Stoddard relates that Andersen has since written other books and that the entire list is quite extensive. He suggests that there may even be works unknown to English readers in view of the fact that the last Leipzig edition comprises thirty-five volumes. He then steps back and surveys Andersen's body of work to date, as known to him: "Andersen stands before the public in the fourfold capacity of poet, novelist, traveler, and writer of fairy-lore. With his poetry we are unacquainted, it not being 'done into' English yet; one specimen we remember to have seen, in, if we are not mistaken, the memoir prefixed to Mary Howitt's translation of 'The Improvisatore,' and very beautiful it was, full of nature and feeling; a pastoral on a young miller's love for his master's daughter.[39] Earlier in the article Stoddard opines that *The Improvisatore*, which is "part truth and part fiction" and "painted the events of [Andersen's] early life in gorgeous colors, with a proper haze of imagination," is probably the best, and certainly the best known, of the novels.[40] At this point he writes, "His novels and books of travel are pleasant, light reading. He has considerable skill in portraiture, and his descriptions of nature are vivid and life-like. In 'The Improvisatore,' his warm and glowing fancy riots in gorgeous Italian scenery, showering abroad 'barbaric pearl and gold.' Antonio the improvisator is Andersen himself. Indeed, all his books give us a feeling of the man Andersen, running over with a personality which in any one else would be egotism."[41]

It was already clear to Stoddard that Andersen was best known for his fairy tales and stories and that it was "by them that he will be chiefly known in the future."[42] For, as he states unequivocally, "his fairy tales . . . seem to us the finest ever written."[43] Following a glance at the history of the genre and its antecedents from antiquity to the Grimms brothers, he continues, "Andersen, however, is the master of the school, the very sovereign of the whole realm of fairy-land. We doubt whether his poetry is near so poetical as his tales; certainly it cannot exhibit their creative imagination—the poem proper demanding a severity of treatment wholly at variance with the latitude of the fairy story. To us they read like children's poetry—little prose poems, full of nature and simplicity. The wildest and most extravagant has a certain completion of conception, and a wonderful finish of execution—the perfection of art because it is art concealed. They seem to gush from his head like brooks, to grow from his heart like flowers. No matter what may be their object, whether to inculcate a moral, or to riot in the world of imagination—whether dealing with mortals like ourselves, or with fairies and angels, and the personification of abstract qualities—they are alike excellent, and alike beautiful."[44]

Stoddard's praise of Andersen's fairy tales and stories is praise indeed, for it constitutes the homage of an apprentice, one familiar with the challenges of his craft, to a "master," a word that Stoddard likely used advisedly. We recall from the preceding chapter that he, together with Hawthorne, made 1853 the year of the juvenile for John Esten Cooke, according to an article in the *Southern Literary Messenger*, for it was in that year that his own *Adventures in Fairy-Land* appeared.[45] While *The Improvisatore* exhibits riotous fancy, the fairy tales and stories riot in the even higher power of creative imagination. The longer prose as a whole has individual virtues, but the tales possess a wholeness of design and implementation that conceals the artist at work, lending his creations the dignity of the beautiful, the ultimate goal of the romantic artist. Stoddard likens the stories to children's poetry, but that in no way diminishes their excellence as art for him. Moreover, he is quite cognizant of their double appeal: "[Andersen] wrote them just as he related them to the children of his friends, and with the same expressions [an acknowledgment of his "oral" literary style]; the children made themselves merry with the story, the older folks were interested in the moral. When once their aim was understood, he removed the appendage, 'told for children,' and published them simply as 'Tales.' "[46]

In his *Recollections* Stoddard devotes an entire chapter and numerous additional passages to his close friend Bayard Taylor, who was the next American to write on Andersen in the general interest vein.[47] Born the same year as Stoddard and in similar circumstances, Taylor (1828–78) rose more rapidly than his future friend, publishing poems in the *Saturday Evening Post* beginning in 1841.[48] Over the next some thirty-five years he gained wide recognition for numerous volumes of poetry. Also the author of novels, plays, and criticism, including essays on German literature, his translation of Goethe's *Faust* was long considered the finest in English and remains his best-known work. Inspired by romantic wanderlust and supported particularly by the *New York Tribune,* for which he served as literary editor from 1848 to near his death, Taylor made numerous extended journeys abroad that left their mark on much of his poetry and yielded many newspaper articles as well as several highly popular travel books, for which he became known as the "Great American Traveler." His reputation waned with the advent of realism, but during his day he ranked among the leading writers of the United States. It was in one of his travel books that he wrote on Andersen.

Taylor's trek through Scandinavia in 1856 and 1857 bore fruit in *Northern Travel: Summer and Winter Pictures; Sweden, Denmark, and Lapland.*[49] In chapter 19, which is entitled "Journey to Gottenburg and Copenhagen," Taylor recounts a visit Andersen paid him on the second day of his sojourn in the Danish capital.[50] Having described Andersen's dress, he writes, "[H]is head was thrown back, and his plain, irregular features were an expression of the greatest cheerfulness and kindly humour. I recognized him at once, and forgetting that we had never met—so much did he seem like an old, familiar acquaintance—cried out 'Andersen!' and jumped up to greet him."[51] Taylor continues, tellingly: "One sees the man so plainly in his works, that his readers may almost be said to know him personally. He is thoroughly simple and natural, and those who call him egotistical forget that his egotism is only a naïve and unthinking sincerity, like that of a child. In fact, he is the youngest man for his years that I ever knew."[52] After relating the further course of the conversation, in which Andersen stated that he might come to America despite the possibility of seasickness, Taylor concludes, "God bless you, Andersen! I said, in my thoughts. It is so cheering to meet a man whose very weaknesses are made attractive through the perfect candour of his nature!"[53]

On the whole, Taylor's reminiscence of his meeting with Andersen is unremarkable.[54] For present purposes, however, one should note his observation of Andersen's endearing artlessness as well as his identification of the man and his work, if only as signs of an emerging stereotype. More striking, because less commonly expressed, is the intimate sense of fellowship that Taylor had felt for Andersen even before meeting him and which then burst upon his awareness as soon as he caught sight of his visitor. Such a response surely derived ultimately from the peculiar humanity of the two individuals, but it may have also stemmed from Taylor's awareness of being in the presence of a kindred sensibility. We saw earlier that he was one with Stoddard, Stedman, and other New York writers in his notion of the exalted role of imaginative art and the high vocation of the creative artist. As with Rosenberg and other travelers, in any case, the mere fact that he deemed Andersen worthy of a visit, a newspaper article, and a substantial passage in a book attests to Andersen's renown and appeal in the United States during the period under examination. Most of Taylor's commentators, including Hansen-Taylor and Scudder, oddly enough, merely register the fact that his conversation with Andersen took place.[55] In 1879, the year after his death and only four years after Andersen's passing, however, his first biographer paused to write, "At Copenhagen he [Taylor] met Hans Christian Andersen, the great Danish poet, by whom Mr. Taylor was received most cordially. Thus, one after another, the great men of the world were added to the list of friends found by this son of an humble American farmer [another reason for Taylor's sympathetic reaction to Andersen?]. Andersen afterwards sent Mr. Taylor copies of his poems and essays before they were printed, and in many ways showed his regard for the American poet."[56]

In early 1863 *Harper's New Monthly Magazine* published a three-part article entitled "A Californian in Iceland," which was written by another world traveler and writer of travel books, J. Ross Browne.[57] Born in Ireland, Browne (1821–75) came to the United States at age twelve and, having survived a youth of financial vicissitude and meager formal education near Cincinnati and in Louisville, launched a successful career as a newspaper writer and author before turning twenty.[58] Beginning with stories in the *Southern Literary Messenger* and Poe's *Graham's Magazine*, this soldier of fortune turned an eleven-month stint aboard a whaler and journeys through various parts of

five continents into highly popular books that combine features of
the travel narrative and the novel.[59] Browne was an early realist and
humorist who satirized romanticism as well as the related American
idealization of European culture, exerting an influence on both
Herman Melville and Mark Twain. Already the author of travel
sketches published in *Harper's* in 1853, Browne was able to translate
the popularity of his best-known book (*Yusef; Or the Journey of the
Frangi, A Crusade in the East,* 1853) into a number of lead articles for
the same magazine in the 1860s. "A Californian in Iceland" is one of
these.

At the beginning of the first installment the "Californian," which
Browne in fact was for parts of his life, states his intention to present
a portrayal of Iceland and its people to the "five hundred thousand
of my fellow-citizens, who do their traveling through these illuminated pages. . . ."[60] His first station in Scandinavia was Copenhagen,
where he gathered information in preparation for the trip west. Having expressed his admiration for the Danes and their capital, he
writes, "I could not do myself the injustice to leave Copenhagen without forming the personal acquaintance of a man to whom a debt of
gratitude is due by the young and the old in all countries—the ram-
blers in fairy-land, the lovers of romance, and the friends of humanity—all who can feel the divine influence of genius, and learn,
through the teachings of a kindly heart, that the inhabitants of earth
are 'Kindred by one holy tie'—the quaint, pathetic, genial Hans
Christian Anderssen [*sic*]."[61] Few of Andersen's American commentators compress so much into one sentence as Browne does here, for
he suggests at once familiarity with the novels as well as the fairy tales
and stories, the sophistication of the latter, and the humane spirit
that pervades them all, and he does so in an emotive tonality that
belies the realist in him. However, Browne's characteristic social con-
science manifests itself in his appreciation of the neighborhood and
type of lodging in which the "great Danish author" has chosen to live,
namely, the "second story of a dingy and dilapidated house, fronting
one of those unsavory canals, a confused pile of dirty, shambling ten-
ements in the rear, and a curious medley of fish and fishermen,
sloops and schooners, mud-scows and skiffs in front. . . . It is purely a
labor of love in which he spends his life. The products of his pen have
furnished him with ample means to live in elegant style, surrounded
by all the allurements of rank and fashion, but he prefers the obscurity of a plain lodging amidst the haunts of those classes whose lives
and pursuits he so well portrays."[62]

Notwithstanding his keen eye for concrete reality, Browne appears to have been inspired by the prevailing spirit of caprice he sensed in Andersen's quarters. He describes the two old women employed by his host as domestics as "decrepit old creatures, with faces and forms very much like a pair of antiquated nut-crackers."[63] To his mind Andersen himself has a face "that might have been mistaken for the dreadful child-trap of an ogre but for the sunny beams of benevolence that lurked around the lips and the genial humanity that glimmered from every nook and turn."[64] In Andersen, Browne detects a vitality that is like a force of nature, "a voice bubbling up from the vast depths below with cheery, spasmodic, and unintelligible words of welcome"; Andersen is for him "the great Danish improvisator, the lover of little children, the gentle Caliban who dwells among fairies and holds sweet converse with fishes and frogs and beetles!"[65] Browne writes that he would have picked Andersen out of a thousand Americans as a candidate for Congress[66] or the owner of a tavern, but his initial impression soon yielded to discernment of a "certain refinement" in Andersen's awkward gestures and simple speech "not usually found among men of that class."[67] However, it was the "spontaneous and almost childlike cordiality of his greeting" and "the unworldly impulsiveness of his nature, as he grasped both my hands in his, patted me affectionately on the shoulder, and bade me welcome" that convinced Browne that "this was no other and could be no other" than Andersen.[68]

Browne's relation of his conversation with Andersen, which, leaping from one subject to the next according to Andersen's whims, covers over half of the lengthy passage in the article, is less revealing than the vividly imaginative and affective brushwork that precedes and follows it. Near the end Browne characterizes Andersen's varied effusions by saying that they were "all in such mixed up broken English that the meaning must have been utterly lost but for the wonderful expressiveness of his face and the striking oddity of his motions. It came to me mesmerically. He seemed like one who glowed all over with bright and happy thoughts, which permeated all around him with a new intelligence. His presence shed a light upon others like the rays that beamed from the eyes of 'Little Sunshine.'"[69] Browne writes that he took his leave of Andersen "more delighted, if possible, with the author than I had ever before been with his books," but it is evident that his experience of Andersen, the "new intelligence" with which the author infused him, was very much conditioned by Andersen's books, first and foremost the fairy tales and stories.[70]

Another general interest article on Andersen appeared under the title "The Story-Teller of Copenhagen" in the January issue of *Putnam's Magazine* in 1869.[71] Like Stoddard's piece, it adheres closely to *The True Story of My Life* but cannot be considered a review of the book, the most recent English edition having been published seventeen years earlier. Few traces of the author, Theodore Johnson, appear to remain, but available evidence indicates that he was an individual of sophistication and learning. The Web site "The Nineteenth Century in Print," for example, reveals that he wrote several articles on French life and culture for *Putnam's* and *Harper's* and translated a book relating to Madame de Staël.

Like many others, Johnson places greater emphasis on Andersen's trials than on his triumphs, recounting his youthful statement on the necessity of suffering before becoming famous, the matter of his confirmation suit and new boots, and other episodes that were by now part and parcel of Andersen lore. He assigns a prominent position to *The Improvisatore*, "a novel, whose scene lies under the sunny sky of Italy, depicting in glowing and striking colors the national life of the Peninsula. It is on this account, and, above all, owing to its artistic composition and the grace and purity of its style, that it is even now considered Andersen's most successful production."[72] Johnson notes the continuing popularity of *O. T.* in Denmark, where many critics allegedly continue to call it Andersen's best book.[73] He finds *Only a Fiddler* inferior to *The Improvisatore* in "artistic arrangement" but feels that it, too, was written with the poet's heartblood, for "[i]n all his books Andersen turns the history of his own life to account."[74] Indeed, Johnson feels that there is more of Andersen in the fiddler Christian than in Antonio, the improvisatore.

Perhaps most interesting about Johnson's remarks is that they appear to rest on a broader acquaintance with Andersen's work than those made by the majority of his peers. He speaks, for example, of the author's "*naïve* self-deception" regarding the theater: "The truth is that he is decidedly wanting in dramatic talent, but that that siren, the Theatre, allured him again and again to try his luck as a dramatist."[75] Broadening his criticism, he continues: "Even his novels are often faulty in arrangement and unity of conception; even there his characters lack well-defined outlines, fire, and strength of action [though Johnson refers to Andersen as well as Dickens as "the two great novelists"]; and these faults are still more conspicuous in his numerous plays, such as 'Agneta and the Merman,' 'The Mulatto,' 'The Moorish Girl,' 'The Flower of Happiness,' etc."[76] For Andersen the lyricist, on the other hand, Johnson has kinder words: "As a lyric poet . . . Andersen is more eminent. There is a certain fragrance, a wonderful charm, a strange, mournful melody, in most of his lyrics, a great many of which have been composed and are exceedingly popular in Denmark."[77] Surprisingly, perhaps, he passes no judgment on the fairy tales and stories. However, he relates that they "were not less eagerly read and listened to by grown persons than by children" and that, when writing them down, Andersen "took pains to preserve their child-like tone," which may be understood as tantamount to an attempt to retain their orality.[78] Similarly, he says nothing about Andersen's personal childlikeness but cites his observation that reading fairy tales with a foreign accent, that is, reading his own works in German, is "least objectionable," since "there is something childlike in the foreign accent, which imparts a characteristic color to the reading."[79]

An article of another cast appeared in *Appleton's Journal* on July 8, 1871, a point when the periodical was in the midst of its heyday as a near topflight magazine.[80] Entitled simply "Hans Christian Andersen," the piece might easily have become yet another personally accentuated retelling of the autobiography. It came out the same year as Scudder's updated version of *The Story of My Life*, and the author, Louis Bagger, was the translator on whom Scudder chiefly relied while editing the second, improved edition of the book and perhaps other volumes of the Author's Edition.[81] Born in Denmark, Bagger appears to have emigrated to the United States as a young man.[82] During the time he was assisting Scudder, he worked as editor of a short-lived newspaper based in Washington, DC, called the *Patriot*.[83] Rather than writing of Andersen's life as a whole, however, he chose to focus on his own personal experience of him.

Bagger begins by pointing to Andersen's universal renown: "Among the galaxy of living authors of world-wide fame, there is, perhaps, hardly one whose writings have, within the past few years, become more generally known, read, and appreciated, than the romances, stories, and fairy-tales of the Danish poet and novelist who forms the subject of the present article."[84] Bagger feels that Andersen has remained youthfully vigorous in mind and body, his genius indeed improving with age. Clearly revealing his romantic temper, he opines that Andersen's writings "possess, with the most faultless rhetoric, the truthfulness and beauty of feeling, the appreciation of every thing in Nature which is good and beautiful, that only a pure and undefiled talent can produce. Hence his success, and hence the fact that everybody that reads his books not only admires the genius that produced them, but also loves the man who wrote them."[85]

During a visit to Copenhagen a few years earlier, Bagger relates, he had had the opportunity to meet Andersen frequently both in public and in private, and the two had become "friends in a minute" and remained such.[86] Though Andersen was known throughout the world principally as an eminent novelist and storyteller, Bagger stresses the apparently little-known fact that at home and in Norway and Sweden (and, one should add, in Germany as well) he had gained great acclaim for his public readings. In this regard Bagger compares Andersen favorably and rather extensively with the highly popular and recently deceased Charles Dickens. "To hear Dickens," he writes, "was, in fact, to see a play—one of his own stories dramatized; but to hear Andersen," at readings for the Danish Workingmen's Society, "is to hear the air whisper you its secrets; the trees and flowers entrance you with delightful stories; the sparrow, the fieldmouse, and the stately 'stork,' converse with you freely, the latter telling you all about her Egyptian experiences; nay, even the old furniture, that you know so well, button-hooks you, and has a sociable chat with you, which makes you open your eyes, and in future look upon old cupboards and chairs with more respect, and with a sense as if there were a soul hidden away in a corner within them, or beneath the worn leather covering. Andersen is the magician who wields the wand that can cause the elements to whisper, and every thing upon earth, animate and inanimate, appear as your bosomfriend, and divulge its secrets."[87] On reading these lines, one familiar with German literature thinks involuntarily of a quatrain by Joseph von Eichendorff called "Divining Rod" (Wünschelrute):

> There's a song in all things, sleeping,
> That now lie in dreams unheard,
> And the world begins its singing,
> If you but find the magic word.[88]

Behind Bagger's sentimental pathos one detects an awareness of the mature experience and artistry that Andersen's stories and his oral delivery of them reveal. For him, the distance, not to say "alienation," created by Andersen's "magical" usage of fabular and folk traditions and even contemporary realism makes the reader or listener more alive to and intimate with the world about him. In other words, the secrets that the air and other elements whisper in Andersen's fairy tales have far less to do with the *Weltgeist* of a Friedrich Schelling, the ultimate source of the motif in Eichendorff's poem, than, as in the poem itself, with a heightened experience of life.

Bagger's Andersen enables his reader or listener not only to experience life more immediately but also to apprehend its "true" nature. Bagger reports having seen people take Andersen's hand with tears in their eyes, thanking him for both the delight he had afforded them and the moral he had taught them, namely, "the conviction that, after all, this is a good world, if we will only see it as it really is, with the eyes that truth and Nature gave us, and not through the dark glasses of dismay and despair."[89] The depressed and dejected, the hopeless and misanthropic "have come away converted, and commenced life anew, and many a household has been made happy, and many a dull heart brightened, by Hans Christian Andersen."[90] While Bagger's biblical allusiveness and virtually missionary tone may seem overwrought by today's standards, one must nonetheless assume that they reflect lived experience and that this, or similar, experience was not isolated, either in the Denmark of Andersen's latter days or in the United States, at least among those Americans who experienced Andersen's readings directly or vicariously through the writing of Bagger and others.

One who belonged to both categories of Americans was G. W. (Gilderoy Wells) Griffin, who sometime between Andersen's death in August and the end of 1875 published a book bearing the title *My Danish Days: With a Glance at the History, Traditions, and Literature of the Old Northern Country*.[91] Trained as a lawyer, Griffin (1840–91) met Andersen during his term as U.S. Consul in Copenhagen from 1871 to 1875, after which he served in the same capacity in the Samoan Islands, Auckland, New Zealand, and Sydney, Australia.[92] Having engaged in journalism prior to his first consular appointment, he later wrote, in addition to *My Danish Days*, other books resulting from his travel abroad as well as biography and literary studies. During his time in Copenhagen Griffin exchanged visits with Andersen on at least three occasions, corresponded with him, and received a gift copy of the autobiography from him.[93] As we shall see, he also heard Andersen give a public reading of his works at least once.

Griffin treats Andersen in the rather lengthy tenth chapter of *My Danish Days*, in which he intersperses personal reminiscences, observations, and the like in an account of Andersen's life, including extensive passages from the autobiography and related texts.[94] He joins the already large number of those who dwell on Andersen's early poverty, rehearsing in all earnest Andersen's youthful declaration on adversity and fame, the wise woman's prediction of Andersen's celebrity, and, later, its fulfillment, and so on. He is indeed so impressed by such a rise above circumstance that his recollection of seeing Tordenskjold's picture in Andersen's apartment inspires a digression on a similar life curve.[95] For reasons about which one can only speculate, Griffin relies on Bagger's article for certain turns of phrase in his description of Andersen and his comparison of Andersen's public reading style with that of Dickens, whom he had also heard. Less pious than Bagger, he is quite as sentimental: "[B]ut when I heard Andersen read the story of the Little Girl with the Matches, I did not think of the author at all, but wept like a child, unconscious of everything about me."[96] Griffin also lingers less, and less lyrically, on the nature and impact of Andersen's reading from his works, choosing instead to reproduce the statement on the purpose of poetry—to open "our eyes and our hearts to the beautiful, the true, and the good"—with which Andersen prefaced his readings before the Workingmen's Society.[97]

Early in the chapter, Griffin writes that he had been anxious to meet Andersen upon arriving in Copenhagen, having been an admirer of the Dane from his earliest recollection. Born in 1840, he belonged to the first generation of Americans who grew up with Andersen's fairy tales and stories and who thus most naturally associated the author and his work with childhood. It is perhaps for this reason that he is sensitive, perhaps unwarrantedly so, to Andersen's childlikeness and relationship to children. He portrays his initial meeting with Andersen as follows: "I shall never forget the first visit he paid me. His entrance into my room was like the breath of summer, a glimpse of sunshine. I could hardly keep from throwing my arms about him. He reminded me of one of my early schoolmates with whom I used to play leap-frog. Although he was nearly seventy years of age, I could only think of him as a boy."[98] Subsequently, Griffin relates that Andersen, on nearing the Griffins' home, had met the consul's wife and little daughter, taking the latter in his arms and kissing her, "perhaps the only stranger that she ever saw in her life that she did not shrink from."[99] Over the next two pages Griffin recounts a series of anecdotes demonstrating Andersen's fondness for children and their love for him, one of which he had told to Andersen. On hearing this story, Andersen had said to him, "I can have no better friends than the children. Our Saviour said: 'Suffer little children to come unto me, and forbid them not, for such is the kingdom of

God.'"[100] Here, the allusive equation of Andersen with Christ, even if originating with the author himself, is even more transparent than in Bagger's article.

Griffin obviously considered Andersen's childlikeness an "adult" virtue, much as Andersen thought of the attribute himself.[101] He both witnessed and experienced the impact Andersen's public reading of his stories had on adult audiences. However, his relative emphasis clearly identifies "Andersen" and, however implicitly, "Andersen's fairy tales" literally as things of the child, perhaps obscuring their adult moment. It seems unlikely that his book chapter had any more than a minor, passing effect on a certain few Americans' perception of Andersen. All the same, such portrayals of the Dane and his stories, perhaps especially by and for Griffin's generation, surely served in aggregate to create one of the constituent elements of the current Andersen myth.

As we saw in chapter 3, *Potter's American Monthly* was one of the periodicals that published a tribute to Andersen on his death in 1875. The editor must have felt the afterglow of his life to be powerful, for some three years later, in July 1878, the magazine carried an article by one D. G. Hubbard entitled "The Last Days of Hans Christian Andersen."[102] The piece chronicles not only Andersen's last days but also the stages of decline he went through over the final three years of his life and his accompanying thoughts, as expressed to friends. The article is instructive for present purposes chiefly for its final paragraph: "And we, too, say that Andersen is not dead; in his tales and stories he will live on; they are the blossoms which have sprung 'from all his limbs' [a reference to Andersen's dream that he had died and that flowers had blossomed from his arms and legs], from his inmost being, and in ever-enduring spring will keep alive his memory in the hearts of thousands from generation to generation."[103] The article's existence and its last paragraph reinforce the fact that Andersen— nota bene! The Andersen of the fairy tales—had become an institution. The final lines also evince the religious piety of Bagger's and Griffin's articles, albeit in the more secular sense of the ancients and many in the West since the eighteenth century.

One of the most mature pieces of writing on Andersen to appear in the United States or, for that matter, anywhere during the nineteenth century came out under the title "Reminiscences of H. C. Andersen" in the February issue of *Scandinavia* in 1885.[104] According to Mott's sparse comments, the Chicago-based magazine was one of the best periodicals representing a European culture in the coun-

Scandinavia

Terms:
Per Year, $2.00.

CHICAGO, FEBRUARY, 1885.

Single Number
Twenty Cents.

CONTENTS.

FROM HOME.

The political situation of the Scandinavian countries can be understood only when it is realized that a great social question underlies the whole conflict. This is generally overlooked, but has several times been set forth in this paper. It is the difference between the bureaucracy with the several classes connected with it, on one side, and the great majority of peasant farmers, on the other side, which causes the conflict. If we do not see how this difference arose, as the natural outcome of the history of the country, of the whole development, it is impossible to understand either the character of the difficulty, or the necessary means of ending it. Nor could it in any other way be explained how men of this character and these opinions could occupy those positions which they at present hold in the strife.

There are, for instance, the members of the present unpopular cabinet. In fact, Mr. Estrup, the premier and actual leader of the ministry and of the whole conservative party, is a man of liberal views, gifted, and favorable to modern ideas, himself a good debater and parliamentarian, and, more especially, early prominent as one of the most advanced among the great landed proprietors. Son of one of the best men in the country, the historian Estrup, he was himself, although socially connected with the rather con-servative class, one of the men who in his parliamentary beginnings promised best as a friend of the liberty and the progressive movement of the people. Or take his colleague, Nellemann, minister of justice, formerly professor at the University, and probably the best versed man in national history of law in the country. He was early sent to the first chamber, the *Landsthing*, because he was the upholder of the great judicial reforms needed after the great change in the constitution, juries, public and oral proceedings in the courts, with all the important reforms connected therewith. Mr. Nellemann has the liberal progressive ideas of the higher middle class. He is not only a friend of constitutional liberty, but also, for instance, of the Scandinavian unity, and merely his position as prominent judicial member of the Upper House happened to bring him in personal connection with a circle of men from whom emanated the present cabinet. Or take the present minister of marine, Commodore Ravn, one of the ablest and most popular members of the Lower House, the *Folkething*. Or, finally, the recently appointed minister of the interior, Hilmar Finsen, once the pronounced Danish chief of the police of the town of Sonderburg, Alsen, Sleswick, later Landshøvding of Iceland, and finally Mayor of Copenhagen ; everywhere known as an able and liberal official of the highest standing. It is possible that he, as others before him, owes his membership in the cabinet to his personal connection with a number of great landed proprietors and other prominent men from the Academy of Sorø, the Eton of Denmark. Or take the prominent member of the conservative party outside of the government, Carl Ploug, the great poet and journalist, and formerly the liberal of the liberals, the expounder of the Scandinavian idea, and the champion of the Danish nationality in Sleswick. He was never a great newspaper man in our sense of the word, but he was a journalist of such excellence that he was justly called the Armand Carrell of our young constitu-

Front page of *Scandinavia* for February, 1885.

try.[105] Indeed, a contemporary Danish immigrant, complaining about Norwegian control of most important Dano-Norwegian newspapers in the city, writes, "One exception is the monthly, *Scandinavia*. Published by a group of Danes, it gets attention and respect from the Americans."[106] The magazine offered numerous notes on politics and literature, some translations, and, in 1885, a department containing letters "From Home." Perhaps due to the small number of Danes in Chicago, however, its high quality did not enable it to survive beyond its third year.[107]

The article on Andersen was anonymous, but it was most likely written by a Danish American, perhaps the editor of the periodical, N. C. Frederiksen (1840–1905), who, prior to emigrating to the United States, was a member of the Danish parliament and a professor of economics at the University of Copenhagen.[108] For the author reveals an intimate knowledge of things Danish as well as experiences that suggest residence in the United States, very possibly in Chicago.[109] It is clear from the article that he knew Andersen and had heard him read aloud.[110] Unlike Griffin and others, however, he does not focus on visits or readings, in the manner of the travelogue. Instead, he renders a character study of Andersen the man and artist, in part as reflected in his art, and he does so in a manner that warrants more extensive quotation than heretofore.

The author begins by relating an anecdote that illustrates both Danes' ambivalence toward Andersen and his selfless, virtually Christlike response to it: "Not one word about lying or slandering. Not one word about forgiving and forgetting. Nothing, absolutely nothing, but the intensest anxiety, the tenderest exertions, to blot out forever the evil which had been done, and restore the evildoer to his own true self."[111] A few lines later he acknowledges Andersen's determination not to slight anyone owing to the pain he himself had suffered from others, but then himself takes with one hand what he has just given with the other: "But he exaggerated the disappointment it would be to his friends, not to get a smile from H. C. Andersen."[112] He then continues in a similar manner: "Nevertheless, Andersen was not what we call a great character. Entirely free from hatred, from envy, from that egotism which allows a man to put his foot noiselessly on his neighbor's right; entirely free from the least taint of anything odious or vicious, he lacked something of that positive force which we cannot help admiring even in cases in which it would be more proper simply to fear it. In his soul, as with a revolving light, there was something intermittent, which made him intense and striking in the moment, but which prevented him from fully realizing that which grows through years and years in silent continuity, without having any special hour of manifestation. Once when he heard the sailor boys of the neighborhood call him 'Our ape,' he exclaimed indignantly: 'I am such as the Lord has made me.' It was true, but it was a little too true. He remained a child to his death. His life expresses a beautiful destiny, but there is no history in it. It was marked with great gifts and singular vicissitudes, with perfect faith and unflinching persever- ance, but there was no trace in it of that self-training toward an inborn ideal, which constitutes the great character. It looks more like the life of a flower; nature said, blossom, and it blossomed."[113]

The author attempts to portray Andersen dispassionately, present- ing several instances of his moral superiority over his detractors, but he is essentially of one cloth with them, if not for all the same rea- sons.[114] At one level, he is unhappy with Andersen simply because he was not a "man's man," and one may question his association of admi- ration with fear. At another level, he exhibits recognition, but little understanding, of Andersen's personal and artistic nature, the fact, to speak with Schiller, that Andersen was a "naive" personality type and poet—"nature said, blossom, and [the flower] blossomed"— rather than a "sentimental" one such as the author himself. One senses the incredulity with which he notes how Andersen viewed the origin of his art: "[W]hen he spoke of his power he always spoke of it as a 'gift,' in a thankful way. To himself he was 'Lykkepeer' [Lucky Peer]; he believed in his star, or better, as he himself puts it in one of his poems to his mother, in his mother's prayers."[115]

Nonetheless, the author is able to appreciate the nature and power of Andersen's imagination, if not without reservations that betray an awe verging on fear of the uncanny: "The principal force in him was his imagination. The boldness with which Andersen's imagination attacked the strangest objects, the precision with which it struck them, the energy with which it handled them, the voracity with which it fed upon them, actually reminded one of that most audacious, most obstinate, most cruel of all birds of prey, the sparrow-hawk. . . . In another of his novels he describes the sound frozen and the ice break- ing up on account of a change in the current. The description is very elaborate and minute; it occupies a whole chapter. I have had that chapter examined by scientists who were fully conversant both with the relation between ice and running water, and with the relation between atmospheric changes and the corresponding changes of marine currents; and I have had it examined by old pilots who knew

the sound as a mother knows the cradle of her baby, and who had witnessed the phenomenon more than once, and with danger to their
lives. In all cases the examination began with a little smile, and in all
it ended with amazement and enthusiasm. The description is true. To
this may be added first, that it contains not one scientific observation,
not one scientific term, but moves on, giving only that which would
present itself to the eye and ear of any spectator; next it is as rich to
the ear as to the eye. The sucking, heaving, sighing, clicking, boom-
ing, bellowing of the water below, the fluttering, whistling, whining,
yelling, roaring of the wind above, fills the imagination to the very
brim; and this is a merit which even now [in the early years of natu-
ralism] is very rare, and which, at the time when the description was
made, was an astonishing innovation."[116]

For the author, Andersen's imagination is no less remarkable when
addressed to the small but often complex things of everyday life in
the fairy tales and stories, where it discloses subtle yet keen perceptiveness and exercises a powerful influence on readers: "The philosophy of the old ducks under the nettle-ferns, the criticism of the wise
hens of the barnyard, the lectures of the sparrow-mother under the
eaves, the love affairs between the leaden soldier from the play-box
and the dancer cut out of a piece of paper, etc., etc.,—often by a single queer word, as if by a twinkling of the eye, they flash upon the
reader—an insight in real life, in its truth and its follies, in its beauty
and its shortcomings, in its whole moral order, such as it is and such
as it ought to be, which is sought for in vain in the cumbrous descriptions of the naturalists of our time. I have seen children flushed with
excitement by reading about the first sun-ray of spring; how 'it
knocked at the door,' and how the seed under the ground cried out:
'Come in! come in!' I have seen old men startled by that trenchant
satire which, from the antics of all those fire-pokers and candle-
snuffers, fell upon themselves and their surroundings. I have more
than once heard a dispute settled, under a roar of laughter, by a few
sentences of Andersen, which opened a window where everybody
imagined a solid wall, and let in a flood of unexpected light."[117]

Despite his wonder over Andersen's imagination, expressed here
in tones reminiscent of the religious testimony, the author perceives
what he considers to be its limitations, which, however, are attributable in part to the "sentimental" turn of his own mind: "But even
Andersen's imagination was intermittent. It came and went like
good luck; nobody knew when or why. In his writings, the charm lies
in the style rather than in the composition, in the details rather than

in the total conception. A single side of human nature, or a single occurrence in human life he might exhaust in all its depth. But a whole man, or a whole destiny, he looked upon as a kind of enigma, whose solution he expected to find hereafter. This peculiarity, however, which, with many another author, would indicate a lack of depth, was with him simply expressive of the peculiar character of his powers. They might flame up into a huge conflagration, but they seldom, if ever, burned with a steady fire. Sometimes his imagination was dead, so that even the stars shone in vain, and at other times it became completely uncontrollable."[118]

Despite such perceived shortcomings the very power of Andersen's imagination inspires the author to dissuade readers from regarding *The Story of My Life* as a source of insight into the nature of the man, for "[h]e has given us his life, his feelings, everything that was his, in his works."[119] For similar reasons he indeed rejects the autobiography as a whole, drawing on the original "naïve" poet to admonish the even more "naïve" poet: "The words of Goethe, 'Candid only when unconscious, as a child, thy consciousness is death to thee,' ought to have kept Andersen from writing that book. He had a sharp eye for the odd eccentric, occurrences of life, and when told by him, in his naive graphic way, without other commentaries than a bright gleam of the eye, they were witty, but when retold, and put down in dead letters, they often became absurd."[120]

It is in this context that the author makes most of his few explicit comments on Andersen's creative works: "His true story is in his books. He had an open eye for the natural character and the customs of the different people he visited, he delighted in folklore traditions, and tells us about them in a picturesque, fascinating way. Andersen is an able cicerone. He takes us to Italy, Greece, Spain, Denmark, and his novels may obtain historical interest when those customs and pageants he describes are disappearing, and are no more."[121] The author then likens Andersen's description of Jægersborg Deer Park (Jægersborg Dyrehave) near Copenhagen to a painting reminiscent of Brueghel, averring that Andersen's stories make life in those countries real to the reader.

The author asserts unequivocally that "Andersen was in an eminent sense of the word the children's poet"[122]—this, as with a number of other commentators, despite himself having been enraptured as an adult on hearing Andersen read[123] and notwithstanding his knowledge of Andersen's startling and salutary effect on grown men as well as his perceptiveness and realism. However, he seeks to substantiate his claim not by scrutinizing the fairy tales and stories per se but rather by exploring why Andersen appeals to children and how he affects them. On the first count, he finds an explanation in what he calls Andersen's power of condensation: "Some people think that all mental food given to children ought first to be ground down to a powder as fine as dust—'abbreviated to the scope of the young understanding'; and then soaked in water until it becomes a slippery palaver—'accommodated to the grasp of the young understanding.' But this is certainly a sore mistake [one, as we shall see in the next chapter, that was perceived earlier by another of Andersen's keenest observers]. It is just the short and clear-cut sentence of Andersen's style, and the strange and shocking condensation of his statement, which make his tales a charm to all children."[124] The author also points to Andersen's "astonishing power of imitation" as a source of his appeal: "His tales are full of chirping birds and whistling winds and rustling leaves, and when he read them aloud he would make the whole room living with the voices of nature. But there was in his imitations nothing of that gross mechanical counterfeiting which may deceive and even frighten, but which also provokes and irritates. Nobody ever mistook his imitations for realities, and yet the images were so vivid and so exact that they never failed to produce intense delight."[125]

On the other count, the author is convinced that reading Andersen's fairy tales and stories can strengthen children in their religious faith and morality: "A mother asked, some time ago, 'What shall I do to educate, to form, to cultivate my children's imagination.' She was answered, 'Give them Andersen's stories.' What quantity of trashy books do not the children read! Some of those so-called Sunday-school books are often nothing but a sad mixture of millinery and Bible text. Andersen teaches children that they have a Father in heaven who cares for them personally, cares for every animal and plant as well; that crime, untruth, wickedness, vanity are always found out; or, rather, that they carry their own punishment. And have you anything better to offer? In Andersen's novels, if sin is spoken of, it is never made attractive. The stories are so well told that they will interest the young, and teach them a good deal besides."[126]

The author is one of exceedingly few commentators who know of Andersen's ambivalent relationship to children, his sense of ease with groups of them and discomfort with individual ones. He considers Andersen's association of the child with innocence to be the product of a provincial upbringing in a provincial country: "It is, however, no use denying it: there are people, and there are many of them, to whom innocence is not the heaven from which they fell, not a dream which has vanished, and upon which they look back with sorrow, but an acquired ideal which they feel should be reached sometime and somehow, and towards which they perhaps are striving with bent back; and this means that there are children, and many of them, whose very first act of self-consciousness is a crime, in the full psychological and moral meaning of the word. A child is a bundle of possibilities, and its whole innocence consists in its possibilities not yet having become realities. But if ever we shall have a psychology which is competent to explain anything, and a moral which is able to take the command, we must do away with this idea of a natural innocence born to develop by falling."[127] All the same, in spite of himself and with all reservations, the author affirms the power and the powerful impact of the provincial poet.

The last three general interest articles on Andersen were written by the same individual, and, although they appeared over a span of eleven years, their common point of view and considerable overlap make it reasonable to discuss them together. Two of them appeared in magazines, while the third was published in a collection of essays. The earliest came out in the *Dial* of Chicago in November 1884.[128] The *Dial* was for a time a radical journal of opinion and later an organ for modernist literature, criticism, and art, publishing works by many of the leading writers of both the United States and Europe.[129] For its first three and a half decades, however, it was a magazine of literary criticism about which Mott asks rhetorically, "Has any other American periodical so well represented the scholarly and conservative point of view in literary criticism as the *Dial* in its first phase?"[130] Despite its high quality and reputation the magazine ultimately went the way of many such publications, never exceeding a circulation of 5,000 during the stewardship of its first editor, who published the piece on Andersen.[131] The second article came out in March 1892, in the *Century*.[132] Although founding editor Josiah Gilbert Holland had died in 1881, his successor, genteel poet Richard Watson Gilder, maintained the periodical's general policies and status as a quality magazine.[133] By 1892, it had slipped somewhat below the circulation of 200,000 it reached in the late eighties, its highest point ever, but it retained its popularity as well as its quality. The third piece appeared in 1895 in a volume entitled *Essays on Scandinavian Literature*, which was written by the author of all three, Hjalmar Hjorth Boyesen.[134]

Hjalmar Hjorth Boyesen. By permission of the Houghton Library, Harvard University.

Born to a prosperous family in Norway and university educated in his home country, Boyesen (1848–95) emigrated to the United States in 1869 to pursue a career as a writer in what he considered to be the "land of literary opportunity."[135] First teaching at a college in Ohio and then editing a Norwegian-language weekly in Chicago, he traveled to Boston in 1871, where he met William Dean Howells and, through him, secured a position as an instructor of modern foreign languages at Cornell University, which he retained until 1880. The following year he received an appointment as instructor, and a year later as full professor, of Germanic languages and literatures at Columbia University, where he remained until his death at age forty-seven. During his relatively short career Boyesen wrote eight novels, ranging from the idyllic story of a Norwegian cattle herder turned artist (*Gunnar*, 1874) and a Norwegian immigrant success story (*Falconberg*, 1879) to a contrastive study of social idealism and political ambition (*The Mammon of Unrighteousness*, 1891) and an examination of the impact of wealth on ideals (*The Golden Calf*, 1892). He also wrote eight collections of short stories and eight other volumes, including children's books and literary scholarship, as well as numerous poems, essays, and reviews that appeared in periodicals.[136] Though preserving much of the sentimentalism of his romantic beginnings, Boyesen's work became increasingly realistic as he embraced Darwinism of a more optimistic brand that admitted of moral evolution.[137] He is remembered today principally for his application of these ideas to literary criticism and therefore as an advocate of realism and a precursor of naturalism.

The appearance of an article on a foreign author in the *Dial* was not a matter of course. The magazine showed little interest in literature abroad and was unkind to Ibsen, the one writer to whom it did pay attention.[138] Surely, Andersen's continuing popularity as well, perhaps, as Boyesen's own familiarity in Chicago's literary circles led to the publication of "Hans Christian Andersen" in 1884. Although the article was the first of the three by Boyesen to appear, in any event, it cannot truly be assigned precedence, for the piece published in the *Century* a few years later, entitled "An Acquaintance with Hans Christian Andersen," recounts visits the author paid Andersen in 1873. As he relates in the *Dial* article, indeed, Boyesen's attitude toward Andersen was influenced by these visits.[139] The essay contained in the volume on Scandinavian literature was a reprint of the article in the *Dial*, followed by an overview of Andersen's life and character with emphasis on the works, their reception, and Andersen's response to it. Consequently, Boyesen's writings do not go so far beyond the temporal bounds of this study as might initially appear to be the case. They share a number of features with the article in *Scandinavia,* not least of all maturity and length, both individually and, of course, in aggregate, and thus also call for extensive quotation.

At the beginning of both magazine articles Boyesen emphasizes Andersen's continuing popularity as well as his originality. In his reminiscence he writes, "Hans Christian Andersen has been dead for seventeen years, but his fame shows a vitality which suffers no diminution with the lapse of time. It is born anew with every fresh generation of children, and it is cherished by adults with the tenderness which clings to every memory of childhood."[140] Much in the manner of another American thirty years earlier, as we shall see, he continues, "His 'Wonder Stories' are the only books belonging to the pinafore period which are not discarded with advancing years; nay, which gain a new significance with maturing age. We read 'The Ugly Duckling' with the same delight at thirty that we did at ten; for we discover a new substratum of meaning which escaped our infantine eyes. 'The Emperor's New Clothes,' which fascinates a child by the mere absurdity of its principal situation, recalls to the adult a charming bit of satire for which he finds daily application in his own experience. . . . Father Time, as we all know, is the author's worst enemy; and an author who, though dead, can make such a vigorous fight against the ruthless old iconoclast has evidently the stuff in him for a long post-mortem career. He may be said to have made a successful launch toward immortality."[141]

In his article in the *Dial* Boyesen brings out Andersen's distinctiveness by contrasting him with the Grimms Brothers, as they were understood at the time: "Hans Christian Andersen was a unique figure in Danish literature, and a solitary phenomenon in the literature of the world. Superficial critics have compared him with the Brothers Grimm; they might with equal propriety have compared him with Voltaire or with the man in the moon. Jacob and Wilhelm Grimm were scientific collectors of folk-lore, and rendered as faithfully as possible the simple language of the peasants from whose lips they gathered their stories. It was the ethnological and philological value of the fairy-tale which stimulated their zeal; its poetic value was of quite secondary significance. With Andersen the case was exactly the reverse. He was as innocent of scientific intention as the hen who finds a diamond on a dunghill is of mineralogy. It was the poetic phase alone of the fairy-tale which attracted him; and what is more, he saw poetic possibilities where no one before him had ever discovered them. By the alchemy of genius . . . he transformed the common neglected nonsense of the nursery into rare poetic treasure."[142]

Although Boyesen paints a generally flattering picture in these lines, his comparison of Andersen to a hen and its phraseology might well have made the hypersensitive poet squirm. At one point in the book essay, while assigning Andersen a place in literary history, Boyesen scarcely conceals his fundamental ambivalence toward him: "I have no doubt it would have alarmed the gentle poet very much, if he had been told that he belonged to the Romantic School. To be classified in literature and be bracketed with a lot of men with whom you are not even on speaking terms, and whom, more than likely, you don't admire, would have seemed to him an unpleasant prospect. That he drew much of his inspiration from the German Romanticists, notably Heine and Hoffmann, he would perhaps have admitted; but he would have thought it unkind of you to comment upon his indebtedness."[143]

Boyesen shows his ambivalence toward Andersen in several ways, and at times he does so more obviously than in the passages previously cited, if not always voluntarily. In the *Century* article, for example, he relates an anecdote designed to put Andersen's tenderheartedness and simplicity of spirit in a favorable light, yet only a paragraph later, while recounting his first visit with the poet, he pokes genteel fun at Andersen's mispronunciation of Horace Scudder's surname.[144] During Boyesen's second visit Andersen had voiced a number of negative impressions about America, including his belief that Americans were unfeeling toward Indians. Boyesen had sought to disabuse him of most of these notions, but of the latter he writes, "I shall not reproduce my special plea in the case of The White Man *versus* The Red Man. We had a very animated discussion; and Andersen, who scarcely knew by name the pitiless doctrine of the survival of the fittest, grew quite alarmed at the novelty of the theory which I advanced. He had heard of Darwin, and took him to be a very absurd and insignificant crank who believed that he was descended from a monkey. It surprised him to hear me speak of him with respect as the greatest naturalist of the age. 'Oh, it is very sad,' he said, with a naïveté which laid bare his simple, childlike soul, 'that men cannot be satisfied with what God has taught them, but must question his word as if they knew better than he. Useful inventions which make life easier and happier, those I approve of with all my heart, and to them the scientists ought to confine their labors. But when they come to me and want to deprive me of my faith in God and his word, then I say to them, "Excuse me, gentlemen, I know as much about this as you do, and cannot accept you as guides."' I did not choose to take up the cudgels for Darwin just then. . . ."[145] Boyesen's social Darwinism is perhaps only the most unsavory aspect of his fundamental intellectual elitism and aristocratic sensibility, which one detects in the most unlikely contexts, as when he describes Andersen's appearance on their second meeting: "He was pale and emaciated; but his face seemed ennobled by suffering, and had lost the plebeian look which is characteristic of all the portraits taken during the earlier periods of his life."[146]

Much like the author of the article in *Scandinavia*, Boyesen is repulsed at a visceral level by Andersen the man, perhaps subliminally and not without self-contradiction. He finds Andersen's "plebianism" repugnant and takes him to task for his excessive humility toward the aristocracy, which "seemed unbecoming in a man who by dint of genius had risen from the lowest origin to a world-wide fame."[147] Himself a "sentimental" writer, he speaks of Andersen's "morbid sensibility" and the "unmasculine character of his mind," asserting that he was "[u]ltimately devoid . . . of self-criticism."[148] This all reflects Andersen's "immaturity of intellect," the fact that "intellectually he never outgrew his childhood."[149] "Yet in spite of all these limitations," Boyesen continues, "he was a poet of rare power; nay, I may say in consequence of them."[150] Indeed, Boyesen's characterization of Andersen as an artist calls to mind the idiot savant: "The vitality which in other authors goes toward intellectual development, produced in him strength and intensity of imagination. Everything which his imagination touched it invested with life and beauty."[151]

With regard to Andersen's imagination per se Boyesen stands in unqualified awe: "It divined the secret soul of bird and beast and inanimate things. His hens and ducks and donkeys speak as hens and ducks and donkeys would speak if they could speak. Their temperaments and characters are scrupulously respected. Even shirt-collars, gingerbread men, darning-needles, flowers, and sunbeams, he endowed with rational physiognomies and speech, consistent with their ruling characteristics. This personification, especially of inanimate objects, may at first appear arbitrary; but it is part of the beautiful consistency of Andersen's genius that it never stoops to mere amusing and fantastic trickery. The character of the darning-needle is the character which a child would naturally attribute to a darning-needle, and the whole multitude of vivid personifications which fills his tales is governed by the same consistent but dimly apprehended law. Of course, I do not pretend that he was conscious of any such consistence; creative processes rarely are conscious. But he needed no reflection in order to discover the child's view of its own world. He never ceased to regard the world from the child's point of view, and his personification of an old clothes-press or a darning-needle was therefore as natural as that of a child who strikes the chair against which it bumped its head."[152]

In his book essay the realist even waxes romantic: "All the jumbled, distorted proportions of things (like the reflection of a landscape in a crystal ball) is capitally reproduced. The fantastically personifying fancy of childhood, where does it have more delightful play? The radiance of an enchanted fairy realm that bursts like an iridescent soap-bubble at the touch of the finger of reason, where does it linger in more alluring beauty than in 'Ole Luköie' . . . 'The Little Mermaid,' or 'The Ice-Maiden'? There is a bloom, an indefinable, dewy freshness about the grass, the flowers, the very light, and the children's sweet faces. And so vivid—so marvellously vivid—as it all is."[153] Offering by way of example the passage where Ole Lukoie speaks with the recalcitrant letters in Hjalmar's copybook, Boyesen continues, "This strikes me as having the very movement and all the delicious whimsicality of a school-boy's troubled dream. It has the delectable absurdity of the dream's inverted logic. You feel with what beautiful zest it was written; how childishly the author himself relished it. The illusion is therefore perfect. The big child who played with his puppet theatre until after he was grown up is quite visible in every line. He is as much absorbed in the story as any of his hearers. He is all in the game with the intense engrossment of a lad I knew, who, while playing Robinson Crusoe, ate snails with relish for oysters."[154] As Boyesen demonstrates, one can read such passages with great relish even as a grown man, and apparently a quite masculine one at that.

Despite his distaste for Andersen's "intellectual immaturity" and "childishness," Boyesen has a sharp eye for the Dane's artistry—and intellectual maturity. Having described Andersen's many variations on the prototypical plot of the folktale, in which the hero kills the ogre and marries the princess, he writes, "In another species of fairy-tale, which Andersen may be said to have invented, incident seems to be secondary to the moral purpose, which is yet so artfully hidden that it requires a certain maturity of intellect to detect it. In this field Andersen has done his noblest work and earned his immortality. Who can read that marvellous little tale, 'The Ugly Duckling,' without per-

ceiving that it is a subtle, most exquisite revenge which the poet is taking upon the humdrum Philistine world, which despised and humil-
iated him before he lifted his wings and flew away with the swans, who
knew him as their brother? And yet, as a child, I remember reading
this tale with ever fresh delight, though I never for a moment suspected its moral. The hens and the ducks and the geese were all so
delightfully individualized, and the incidents were so familiar to my
own experience, that I demanded nothing more for my entertainment. Likewise in 'The Goloshes of Fortune' there is a wealth of
amusing adventures, all within the reach of a child's comprehension,
which more than suffices to fascinate the reader who fails to penetrate beneath the surface. The delightful satire which is especially
applicable to Danish society, is undoubtedly lost to nine out of ten of
the author's foreign readers, but so prodigal is he both of humorous
and pathetic meaning, that every one is charmed with what he finds,
without suspecting how much he has missed."[155]

Boyesen has reservations toward one of Andersen's most beloved
fairy tales: "'The Little Sea-maid' belongs to the same order of stories
[as 'The Ugly Duckling' and 'The Galoshes of Fortune'], though the
pathos here predominates, and the resemblance to De La Motte
Fouqué's 'Undine' is rather too striking."[156] However, he has nothing
but praise for another of Andersen's best-known works: "But the gem
of the whole collection [the *Wonder Stories Told for Children* in the
Author's Edition], I am inclined to think, is 'The Emperor's New
Clothes,' which in subtlety of intention and universality of application
rises above age and nationality. Respect for the world's opinion and
the tyranny of fashion have never been satirized with more exquisite
humor than in the figure of the emperor who walks through the
streets of his capital in *robe de nuit,* followed by a procession of
courtiers, who all go into ecstasies over the splendor of his attire."[157]

Moreover, Boyesen continues, "It was not only in the choice of his
theme that Andersen was original. He also created his style, though
he borrowed much of it from the nursery. 'It was perfectly wonderful,' 'You would scarcely have believed it,' 'One would have supposed
that there was something the matter in the poultry-yard, but there
was nothing at all the matter,'—such beginnings are not what we
expect to meet in dignified literature. They lack the conventional
style and deportment. No one but Andersen has ever dared to employ
them. But then, no one has ever attempted, before him, to transfer
the vivid mimicry and gesticulation which accompany a nursery tale
to the printed page. . . . The more successfully you crow, roar, grunt

and mew, the more vividly you call up the image and demeanor of the animal you wish to represent, and the more impressed is your juvenile [adult, or at least cultivated adult?] audience. Now, Andersen does all these things in print: a truly wonderful feat. Every variation in the pitch of the voice,—I am almost tempted to say every change of expression in the story-teller's features—is contained in the text. He does not write his story, he tells it; and all the children of the whole wide world sit about him and listen with eager, wide-eyed wonder to his marvellous improvisations."[158]

Boyesen prefers the earlier fairy tales and stories, expressing reservations toward some of the later ones. In the essay he writes, "Throughout the first series of 'Wonder Tales' there is a capital air of make-believe, which imposes upon you most delightfully, and makes you accept the most incredible doings, as you accept them in a dream, as the most natural thing in the world. In the later series, where the didactic tale becomes more frequent ('The Pine Tree,' 'The Wind's Tale,' 'The Buckwheat'), there is an occasional forced note. The story-teller becomes a benevolent, moralizing uncle, who takes the child upon his knee, in order to instruct while entertaining it. But he is no more in the game. A cloying sweetness of tone, such as sentimental people often adopt toward children, spoils more than one of the fables; and when occasionally he ventures upon a love story ('The Rose-Elf,' 'The Old Bachelor's Nightcap,' 'The Porter's Son'), he is apt to be as unintentionally amusing as he is in telling his own love episode in 'The Fairy-Tale of My Life.'"[159] "However," Boyesen concedes, "no man can unite the advantages of adult age and childhood, and we all feel that there is something incongruous in a child's talking of love."[160]

While overwhelmingly enthusiastic about the fairy tales and stories, Boyesen's response to Andersen's novels and other works is ambivalent. In "An Acquaintance," he affirms the continuing popularity of *The Improvisatore*: "The novel. . . , though it is fifty-seven years since it was written, is yet exhibited in the booksellers' windows on the Piazza di Spagna side by side with the latest Parisian successes; it is found in the satchels of nearly every tourist who crosses the Alps; and it was republished a few years ago, in a complete set of the author's works, by a well-known Boston publishing house."[161] But in the *Dial* article Boyesen had already given *The Improvisatore* a mixed review: "In reading Andersen's collected works . . . one is particularly impressed with the fact that what he did outside of his chosen field is of inferior quality—inferior, I mean, judged by his own high standard, though in itself often highly valuable and interesting. 'The Improvisatore,' upon which, next to 'The Wonder-Tales,' his fame rests, is a kind of disguised autobiography. . . . To appeal to the reader's pity in your hero's behalf is a daring experiment, and it cannot, except in brief scenes, be successful. A prolonged strain of compassion soon becomes wearisome, and not the worthiest object in the world can keep one's charity interested through four hundred pages. Antonio, in 'The Improvisatore,' is too much of a milk-sop to be agreeable, and without being agreeable he cannot, outside of Zola's novels, aspire to the part of a hero. That the book nevertheless remains unfailingly popular . . . is chiefly due to the poetic intensity with which the author absorbed and portrayed every Roman sight and sound. Italy throbs and glows in the pages of 'The Improvisatore' . . . Story's 'Roba di Roma,' Augustus Hare's 'Walks in Rome,' and all the other descriptions of the Eternal City, are but disguised guide-books, feeble and pale performances, when compared with Andersen's beautiful romance."[162]

Two of the other novels fare worse than their predecessor: "The same feminine sentimentality, which in spite of its picturesqueness makes 'The Improvisatore' unpalatable to many readers[,] is still more glaringly exhibited in 'O. T.' and 'The Two Baronesses.'"[163] According to Boyesen, the autobiography suffers from the identical flaw, though it has redeeming features as well: "In 'The Story of My Life' the same quality asserts itself on every page in the most unpleasant manner. The author makes no effort to excite the reader's admiration, but he makes constant appeals to his sympathy. Nevertheless this autobiography rivals in historic and poetic worth Rousseau's 'Confessions' and Benvenuto Cellini's 'Life.' The absolute candor with which Andersen lays bare his soul, the complete intentional or unintentional self-revelation, gives a psychological value to the book which no mere literary graces could bestow."[164]

In the later passages of the essay Boyesen turns to Andersen's theatrical works: "It is a curious fact that his world-wide fame as the poet of childhood never quite satisfied Andersen. . . . He was especially eager to win laurels as a dramatist; and in 1839 celebrated his first dramatic success by a farcical vaudeville entitled 'The Invisible at Sprogöe' [*Den Usynlige på Sprogø*]. Then followed the romantic drama 'The Mulatto' [*Mulatten*] (1840), which charmed the public and disgusted the critics; and 'The Moorish Maiden' [*Maurerpigen*], which disgusted both. These plays are slipshod in construction, but emotionally effective. The characters are loose-fibred and vague, and have no more backbone than their author himself."[165] While dis-

cussing a number of other works for the theater, however, Boyesen
has to give Andersen credit: "But his highest dramatic triumph he celebrated in the anonymous comedy 'The New Lying-in Room' [*Den
nye Barselstue*], which in a measure proved his contention that it was
personal hostility and not critical scruples which made so large a portion of the Copenhagen literati persecute him. For the very men who
would have been the first to hold his play up to scorn were the harti-
est in their applause, as long as they did not know that Andersen was
its author."[166] *Little Kirsten* (*Liden Kirsten*), however, was less successful, and *Ahasverus* was a virtual failure.

Boyesen's general ambivalence toward Andersen's lifework is especially pronounced in his judgment of *To Be or Not to Be*, less so with
regard to *Picture Book Without Pictures*. Of the former he writes, with
poorly concealed sarcasm, "But the most amusing thing he did, showing how incapable he was of taking the measure of his faculties, was
to write the novel, 'To Be or Not to Be' (1857), in which he proposed
once and forever to down the giant Unbelief, prove the immortality
of the soul, and produce 'peace and reconciliation between Nature
and the Bible.' It was nothing less than the evidences of Christianity
in novelistic form with which he designed to favor an expectant
world. 'If I can solve this problem,' he naïvely wrote to a friend, 'then
the monster materialism, devouring everything divine, will die.' But
rarely was a bigger Gulliver tackled by a tinier Liliputian [*sic*]. The
book not only fell flat, but it was only the world-wide renown and the
good intention of its author which saved it from derision."[167] However, he again waxes poetic over *Picture Book*, overcoming characteristic reservations: "The moon's pathetic and humorous observations
on the world she looks down upon every evening of her thirty nights'
circuit have already become classic in half-a-dozen languages. . . . The
tenderest, the softest, the most virginal spirit breathes through all
these sketches. They are sentimental, no doubt, and a trifle too sweet.
But then they belong to a period of our lives when a little excess in
that direction does not trouble us."[168]

The last paragraph of the essay summarizes Boyesen's reflections
on Andersen and represents his final word on the poet: "The softness,
the sweetness, the juvenile innocence of Danish romanticism found
their happiest expression in him; but also the superficiality, the lack
of steel in the will, the lyrical vagueness and irresponsibility. If he did
not invent a new literary form he at all events enriched and dignified
an old one, and revealed in it a world of unsuspected beauty. He was
great in little things, and little in great things. He had a heart of gold,

a silver tongue, and the spine of a mollusk. Like a flaw in a diamond, a curious plebeian streak cut straight across his nature. With all his virtues he lacked that higher self-esteem which we call nobility."[169]

After reading this résumé, one may be inclined to doubt whether personal acquaintance indeed provided Boyesen with greater insight into Andersen's character and to think rather that it made him incapable of judging the man and his work objectively. It is interesting to note that most of the pejorative labels he attaches to Andersen— "superficiality," "lack of steel in the will," "irresponsibility," "the spine of a mollusk," and "a curious plebeian streak"—are personal or social rather than aesthetic in nature. As a result, one might venture to say, not altogether facetiously, that Boyesen would have been happier with Andersen had he been a woman of polite birth. That, at least, would have made his "naïveté" understandable, perhaps even acceptable, if not desirable. For Boyesen's ambivalence toward Andersen surely derived not only from strictly personal predilections but also from the realist's intellectual and aesthetic rejection of the perceived effeteness of the romantic sensibility and the genuinely feminine culture that had arisen in the United States in the 1840s and remained influential in "genteel" writers such as Taylor and Stoddard until around the turn of the twentieth century.[170] Unfortunately, his own ideological orientation beguiled him into branding Andersen "the children's poet"[171] and terming the fairy tale his "chosen field," even though he obviously knew better.[172] It also blinded him to the difference between real or supposed simplicity and "childishness," or simplemindedness—that is, in his overall assessment of Andersen. For in his, in part, lyrical consideration of individual works, especially the fairy tales and stories, he discloses deep appreciation for the originality or sophistication of both their form and content. If not the first to perceive the orality of Andersen's narrative style, he discusses it at greater length than any of the commentators examined heretofore and is the only one to mention its seemingly impromptu nature. Embracing the theatrical works, though, curiously, not the poetry, indeed, his articles are unique for the breadth and depth in which they treat Andersen.[173]

~

Of the some dozen and a half individuals who wrote general interest articles on Andersen, Stoddard and Taylor alone were major figures during their day. Among the remainder only Curtis, Boyesen, and Browne (and, to a lesser extent, Scudder) appear to have enjoyed considerable esteem for a time. With the possible exception of the author of the article in *Scandinavia*, all of the others were apparently either leisure-hour authors with other primary pursuits or competent but, as it were, workaday writers who long ago slipped beyond the reach of cultural memory. Most were romantic in sensibility. Bagger, who wrote his piece in 1871, is a late, if not truly anachronistic, example. Browne, the author of the *Scandinavia* article, and Boyesen, on the other hand, belong in the realist or naturalist camp. Writing in 1863, Browne was clearly ahead of his time. However, all three were quite capable of responding virtually rhapsodically to the most exuberant of Andersen's imaginative sallies as well, no less significantly, to his sense for, and ability to sustain, realistic detail.

A number of the magazines in which the articles appeared—the *National*, *Potter's*, and *Scandinavia*—attracted few readers and were therefore short-lived. This is particularly unfortunate with regard to the article in *Scandinavia*, for its author is at least the equal of Boyesen in knowledge of Andersen and intellectual refinement and perhaps surpasses him in psychological sophistication. Three of the articles had the good fortune to appear in high-class literary magazines with relatively or exceedingly large readerships—*Putnam's*, *Harper's*, and the *Century*. In the latter, Boyesen's "Acquaintance" potentially found what was for the time a massive number of readers. It is a shame that his more ambitious article in the *Dial* did not even remotely fare so well, though there is evidence that the expanded version included in his volume of essays on Scandinavian literature reached a large number of people.[174] Of the four pieces that appeared as book chapters, one suspects that the renowned Taylor's found the most readers.

It is no wonder that the authors of the general interest articles, like many reviewers, took an interest in Andersen the man as well as the artist. From a social point of view his life and career were indeed exceptional, and he expanded on them in an autobiography which, like his strictly literary work, attained great notoriety in an age that delighted in confession and voyeurism. In the wake of historicism and positivism during the final third of the century, moreover, there arose a genetic notion of the relationship between author and work, a biographism based on the assumption that understanding of writing presupposes understanding of the author's life and vice versa. It also comes as no surprise that the seven writers who actually met Andersen exhibit the greatest interest in him as an individual. Most of them express awareness of a discrepancy between, on the one hand, his ungainly appearance and artlessness, which some attribute to his social background, and, on the other hand, the stylistic and even intellectual sophistication of his work, especially the fairy tales and stories. With Rosenberg and particularly the *Scandinavia* author and Boyesen, writing several decades after Q., this incongruity elicits distinct incredulity. At least the two Scandinavian Americans cannot construe Andersen's art as proceeding organically from his social background and character unless first making of him something approaching an idiot savant and/or regarding the fairy tale as the genre most appropriate to him.

In addition to the great artistic success of the fairy tales and stories such factors surely contributed to the increasingly narrow view of Andersen's lifework. To be sure, the notion of his homeliness and lack of sophistication did not prevent writers from appreciating his novels, travel books, and other works, if not uncritically, to the extent that they were aware of them. Nor were these deficits able to keep those who met him and/or heard him read from his works from experiencing a warm sense of fellowship with him or from admiring his oral vivification of the tales, which to their minds already lies in the language of the texts itself. The descriptive power he exhibits in his longer prose remains imposing even in the age of naturalism. However, the impression of Andersen's childlikeness, or, occasionally, childishness, whether gleaned from his autobiography, personal acquaintance, or both, led to an increasing focus on the fairy tale as the literary form most congenial to him and to the idea that he, the "children's poet," wrote principally for children—this even among commentators who reveal an awareness at some level that such was in fact not the case. Modern readers who associate Andersen exclusively with the nursery, with or without historical awareness, will probably register surprise over how many contemporary commentators perceived the mature wisdom and refined artistry of the fairy tales and stories. As the century progressed, however, this perception became clouded by causes that had nothing to do with the works per se and eventually vanished from the awareness of all but a very few.

Another factor would appear to have played a prominent role in this process. The younger writers, those born in the later 1830s and the 1840s, were the first to grow up with "Andersen's fairy tales." In "An Acquaintance," for example, Boyesen relates having told Andersen during one of their conversations that "his stories had been the dearest books of my childhood, and seemed associated with all that was delightful in the memory of it."[175] He was not the only one to make such a statement.[176] Coupled with the circumstances discussed above and to be considered in chapter 7, the apparently almost existential childhood experience of Andersen's fairy tales and stories may well have determined the younger writers' view of the author and probably itself sufficed to determine that of many readers who followed them.

6

Horace E. Scudder: An American "Literary Workman" and His Creative and Critical Response to Andersen

In the introduction to this study I made the seemingly paradoxical statement that book reviewing in the United States during Andersen's lifetime was anonymous even in those many instances where the reviewer's identity was known. Such was obviously not the case if one understands the word "anonymous" in its perhaps most common meanings, "not named or identified" or "of unknown authorship or origin."[1] If one takes the word to mean "lacking individuality, distinction, or recognizability," however, the assertion is valid, for even a name under a review does not in and of itself disclose the personal principles or predilections on which critical judgments are based.[2] Moreover, a reviewer's identity is shaped by historically conditioned national-cultural forces that are at least as likely to remain shrouded as to be revealed in a review, especially when read by later generations of readers. Multiply these identities by, say, the number of Andersen's commentators, and it becomes difficult to gain a picture of the pertinent critical landscape or landscapes that is both coherent and detailed. For these reasons, and due to considerations of space, it makes sense to scrutinize one individual who shared much the same background and many of the same assumptions about life and art as most relevant writers—an "ideal type" of the American Andersen critic, as it were—a person who can thus serve as a point of comparison and contrast and, indeed, give Andersen criticism in the United States a face.

Of course, the choice of Horace E. Scudder or, for varying reasons, anyone else to represent such a large and, in important respects, diverse group is inherently problematic. To the extent that Scudder is currently known at all, he is remembered principally as editor and

Horace E. Scudder. By permission of the Houghton Library, Harvard University.

popularizer of the Fireside Poets and for the many textbooks of literature he edited for the schools; no monograph has ever been written about him. For most readers his name alone will therefore not automatically evoke the range of associations requisite in a study of this sort. Born in 1838, he was only seven years old when reviews of Andersen's works began to come out in American magazines. However, this circumstance is itself less dubious than it appears at first glance. Despite the many important events and developments that occurred in the United States between 1845 and 1875, not to mention the last quarter of the century, the country experienced significant continuity of cultural assumptions as well, particularly in the leading segments of society. Moreover, the dates of Scudder's life and his biography itself offer considerable advantages. A native of Massachusetts, he grew up steeped in precisely those values that dominated the New England mind during the some three decades in question, a mentality which determined much of the critical thought of the time and persisted, with reduced vigor, even beyond it. A good generation younger than Emerson and Longfellow, he also experienced and reflected the shift in values that began after the Civil War. He belonged to the first generation of Americans that grew up with Andersen as a self-evident feature of the Western literary landscape. Significantly, Scudder was himself a creative writer who published, among many other things, a number of children's books that include three volumes of fairy tales and stories. Well received, these books earned him the sobriquet of "the American Andersen."[3] Many of his stories are readable even today, as suggested by the inclusion of one in a recently published anthology entitled *American Fairy Tales*.[4] It is small wonder, then, that Scudder became the principal admirer and most vocal advocate of Andersen in the United States.

In his article on Andersen published in the *Century* in 1892 Hjalmar Hjorth Boyesen spoke for most cultural cognoscenti in the country when he called Scudder a "well-known man of letters."[5] By the time he wrote these words, Scudder had indeed long since become an *homme de lettres* in the broadest sense of the word: as a creative writer; as a journalist writing on a wide variety of subjects; as a critic; as literary adviser to one of the most prestigious publishing houses in the nation; and as editor of several magazines, including one of America's leading literary publications. Especially wearing his hats as critic, literary adviser, and editor, he exerted a powerful influence on American letters. Despite his—I would contend undeserved and quite unfortunate—consignment to the halls of the forgotten, one may well consider Scudder the most felicitous choice to represent "the American Andersen critic." For these reasons, and because of his own inherent interest, the present chapter offers a detailed overview of Scudder's life and work followed by an examination of his critical writing on Andersen.

1

Scudder was born in Boston on October 16, 1838, to parents whose lineage reached all the way back to the Puritan settlement of New England.[6] His mother was a descendent of John Winthrop, the first governor of the Massachusetts Bay Colony, while his father's family arrived in America during the early days of the Colony. His paternal ancestors were seafarers who lived on Cape Cod until his father moved to Boston to become a moderately successful hardware merchant. Over the some two centuries of their presence in the New World neither family had strayed from its original Congregationalism. However, Scudder himself reflects the liberalization of the faith inspired inter alia by Horace Bushnell (1802–76), whose influence reversed the denomination's return to its Calvinist roots around the beginning of the nineteenth century, which occurred in response to the Unitarian "defection" over the course of the preceding century.[7]

In 1846, when Scudder was around eight, his family of nine moved to a farm near Roxbury, like the Bodley family in the first volume of his successful children's series.[8] There, he enjoyed the pleasures of an outdoor life and attended Roxbury Latin School. Following his family's return to Boston in 1853 due to reverses in his father's business, Scudder completed his preparatory training at Boston Latin School and the next year went to Williams College, which his father had chosen for him and his three older brothers because of its religious orthodoxy. Sometime after graduating, Scudder wrote matter-of-factly of the limitations of his education at Williams, citing among other things the virtual absence of "acquaintance with general literature" and the absolute lack of "thorough scholarship in the classics."[9] At the same time he felt that the college had provided its students with the habit of "independent, vigorous thought."[10] Whatever the shortcomings of his typically middle-class classical education may have been, Scudder later maintained a strict regimen of private study, including daily reading in his Greek New Testament, and demonstrated a remarkable appetite for creative, scholarly, and editorial work of the most varied kinds.

Scudder considered careers in the ministry and teaching but rejected both, in part because of intermittent deafness of varying intensity that plagued him his entire life. Having written for his college magazine and served as editor for a time, he determined to earn his livelihood by the pen and within a year of graduation moved to New York City, which was soon to eclipse Boston as the cultural center of the nation. Over the next few years he succeeded in placing numerous articles and stories in a number of newspapers and religious journals as well as the *New Englander*, the *Atlantic Monthly*, and the *North American Review*, not to mention his seminal article on Andersen, which appeared in the *National Quarterly Review* in 1861—quite an achievement for someone of his still tender years.[11]

Scudder collected seven of his magazine stories, some of which he likely originally wrote for his nieces, in a volume that came out under the title *Seven Little People and Their Friends* in time for the Christmas holidays of 1862. The first review of the book appeared in the *Atlantic* in January of the following year and was written by Henry Mills Alden, a descendent of the John Alden of Longfellow's "The Courtship of Miles Standish" and later the editor of *Harper's (New) Monthly Magazine* for half a century.[12] Alden and Scudder had met at Williams and had lived together in New York for several months in 1861. Their friendship during this time perhaps explains both the kind tone of the review and the parallels drawn between Scudder and Andersen.

Indeed, Scudder discloses his reading of Andersen in the very first story, "The Three Wishes," in which little Effie Gilder finds a marvelous ideal realm at the bottom of the sea. A figure similar to Ole Lukoie named Kleiner Traum (German for Little Dream), who has a wonderful kaleidoscope rather than a magic umbrella, appears in "A Christmas Stocking With a Hole in It," perhaps the most readable of the stories despite its derivative character. In this piece, as in others in the volume, Scudder reveals an even greater debt to Charles Dickens, the final two sections containing unmistakable reminiscences of *A Christmas Carol*.[13] On the whole, Scudder's New York has much the same feel as Dickens's London, and he indulges in the often humorous conceits so typical of Dickens, such as the competition between the kettle and the cricket in *The Cricket on the Hearth*. If beholden to Dickens and Andersen for motifs and stylistic devices, Scudder frequently makes them his own, for instance when he enables inanimate objects to speak, as it were, in character, albeit with less address than his model. There is something of Andersen's magic in Jack Frost's description of his window painting and other elements in "A Faery Surprise Party," and there is an unmistakable bit of "The Wind Tells about Valdemar Daae and His Daughters" in the Northeast Wind's "Wheugh" in the same story.

In his review of the collection Alden points to a more fundamental similarity between Scudder and Andersen when he opines that his friend's stories appeal to adults as well as to children. While one may question whether "there is more depth of idea in their design," Scudder's tales doubtless possess an ideal substance inaccessible to younger readers.[14] The corals dying and becoming part of the undersea castle in "The Three Wishes" are building a society based on love qua respect for the individual and individual responsibility. "The Old Brown Coat" is a parable that depicts timeworn and inhumane convention, read *feudalism*, yielding to the new and humane, read *democracy*. Equally parabolic, "The Rock Elephant" portrays man's fall from grace and the promise of redemption and eternal life. "New Year's Day in the Garden" is at base a little creation myth affirming life despite its sorrows.

Scudder's New York days, which proved to be a sort of moratorium between student life and adulthood, came to an abrupt end in January 1863, when his father's death brought him back to Boston to assume responsibility for the family household. His brother David had died earlier while working as a missionary in India, and Horace now honored his father's wish that he write a memorial biography, which came out in 1864.[15] However, Scudder continued his critical and creative writing even under the new, more restrictive circumstances. The same year, he made a favorable impression with an essay on William Blake published in the *North American Review*, in which he stressed the power of imagination to realize the essence of life and humanity.[16] During the same period he also issued a collection of fourteen stories bearing the title *Dream Children*.[17] In the preface, playing with an allusion to Charles Lamb's piece of the same title, he asserts that the children portrayed in the book are not mere dreamers or creatures of fancy, in the absolute sense.[18] He thinks of them instead as rooted in life and revelatory of "conceptions of spiritual excellence which appear to us most readily through the presence of children, and which reappear, it may be, in our less worldly moods afterward"—a key notion in his thought and writing.[19]

Scudder's reading of Andersen and Dickens is also manifest in his second collection of stories. In a review of his friend's latest work,

DREAM CHILDREN

BY THE AUTHOR OF
"SEVEN LITTLE PEOPLE AND THEIR FRIENDS"

CAMBRIDGE
SEVER AND FRANCIS
1864

Title page of *Dream Children* by Horace E. Scudder.

indeed, Alden speaks of Scudder as the children's Dickens.[20] Though differing entirely in execution, "The Old House in the Wheat Forest" shares with "The Old House" (*Det gamle Huus*) both its central motif and its theme of transience mitigated by the constancy of certain virtues, love here and kindness there. "What Befell the [kitchen] Range," which picks up where the Robinson Crusoe spoof, "The Castaways," in the earlier volume leaves off, recalls "The Red Shoes" inasmuch as both tales feature shoes that are assigned the role of rectifying wrong. One of Scudder's best and most Dickensian stories is "Widow Dorothy's New Year's Eve," in which the title figure and her simpleminded servant prepare for guests long departed from the family home, or earthly life, but not from old Dorothy's clouded, ever hopeful memory. Several additional stories center on the home and deal with the transiency of life. "The Pot of Gold," for example, is a quest myth in which the "Holy Grail" proves to be precisely the home. In most of the stories transience is counterbalanced by a positive value such as the beauty of life or the promise of salvation. The melancholy is unbroken only in "John's Nap," in which a young woman discovers a toy lost during her childhood.[21]

In view of the times and Scudder's predilections it may come as some surprise that only one of the stories takes up the theme of art. "The Two Roses" is a (rather saccharine) tale of love's power, persistence, and fulfillment, in which Scudder presents a conventional romantic image of the poet as creator of beauty and of poetry as confession. Perhaps less unexpected, if hardly self-evident in the early 1860s, is the fact that Scudder treats social foibles and ills. In "The Rich Man's Place" he criticizes ostentation in the form of immoderate pride in travel abroad and its booty, recommending genuineness and simplicity of spirit in its place, not without an implicit comparison of (European) feudalism and (American) democracy. More acutely topical in 1864 was "The Prince's Visit," in which "weak Job" forgoes his long-anticipated opportunity to see the prince in order to help a sick and needy black child on the street. Due to the obliquity of criticism in both tales and the strong moral-religious overtones of the latter these stories are a far cry from what lay around the corner in the 1870s and beyond, but they demonstrate that Scudder was sensitive to what was already in the air.

The year 1864 was pivotal for Scudder. Not only did his second collection of children's stories come out to a friendly critical reception, but its success inspired James T. Fields, part-owner of the famous publishing house of Ticknor and Fields and for a decade editor of the

Atlantic Monthly, to invite him to contribute regularly to the firm's envisioned children's magazine, *Our Young Folks.* Moreover, E. P. Dutton, who had published several of Scudder's stories in his *Church Monthly,* asked the young writer to work for him as an adviser, or editor, with the responsibility of evaluating book manuscripts submitted for publication. In addition to accepting Scudder's essay on Blake for the venerable *North American Review,* editor Charles Eliot Norton proposed that the rapidly rising author write a critical essay on children's literature for the magazine, which led to activity of greater duration and perhaps greater historical import than his creative work for the young.

However, it was an even earlier contact that proved to be most auspicious of all. During his senior year of college Scudder had edited the Williams *Quarterly* and had engaged Henry Oscar Houghton and his Riverside Press to print the publication. Recalling his satisfaction with the work, he had again relied on the firm, which was now called Hurd and Houghton and offered publishing as well as printing services from offices in New York and Boston, to handle his biography of his deceased brother. Before the year was out, Houghton, who ran the Boston office, hired Scudder as literary adviser, not only to evaluate manuscripts but also, inter alia, to collate an edition of British historian, author, and statesman Thomas Macauley, to write a book on croquet, and even to prepare advertising copy. Houghton was keen to enter the burgeoning juveniles market and believed he had found the right man to do the job in the American Andersen.

Scudder's preparations for the magazine were long and arduous, involving a six-month sojourn in England together with Houghton's partner, Melancthon Montgomery Hurd; study of Ticknor and Fields's *Our Young Folks,* from which he withdrew a manuscript and further cooperation; and an endless stream of conferences intended, among other things, to design the magazine and to arrange for contributors and artists. Scudder was able to attract illustrators on the order of political caricaturist Thomas Nast and Winslow Homer and writers such as Jacob Abbot of the popular Rollo series; Unitarian minister and transcendentalist writer and painter Christopher Pearce Cranch; poet of the New Hampshire coast Celia Thaxter; Unitarian clergyman and popular writer Edward Everett Hale (*The Man Without a Country*) and his sister, educator and satirist Lucretia Peabody Hale; as well as Mary Elizabeth Mapes Dodge (*Hans Brinker; or, The Silver Skates*); local colorist Sarah Orne Jewett; poet and friend of Emily Dickinson, Helen Hunt Jackson; and most impressively, of course, Hans Christian Andersen.

The story of Scudder's relationship to Andersen, from his repeated, unsuccessful attempts to establish contact with his distant mentor to his eventual publication of seventeen of Andersen's fairy tales and stories, ten for the first time anywhere, has been treated elsewhere and need not occupy us here.[22] Gaining the best-known and best writer of fairy tales in the world as a contributor was certainly Scudder's greatest coup, both in terms of publicity for the magazine and, as will become apparent later, because of his high estimate of Andersen as a writer for children.[23] The *Riverside Magazine for Young People* debuted in December 1867, to favorable reviews in several papers. Mott later called it "brilliant," and it still receives accolades as the best, or one of the best, publications of its kind during its time.[24] However, despite Andersen's presence and Scudder's best efforts, which included cost-saving measures such as writing a certain number of pages per issue gratis, the magazine was never profitable and ceased publication with the December issue of 1870.

During the *Riverside*'s three-year run Scudder was also busy in other respects, not least of all with preparation of the Author's Edition of Andersen's works. It is interesting to pursue the course of this project in the correspondence between the two men, where it occupies a dominant position beside discussion of the fairy tales and stories that were to appear in the children's magazine and, after its demise, in *Scribner's Monthly*.[25] Initially, for example, Scudder intended to publish only an authorized edition of the tales, but Andersen himself proposed that he update his autobiography for inclusion. Scudder also eventually planned to publish a volume of poetry and plays but ultimately abandoned the idea due to difficulty in finding a translator for the verse and poor sales of volumes already issued. The depression of 1873 to 1879 as well as other factors united to condemn the edition to commercial failure. Nonetheless, it accounted for most of the small amount of money Andersen received for sales of his books outside of Denmark, owing to the absence of an international copyright law, and remains the most extensive edition of his works in the English language.

In 1887, Scudder dedicated a volume of essays to his old friend Alden, writing, "In that former state of existence when we were poets, you wrote verses which I knew by heart and I read dreamy tales to you which you speculated over as if they were already classics. Then you bound your manuscript verses in a full blue calf volume and put it on the shelf, and I woke to find myself at the desk of a literary workman."[26] It is uncertain precisely what point in time Scudder had in

Photograph of Andersen in 1872 at the age of around seventy-two taken by Budtz Müller. Reproduced in agreement with Odense City Museums, Denmark.

mind when he wrote these words, but it may well have been around 1870. It is true that a substantial amount of creative work still lay in the future in that year. And several of the twenty-two texts contained in the volume *Stories From My Attic* of 1869 would have fit nicely in either of the earlier volumes.[27] In one of his letters to Andersen,

THE

STORY OF MY LIFE.

BY

HANS CHRISTIAN ANDERSEN,

AUTHOR OF "THE IMPROVISATORE," "WONDER STORIES TOLD
FOR CHILDREN," ETC.

NOW FIRST TRANSLATED INTO ENGLISH,

AND

CONTAINING CHAPTERS ADDITIONAL TO THOSE PUBLISHED IN THE DANISH EDITION,
BRINGING THE NARRATIVE DOWN TO THE ODENSE FESTIVAL OF 1867.

𝔄𝔲𝔱𝔥𝔬𝔯'𝔰 𝔈𝔡𝔦𝔱𝔦𝔬𝔫.

NEW YORK:

PUBLISHED BY HURD AND HOUGHTON.

𝔠𝔞𝔪𝔟𝔯𝔦𝔡𝔤𝔢: 𝔯𝔦𝔳𝔢𝔯𝔰𝔦𝔡𝔢 𝔭𝔯𝔢𝔰𝔰.

1871.

Title page of Andersen's autobiography as edited by Horace E. Scudder in the Author's
Edition published by Hurd and Houghton.

indeed, he writes that some of the stories could not have been written, had Andersen not taught him "many things."[28] He specifically
mentions "Good and Bad Apples," a little morality tale about a worm
that recommends avoidance of sin even though it feels good, and
"Tom and Jom," a story of two horses who illustrate the virtue of good
humor and the virtuelessness of its opposite. However, he might
equally well have cited "As Good as a Play," in which an odd assort-
ment of knickknacks reminiscent of those in "The Shepherdess and
the Chimneysweep" (*Hyrdinden og Skorstensfeieren*) relate to each
other, each according to its own peculiarity.

Whether Andersenesque or not, several other stories in the collection number among Scudder's most interesting and/or best. "The
Neighbors" tells of two families whose rancor and reconciliation are
anticipated and echoed by their cats. In "Three Wise Little Boys" parents who have withheld the teachings of Christianity from their children to enable them to make a rational decision as adults witness
them unwittingly reenact the Christmas story. As in *Dream Children,*
Scudder takes up sociopolitical themes and treats the nature and role
of art in some of these stories. The religious pathos of "The Vision of
John the Watchman," while likely to offend modern sensibilities, cannot conceal a critical attitude toward working conditions associated
with an increasingly industrial society. In "The Music Party," Scudder
presents a complicated, Hoffmannesque phantasmagoria that evokes
the power of music and suggests both the necessity of receptiveness
for this power to be experienced and the notion that said experience
itself represents a new creation. Though set in a vaguely medieval
past, the romance "Rose and Rosella" unites these two concerns, contrasting rich and poor more starkly than "The Rich Man's Place" and
assigning an important role to the poet, who possesses the "voice that
utters [people's] best thoughts" and from whom they learn a song
"which is now to them their own heart, beating in words."[29]

Like "The Music Party," "The Return of Orpheus" celebrates the
power of music, specifically the then current renewal of music in the
sense of a divinely inspired, romantic art that had deposed an art
"reduced . . . to perfect rules."[30] And the roof garden in "A Story that
I Mean to Write" recalls the one lying between the dormer windows
of Kay's and Gerda's houses in "The Snow Queen," Andersen's classic creative statement on the relationship between imagination and
intellect. However, this text is actually a familiar essay on the rocket
as a symbol of human life rather than a story, and the preceding one
is essentially a retelling of the myth of Orpheus. A substantial num-

ber of the works in the volume are designed less to address the imagination than to serve various didactic purposes, albeit in an entertaining manner, for example, to provide a historical overview of the progress of liberty from the Middle Ages to the American present ("The Sleepy Old Town of Bruges," "The Battle of the Golden Spurs");[31] to portray great artists (William Blake in "Looking at a Picture," "Sir Walter Scott," "Wolfgang Amadeus Mozart"); or to introduce an exemplary personage (the blind Swiss entomologist "Francis Huber"). With "The Singing of the Seirens [*sic*]: As Told by Odysseus" thrown in for good measure, indeed, *Stories From My Attic* is an omnium-gatherum, the contents of which one recent commentator likens, not surprisingly, to those of a magazine.[32]

The volume opens with a sort of introduction entitled "The Attic," which, as Scudder related to Andersen, referred to a real place, perhaps his quarters in New York, but which he now conceives of as a realm of imagination.[33] Describing it accordingly, he writes that he must now leave it for another home, collecting in the book the most fitting of "the fancies and stories and thoughts which have endeared the room to me" to take with him into society.[34] This may have been his way of bidding farewell to the spiritual home of his youth for the less magical but nonetheless congenial and meaningful activity of a "literary workman." That is to say, it may have already dawned on him what course his professional life was to take. He would thus appear to have been on the cusp of the two trends in the vocation of authorship that Lawrence Buell recognizes in nineteenth-century New England: "a movement toward the sense of a specialized vocation, partially countered by the persistence of a generalist ideal of cultural coherence, and a movement toward commercialization, partially countered by the persistence of the ideal of art as a form of cultural service."[35] In any event, the didacticism already evident in several of the texts in *Stories From My Attic* outweighs the imaginative element in most of Scudder's later work.

The didactic cast of these pieces did not seem to disturb William Dean Howells, who reviewed the book in the December issue of the *Atlantic Monthly* in 1869, for he finds both entertainment and unobtrusive religious edification in the parti-colored collection, mildly criticizing only what strikes him as the inadequate closure of certain texts, the heavy-handedness of others, and the overwrought ethereality of "Rose and Rosella."[36] If Scudder was at all disappointed over this review, his feelings must have been permanently assuaged by Andersen's kind and, certainly in part, justified response to the copy of the book Scudder sent him: "I saw in these [stories] something kindred to my own poetic nature, and cannot but be pleased that *you* like my writings. I could not wish for a better translator than a man who is spiritually akin to me."[37] The book must have been quite popular. Although no record of sales or the number of editions was available to me, my personal copy was published in 1900, a generation after the book's debut.

A glance at the publication dates of Scudder's works, original and edited, discloses that the period from around 1870 to 1875 was a fallow, and the reason is clear. The importance of his contributions to the burgeoning business of Hurd and Houghton, operating in Boston from the Old Corner Bookstore, which had become famous during the ownership of Ticknor and Fields, had grown so precipitously that by early 1871 he was made Houghton's second-in-command and, the following year, a partner in the firm. The advancements proved problematic in at least two respects. Tied to the financial fortunes of the house, the no longer salaried Scudder's income suffered a substantial decrease due to the economic woes of the early seventies. Perhaps more importantly, his work for the firm consumed his time and energy to the extent that he was scarcely able to pursue his beloved private study and writing. Consequently, he resigned his position early in 1875 and embarked on an eleven-year period of relative freedom for freelance writing and lecturing—"relative," because later the same year he agreed to work for Houghton part-time for a specified salary and over the next decade or so assumed the editorial reins of the *Atlantic Monthly* during three summer absences of editor Thomas Bailey Aldrich.

Scudder himself possessed in rich measure the "habits of industry and close application" he attributed to Sir Walter Scott.[38] During his years of comparative independence he completed both his work for Houghton and at least twenty volumes that include lives of Noah Webster and Bayard Taylor (the latter coauthored), a history of the nation for the schools, and anthologies of American poetry and prose as well as collections of both for children.[39] The Bodley family had made its initial appearance in a story published in the *Riverside Magazine* in 1867, but Scudder wrote all eight books in the series as well as a similar volume about Boston, his fourth collection of short prose, and his only novel during this period of time. In all nine of the children's books the didactic element observed in *Stories From My Attic* plays a prominent role.

Indeed, Scudder later numbered the Bodley books among those juveniles that "appealed to the understanding rather than to the imagination of the child. . . ."[40] All of them abound with references to, or vignettes about, remarkable people, places, and events, but each has a particular focal point. The first, *Doings of the Bodley Family in Town and Country*, centers on the discovery of life in the country by the three children—Nathan, Phippy (from "Philippa"), and Lucy— following the merchant family's move from Boston to Roxbury. *The Bodleys Telling Stories* revolves around the history of New England, particularly Massachusetts, from Viking times through the colonial period on to the narrated present, the 1850s.[41] One of the "Last Stories," as the final chapter is entitled, deals with Andersen, containing important details of his life and quotations from his autobiography. Earlier, Lucy receives a volume of the fairy tales and stories, which has "proved a source of unending enjoyment" and a "treasure."[42] Lucy is excited to learn that Andersen is still alive and writing more stories every couple of years.

The next two volumes, *The Bodleys on Wheels* and *The Bodleys Afoot*, tell of journeys to important historical sites in New England.[43] In the former the entire family travels to destinations such as Salem and Newberry(port) as well as to Amesbury, which receives a chapter devoted to John Greenleaf Whittier and the Quakers. The latter relates a foot-trip taken by the now teenage Nathan and older cousin Ned from Boston to New York, during which they learn, among many other things, of Medfield, a town partially destroyed during King Philip's War, or Metacom's War (1675–76), one of the earliest conflicts between colonists and Indians; the Charter Oak in Hartford, where colonial government came to an end under a new British governor; and Yale University prior to its move to New Haven.

The Bodley series demonstrates what Scudder thought American children and youth should know about their European as well as American cultural heritages and the ties between the two. *Mr. Bodley Abroad* recounts father Charles Bodley's journey to England, where sites related to the life of Sir Walter Scott figure prominently, and follows him as he continues his travels through the Low Countries and Central Europe, ending with his return home and relation of the story of Joan of Arc and other events in British and French history.[44] In *The Bodley Grandchildren and their Journey in Holland* Scudder leaps forward to his own time and sends the now married Nathan and Phippy, together with their spouses and children, on a tour through

Holland and Dutch (cultural) history, including a chapter entitled "Track of the Pilgrim Fathers."[45] Interestingly, Scudder allows his characters to express their shock and sorrow on learning of the shooting of his friend from Williams days President James Garfield. In the subsequent volume, *The English Bodley Family*, indeed, he has these Americans and worshippers in an English church join in what amounts to an extended tribute to Garfield upon his death.[46]

In *The English Bodley Family* Scudder focuses on the multifaceted and still not unproblematic relationship of the United States to Great Britain, which despite the high standing of France and, most recently, Germany, still exerted the greatest cultural influence of any other country on the nation. This relationship comes to the fore in many of the people and places of various times that the Bodleys discuss or visit, accompanied part of the way by an English family of the same name. While they must see Stratford for principally "English" reasons, a host of personages and sites attracts the travelers' interest because of their connection to the United States. The Battle of Worcester, which assured Cromwell's accession to power, for instance, furnishes an occasion for noting that Massachusetts's successful self-government served as an ideal which English leaders sought to emulate.[47] This example betrays Scudder's desire to show that the influence which passed between America and England was at times reciprocal, even during the colonial period.

Scudder was hardly a political or cultural jingoist, reflecting the binocularity that characterized most contemporary American men of letters. In the passage dealing with Cromwell he makes clear that, though many Englishmen wonder whether they might not be better-off with the American form of government, any reform would proceed organically from present, that is, inherently English, conditions. He also acknowledges the continuity—in the 1880s—between the United States and Europe, especially England, with respect to institutions, laws, customs, and the like.[48] At the same time, he has one of his characters say, "[A] great deal of the best there is in America has grown up out of the life people have led there. . . ."[49] And the country fares well in other explicit or implicit comparisons with England, for example, the alleged superiority of the elected Senate over the hereditary House of Lords and the ascription of the modern rage for travel to the growth of democracy in the world and the interest in men as men rather than as members of a particular class. Moreover, Scudder's Englishmen reveal both interest in and knowledge of American history and culture. At one point in their journey, for instance, the Bodleys witness a performance of English composer John Barnett's (1802–90) cantata based on Longfellow's ode "Building of the Ship."[50] At least from around 1870 on Scudder saw the main purpose of his work as writer and editor in the promotion of sociopolitical and literary culture in the United States and the cultivation of its awareness especially among young Americans.

In the context of this study the most interesting volume in the Bodley series is the last, *The Viking Bodleys: An Excursion into Norway and Denmark*.[51] Roughly a third of the book is devoted to Denmark, and Andersen himself receives two entire chapters, "The Home of Andersen" and "Andersen's Birthplace," also figuring in "Berthel Thorvaldsen" and, at least implicitly, in "Rambles in Copenhagen," which describes the world in which he moved. Scudder went so far as to include illustrations from some of Andersen's stories as well as a painting of the mature poet based on a photograph by Georg E. Hansen and what appear to be a drawing and a watercolor of the statue by August Saabye located in the King's Gardens near Rosenborg Castle, placing the one in the text and the other on the back cover. Nathan renders an accurate assessment of Andersen's attitude toward children based on the Dane's rejection of a design for the statue that depicted children at his knee.

Like England in previous volumes, Denmark provides an impetus for observations about America and Americans. Nathan relates that he once wished to live in a small country such as Denmark, for "[i]t must be so much easier to make one's patriotism cover a small territory, than to spread it over a vast area like the United States, where one cannot possibly know, even in the most cursory fashion, the people of the different parts of the country."[52] When his brother-in-law expresses his preference for a large nation with a great variety of life, Nathan asserts his pride in being an American yet affirms that he still has moments when America is too large for his imagination. In another passage he attributes the absence of class distinctions in Denmark to the virtual homogeneity of Danish society. While there are no longer Dutch and English in New York, he declares, it will be some time before the new Americans lose their association with the countries of their birth, here specifically Germany and Ireland. To this, Phippy says, "I think we shall be all Americans when we play together, and not when we vote together," words that resonate today as at the time the book was written, if for different reasons.[53] On the return trip home Nathan comes back to this topic, observing that history will rank the current migration from Europe to America above "the

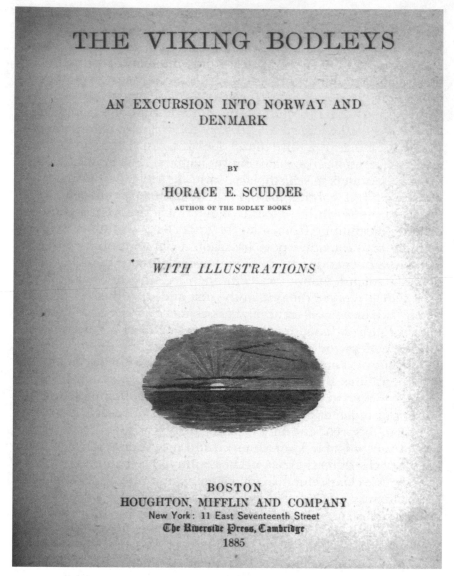

Title page of *The Viking Bodleys* by Horace E. Scudder.

descent of the Northern hordes upon Rome, and second only in importance to the first great migration of the Aryan tribes."[54] While Scudder was at base a cultural pluralist, he was clearly unsettled by the modern *Völkerwanderung*, not least of all because it impinged upon what was for him the crucial question of what constitutes American cultural identity.[55]

Despite Scudder's assertion to the contrary, the role accorded Andersen in the first and especially the last volumes of the Bodley books suggests that imagination figures prominently in the series. In every volume, indeed, the narrative itself often appeals to the imagination through the numerous accompanying illustrations, poems, tales, and even songs, complete with musical notation. Although most of the literary texts are the work of writers now forgotten, Scudder included pieces by major figures such as Blake, Wordsworth, Robert Browning, Oliver Wendell Holmes, and particularly Longfellow, the Bodleys' favorite poet.

The series offers little pabulum, certainly by today's standards and above all in volumes 1–5, which are addressed to younger readers. Surely, the myriad, in part extensive, looks into American and European history and some of the literary works proved challenging as well as stimulating even to Scudder's youth. This was as it should be for Scudder, who in *Childhood in Literature and Art* opines that the distinction between books for the young and books for adults is somewhat arbitrary, especially with regard to the "higher" forms of literature, and pleas for the exposure of children to such writing.[56] Objecting to express subtlety in the newly emerged genre of children's literature, he finds it self-evident that children and adults take different things from their reading of literature and offers "The Ugly Duckling" as a "consummate example" of a narrative that appeals to both on different levels.[57]

The record of the Bodley series' critical reception is far from complete, but reviews in the *Atlantic Monthly*, though perhaps suspect due to Scudder's relationship to both the magazine and its publisher, suggest that it was quite positive. The response to volumes 1 and 2 in the December issue of 1877 shows particular appreciation for the level of realism in the books: "He [Scudder] photographs his scenes on the reader's mind as perfectly as the sun would do it on a prepared plate," presenting "pleasing specimens of every-day humanity and its 'common lot,'" which "find their daily counterparts in thousands of just such American families as the Bodleys."[58] Howells, who reviewed volume 3 in the January issue of 1879, provides a context for his high valuation of "an atmosphere . . . which one breathes like that of our real world," namely, the crowding of the American book market with English juveniles: "We trust that the tide is turned, and that American children are again to form their ideas of life and society and

nature from books that paint our own conditions. . . ."[59] The earlier
reviewer also prizes the fact that the pages of the book are, "yet as if
unconsciously, steeped in the atmosphere of American history,"
which, it is hoped, may counter the "shameful neglect of what should
be the dearest study to us in the world, that of our national history. . . ."—again, words that are in essence as relevant today as when
they were written.[60] That the Bodley series remained profitable at
least a decade or so after its initial appearance is indicated by its
republication in a four-volume edition in 1887.[61]

Scudder's novel, *The Dwellers in Five-Sisters Court* (1876), was based
on a story that appeared in the *Atlantic Monthly* in January 1865.[62]
While the story reads well even today, the novel has serious flaws. The
main problem lies in the fact that the work falls into two halves that
are only tenuously related to each other. It is as if Scudder could not
decide whether he wanted to write a kind of mystery story, an extension of the original piece, or a love story, and thus decided to do both.
Alternatively, it is as if he could not spin the mystery yarn far enough
to warrant the designation "novel," 144 pages representing a distinct
shortness of breath in the Victorian era.

Nicholas Judge comes from his home in a small New England town
to Five-Sisters Court in Boston—so named for houses of similar
appearance that stand clustered together in an out-of-the-way
court—in an attempt to find his long-lost aunt, his only living relative
since the recent death of his father.[63] Confusion over which of two
women residing in the court is his aunt, which governs the original
story, is soon resolved, whereupon the plot turns, plausibly enough,
to the attempts of a severe and self-righteous but bungling would-be
detective to penetrate the mystery surrounding both the elder and
younger Judges' scientific experiments. Manlius, so named in ironic
allusion to the imperious figures of Roman antiquity, is ultimately dis-
credited and moves from the court. Unfortunately, the reader
remains mystified concerning the nature and import of the experiments, a loose end that represents another, not inconsiderable, lapse
on the part of the author. While the continuing presence of most
characters provides a measure of unity between the two halves of the
novel, the narrative focus shifts in the second to the attempts of
Nicholas and a rival to win the affection of the granddaughter of an
elderly resident of the court.

Despite the weaknesses of its plot construction Scudder's novel is
not without redeeming qualities, which was already apparent to some
of his contemporaries. In addition to critical comments, a reviewer

in the *Atlantic Monthly* has kind words for the author's dry humor and reliance on "simple sentiment" as a source of interest.[64] In his memorial appreciation of 1903 Allen writes, "The characters are distinctly drawn. . . , and as a picture of life in New England at the time, with a strong transcendental touch, mixed with pre-Raphaelite fancies, it is not without its interest still."[65] Put differently, Scudder evinces a noteworthy ability to evoke a sense of place as well as a faculty for creating atmosphere, also observable in his earlier stories, that are in certain respects reminiscent of the comic regional grotesque and the provincial Gothic writing of the time.[66] Beyond compensating to some degree for the novel's blemishes, the former skill is quite pertinent in the present context. For in its style, its depiction of a lived reality, if not in its subject matter, which is not ambitious, the novel furnishes additional evidence of the trend toward realism in Scudder's writing, as in American letters on the whole, a trend that he would pursue in his way the rest of his life.[67]

Indeed, the narratives collected in Scudder's *Stories and Romances* (1880) are uniformly mimetic in style.[68] None of the eight pieces, which range in length from twenty to sixty-seven closely printed pages, qualifies as "highly wrought," "heavily plotted," "ornately rhetorical," "tremendously exciting," or "relentlessly exterior," as Nina Baym characterizes the romance in the rare instances when it can be distinguished from the novel, though some of the works are more fanciful and idealistic than others, features also associated with the romance.[69] That is to say, Scudder was no more rigorous in his usage of the term "romance" than other nineteenth-century American writers. In addition to portraying identifiably real-world settings, if hardly the "lower depths" of the next decades, these narratives go beyond his novel, despite their relative brevity, in that they reflect contemporary concerns in both the public and the private spheres.

If the romance is understood to involve romantic love as well as fancy, which was already the case in Scudder's day, one might consider the first piece, "Left Over from the Last Century," a "romance" that metamorphoses into a "story," the latter construed as a "novel" in small.[70] Like *The Dwellers in Five-Sisters Court* the work evinces traces of the comic regional grotesque. The main character, a diffident, sober young man named Antipas Wigglesworth, comes to Cambridge from Kokomo, Indiana, which turns out to be the New England village moved west.[71] Very much in the spirit of the provincial gothic tale, Wigglesworth has immersed himself in the life of his great-grandfather to such an extent that he has virtually resurrected him

STORIES AND ROMANCES

BY

H. E. SCUDDER

BOSTON
HOUGHTON, MIFFLIN AND COMPANY
The Riverside Press, Cambridge
1880

Title page of *Stories and Romances* by Horace E. Scudder.

in himself, or become his doppelgänger. Indeed, he comes to the narrator's home, where his great-grandfather once lived, to absorb the genius loci and repeats the most decisive event in his ancestor's life, the loss of his beloved to a more aggressive rival. Scudder employs this fanciful premise not so much for its own considerable interest as to comment on current questions. His narrator appreciates Wigglesworth's formal manners vis-à-vis the casual deportment of his own son and, more significantly, sympathizes with his valuation of mind and character over material progress. However, he cannot approve of his idolization of historical figures to the great disadvantage of their living progeny. Moreover, he finds that his son's vitality gives him the capacity to grow, whereas Wigglesworth is a "woman" who eventually goes to live among the Shakers and dies an early death.[72] Clearly ambivalent toward moral orthodoxy, Scudder utilizes this bit of social-cultural analysis to cast a decided, if not painless, vote for modernity. And he does so in the realist's manner, presenting Wigglesworth's world as "alien other," as opposed to Wigglesworth's own "romantic" internalization of his reality.[73]

The Shakers, or perhaps religious utopists in general, were apparently of more than casual interest to Scudder, for they play a central role in "A House of Entertainment," representing, much like Wigglesworth, what is essentially a historical past that makes valid, if not absolute, claims on the present. In lengthy, virtually essayistic discussions the protagonist, Alden Holcroft, and the leader of a Shaker settlement weigh the relative value of individualism and a life in and for the community. Holcroft faces the moral dilemma of whether to join the Shakers, less out of conviction than in order to win the hand of the elder's daughter, Ruth, or to continue his present cheerless existence at a physical and psychological remove from the mainstream of life. Ultimately, Ruth leaves the Shakers, deciding in favor of the life she senses in Holcroft and his painting, which in turn enables him to realize the potential for a fuller existence that had lain dormant in him heretofore. In this story, too, Scudder pays his respects to the past but opts for the vitality of the present with its promise for the future. As we shall see below, Holcroft's and Ruth's decision to live in the city reflects a rejection not of the communal ideal per se, but rather of the Shakers' rigid, life-suppressing instantiation of it.

Scudder clearly favored the figure of the retiring young intellectual or artist, which bore unmistakable autobiographical features, and created yet another in "Nobody's Business."[74] The narrator, Edward Brunell, has written a best-selling novel that bears the same title as the story, choosing to publish it anonymously due to the poor figure he cuts in society as well, significantly, as to the fact that "one can flay his dearest friend without being suspected."[75] The very mystery surrounding the authorship of the book has proven to be a chief reason for its great popularity. The model for the main character, an unpromising young man whom Brunell had met at college and disguised in the novel to prevent his identification, has turned out to be a slick opportunist and poseur who, appropriately named Bardwell, subtly creates the impression that he is the author of the novel, in part to impress the young Sadie Denham, in whom Brunell himself becomes interested. Brunell now wishes to reveal his authorship in order to expose Bardwell and gain Sadie's favor. Unfortunately, he had himself insisted on suppressing his identity in his publishing contract, and his publisher refuses to budge from its terms for fear that the revelation would lead to decreased sales. In the end, Brunell reads an announcement of Bardwell's marriage to Sadie in the newspaper and determines to send her a copy of the present story in the vain hope that she will recognize her mistake. The moral he draws from the whole affair applies more to himself than to Bardwell: "Frauds have their partial successes."[76]

Owing to its theme and tone this story must have seemed quite modern around 1880, and not only because of the relation it bears to the "No Name" novels, a series of anonymous works published by Roberts Brothers of Boston beginning in 1876 and made highly popular by Helen Hunt Jackson among others.[77] For in it Scudder proceeded from his already broad experience as writer and editor to take a wry, metaliterary look at art as artifice and at the artist as "artificer," or creator of lies in the sense of a problematic relation to, and depiction of, himself and society.[78] Scudder puts his narrator self-consciously to work, for example, when he has him speak of Bardwell as "my character" and allows him to write at the end, "It would not be very difficult for me to give a turn to this story, and show how I discomfited that fraud Bardwell, and married Miss Denham myself. That would be poetic justice. But the prose outcome is that I did not discomfit Bardwell." Scudder's narrative posture is not original, but his attitude toward imagination and its role in the world is nonetheless far less sanguine than that of still faithful romantics such as Stoddard, Stedman, and, certainly, the younger Scudder himself.[79] That is to say, it is late romantic in inspiration, tending in expression and social contextualization toward realism.

A number of other stories in the volume of 1880 reflect Scudder's belief that traditional values continue to be relevant in the modern age. In "A Hard Bargain," which offers perhaps the most imaginatively inhabitable of Scudder's narrative spaces, a businessman who sold his soul to gain the world seeks, unsuccessfully, to "sell" the world to regain his soul. And in "Matthew, Mark, Luke, and John" a minister who lost his vocation to the claims of the world recovers it through the example of simple but genuine practical religiosity. On the other hand, "Accidentally Overheard" is thoroughly modern in character. While strolling down a crowded Broadway Avenue in New York City, another of Scudder's young artist-intellectuals chances to hear a young woman confide to another that she is in love with him, whereupon, startled, he presses on without turning to see who she is. Through his subsequent attempts to uncover her identity Scudder portrays the frivolity of the young in fashionable society.

Sedgwick writes that Scudder and the *Atlantic Monthly* during his editorship (see below) failed to keep pace with the development of American culture, that he and the magazine "stopped evolving and turned their attention to preserving."[80] This was patently not the case in 1880. Especially if one considers the first and final stories of a collection as framing devices that establish a teleology for the book, then "Left Over from the Last Century" and "Nobody's Business" leave one little choice but to see in *Stories and Romances* a growing commitment to the realist present.[81]

Available bibliographical sources suggest that this volume represents the end of Scudder's purely creative work. While three of the Bodley books appeared during the first lustrum of the 1880s, his return to (near) fulltime work for Houghton Mifflin in 1886 marked the true beginning of his life as a literary workman. Scudder had long since proven himself as a review critic. As editor of the short-lived *Riverside Bulletin,* a position he received as consolation for the demise of the *Riverside Magazine,* for example, he wrote both notices of new books and a monthly editorial article. When this periodical also went under in 1873, he continued his critical writing for other publications, particularly the *Atlantic Monthly.* One contemporary later wrote that "[n]o one had a larger knowledge than he of contemporary literature."[82]

Beginning in 1886, Scudder threw himself into his work as literary adviser to Houghton Mifflin. Even in the early seventies he had been largely responsible for developing a balanced general list of books, and he now played a role in all departments of the firm, himself writing or cowriting two readers.[83] He proposed and then edited two series, American Commonwealths and American Religious Leaders, contributing a biography of George Washington to a third, American Men of Letters, and revising the volume on Longfellow in the same series. His crowning achievement as a biographer was his two-volume *James Russell Lowell* (1901), which has been called "as great as any [biography] by the Victorian masters" and "a history of American literature in the nineteenth century."[84]

It comes as no surprise that Scudder had his greatest impact in the area of literature. Even before 1886 his position as literary adviser had brought him principle responsibility for determining which contemporary writers would be published by one of the most prestigious firms in the country, thereby exerting, in Sedgwick's words, a "pervasive influence on . . . literature . . . during the last quarter of the nineteenth century."[85] He exercised this influence in even more concentrated form during his eight years as full-time editor of the *Atlantic Monthly* (1890–98), in which capacity he supported authors such as Frank Stockton, Sarah Orne Jewett, Henry James, William Vaughn Moody, and George Santayana. He would have also published Howells, Mark Twain, and other mainstream realists if he could have afforded them. For the work he accepted and particularly his review philosophy, which is manifest not least of all in the forty-two reviews he wrote during his editorship, reflect a commitment to a realism informed by ethical and aesthetic considerations.[86]

Alongside his work with contemporary writers Scudder continued his editorial activity in older and recent literature, publishing, among other things, collections of masterpieces of American and British literature and his Cambridge Editions of Hawthorne, Holmes, Longfellow, Lowell, Thoreau, and Whittier as well as Robert Browning, Keats, and Scott. His enduring interest in literature for children led to four volumes of stories, fables, and legends to accompany the two collections that had appeared prior to 1886. He also conceived the Riverside Literature Series for Young People, which exhibited his belief in the superiority of world masterpieces over the new "children's literature" as reading material for youth.

Scudder's views on life and literature emerge at least in outline from his creative work as well as his scholarly and editorial activity. His various enterprises reveal an individual who was infused with the religious and moral, sociopolitical, and cultural values of the Western European and American past, but who was also open in principle and, often, in fact, to modern developments. Scudder maintained his family's practices of regular church attendance and daily prayer, but his form of Congregationalism, if conservative vis-à-vis anti-Trinitarian and anthropocentric movements, was quite generous. In his *Men and Letters* (1887), in which a contemporary found "some of the very best of American thought and criticism," for example, he criticizes English theologian Frederick D. Maurice for failing to associate eternity with futurity, that is, for his departure from traditional Christian eschatology.[87] However, he reportedly followed Maurice as the founder of Christian socialism with the devotion of a disciple, which attests to his general development from Emersonian individualism and the Protestant past toward the collectivism and institutionalism that assumed various forms in the United States during the second half of the nineteenth century, here what one might call a practical Christian humanism or, more specifically, the social gospel.[88]

In Scudder's "A Story of the Siege of Boston," which appeared in *Stories and Romances,* a young British officer switches allegiance out of love for an American woman and because he "became convinced that the principle was on your side," thereby imaginatively demonstrating the author's understanding of America's role, better, mission in the world.[89] Scudder disagreed with those who believed that American history was exceptional, unfolding according to the givens of American life independently of European history, as he indicates in an essay in *Men and Letters* entitled "Aspects of Historical Work."[90] He felt that American history was part of European history through the War of 1812 and that subsequent developments in the country could be understood only before that background. However, he distinguishes between "the England of history and of personal affection and the England that registered in the nineteenth century the prejudices of a lingering bureaucratic régime," meaning perhaps the England of the "Glorious Revolution" of 1689 and of English literature, certainly the political England of the first two-thirds of the current century with its cumbrous rule of wealth.[91] While in England there is a distinction between the people and the government, Scudder writes, the people of the United States constitutes the nation, and there is no political order external to it.[92] Scudder adopted the ultimately romantic notion of an organic unity of national life in the United States, which arose in the 1840s and which manifested itself to his mind in the realization of freedom.[93] For him, as for Brahmin historians William Hickling Prescott, George Bancroft, John Lothrop Motley, and Francis Parkman, the United States had taken up the standard long borne by England and continued to carry it along a path of development that "looks away from Europe."[94] It is clear from his essay "Emerson's Self" that Scudder linked social consciousness as a sense of national community with "ethical apprehension," for he criticized both Emerson and Goethe for not possessing it.[95]

Sharing much in common with the Brahmin poets, Scudder possessed a desire for a literature national in expression, yet related to other national expressions of the humanity common to all nations.[96] He wrote from his own heart when in his explanation of the motivation behind Lowell's magazine, the *Pioneer*, he declared that the editor was "ambitious to bear his testimony to the ideal of a national literature springing from the soil of political independence, and akin to great literature the world over."[97] For Scudder, great literature is both implicitly moral and aesthetically refined. He himself professed Lowell's [and other Romantics'] notion of the poet as *vates:* "[H]e felt the stirring in his nature of that high vocation of the poet which makes him a seer and an interpreter."[98] However, he perceived a tension in Lowell between a poetic impulse as "an end in itself" and a "merely utilitarian notion of his high calling," the word "merely" suggesting a valuation.[99] Averse to overt didacticism in literature, indeed, he goes so far as to criticize Lowell gently for his inability to "detach poetry from character."[100] Given Scudder's adherence to romantic ideas of America's sociopolitical destiny and related view of the task of American literature, it is hardly surprising that he saw conditions in the New England of Lowell's youth as "Arcadian" and could speak, with an uncharacteristic lack of charity, of the "waste of [Southern and Eastern] Europe which inevitably accompanied the sturdy peasants as they immigrated to the country" beginning around 1890.[101]

However, Scudder was what one might call a "sensible" formalist.[102] First and perhaps foremost, he participated in the historical sensibility that emerged in the eighteenth century and dominated thinking increasingly in the nineteenth. In his essay on Longfellow in *Men and Letters,* for example, he displays a keen awareness that an age in American culture is coming to an end.[103] He both espoused and practiced the positivistic, that is, genetic, or historical, approach to biography, though recognizing its limitations.[104] He uses his essay "The Future of Shakespeare" in *Men and Letters* as an opportunity to suggest the appeal of what today is called reader response theory, or reception theory, that is, "the problem of discovering not what Shakespeare was by himself, but what he was in the consciousness of other men,—the men of his own time, the men of Pope's time, the men of Coleridge's time, the men of Matthew Arnold's time."[105] On the other hand, Scudder felt that Shakespeare possessed universal qualities: "To the mind seeking the solution of the great problems of human life, and asking for some definite expression of the problems themselves, there is always Shakespeare."[106] At least by the time he wrote his biography of Lowell he had reservations toward confessional poetry, or *Erlebnislyrik*. In connection with the young Lowell's poetic journal, he writes, "It is hard for most of us to escape the lurking judgment that the man, or boy either, who throws his spiritual experience into verse is more or less consciously dramatizing, and we are apt to credit greater honesty to one who does not than to the one who does poeticize his disappointments. . . ."[107]

Combined with his sensitivity to history and, perhaps, advancing years, Scudder's strong moral-ethical and religious values prevented him from allowing his powerful aestheticist impulse to dominate his thinking. As we have already seen, his earliest creative writing reveals signs of Dickensian realism, and his realistic tendency only grew more pronounced in his short fiction of around 1880. From the seventies on, he supported the realism of Howells as critic and editor. To be sure, he had little sympathy for the deterministic naturalism of Hamlin Garland and Stephen Crane and at times regretted the increasing psychologism of Henry James.[108] Beginning around 1890, he therefore receded from the vanguard of American letters.[109] However, he was moderately progressive over much of his career and, in view of the monolithic claims currently made by postmodern theories and Theory, one may well be inclined to appreciate his plea for literary pluralism.[110]

Scudder was truly progressive in his views on education, particularly with respect to children. His prominence as an educator was reflected by an invitation to address the National Teachers' Association at its annual meeting in 1888 in San Francisco, where he presented the following challenge: "Unless the definite end of ennobling the mind through familiarity with literature of the spirit is recognized in our school curriculum, the finest results of education will be lost."[111] In 1882, he presented a series of lectures at the Lowell Institute in Boston on the portrayal of children in Western literature and art, publishing them in revised form twelve years later in the volume entitled *Childhood in Literature and Art*. Here, as in his editorial practice, he revealed his faith in the "power of noble literature when brought into simple contact with the child's mind, always assuming that it is the literature that deals with elemental feeling, thought, and action which is so presented"—literature such as the stories of Hans

Christian Andersen, which are the subject of the penultimate chapter of the book.[112]

Scudder received numerous distinctions and honors during his lifetime. He was invited to serve as a trustee of the Massachusetts State Board of Education as well as of St. John's Theological School in Cambridge, his own Williams College, and Wellesley College. In 1889 he was inducted into the American Academy of Arts and Sciences and was awarded the honorary degree of Doctor of Letters by Princeton University in 1896. He was offered a professorship at Williams and a position as literary adviser for the *New York World* of Joseph Pulitzer but declined both in order to remain in his beloved Boston with Houghton Mifflin.

In his eulogy to Scudder in 1902, writer and biographer Thomas Wentworth Higginson perhaps spoke for many when he expressed a certain ambivalence toward the recently deceased's achievements. Proceeding from Scudder's self-appellation as a literary workman, he writes, "What other distinction he might have won if he had shown less of modesty or self-restraint, we can never know. It is certain that his few thoroughly original volumes show something beyond what is described in the limited term, workmanship."[113] In another passage Higginson speaks of Scudder's "gift of higher literature."[114] He attributes Scudder's ultimate choice of profession to the New England spirit of self-sacrifice and declares that if one believes that character ennobles life more than "mere talent" then one may find Scudder's "devotion to modest duty" exemplary rather than something to criticize.[115] While his view of the relative value of literary creativity and literary stewardship is patent, Higginson nonetheless has great admiration for Scudder as steward: "But that he brought simple workmanship up into the realm of art is as certain as that we may call the cabinet-maker of the middle ages an artist."[116]

In a tribute that appeared in the *Atlantic Monthly* a couple of months after Scudder's death, the anonymous author writes, "In this brief record of the respect and affection of Mr. Scudder's successors in the conduct of the Atlantic, and of his associates in the publishing house where so large a portion of his life was passed, it is needless to comment upon the characteristics of his original contributions to our literature."[117] However, even the lengthy appreciation published in the magazine a year later disregards Scudder's creative work in its evaluative passages. While a few of his books receive kind words, they are brief and essentially insignificant, extended, as they are, in an enumeration of his various professional activities. As far as "might-have-beens" are concerned, the author focuses on Scudder as a critic: "He might have carried much farther than he did his achievements in literary criticism, although what he accomplished in this direction entitled him to a place among the few very best literary critics whom America has produced. His beautiful essays only filled up the interstices of his more continuous labor."[118]

Scudder's contemporaries apparently failed to recognize, due to a lack of historical distance, the role his editorial work played in establishing the canon of American literature. With exceedingly few exceptions, however, their successors appear to have been no more perceptive.[119] It is altogether possible that his eulogists, again like following generations, downplayed or overlooked his creative work as well as his criticism because much of it was written in the service of children. This neglect would represent yet another similarity between Scudder and his Danish master.

2

Scudder commented on Andersen variously in forms of publication ranging from his own stories and the *Riverside Magazine* to "advertisements," or prefaces, to volumes of the Author's Edition and a couple of the Bodley books. While frequently illuminating, the allusions and observations recorded in these writings are nonetheless random in nature. Scudder presented his thoughts on Andersen most systematically in magazine articles that appeared at the beginning and then in the middle of his career.

The first, written in 1861, when Scudder was only twenty-one, came out in the *National Quarterly Review*.[120] This periodical was founded and written in large part by Edward I. Sears, a professor of languages at Catholic Manhattan College, who modeled it unabashedly on the famous English reviews and sought to make it truly national in scope, in contrast to the "merely Bostonian" *North American Review*.[121] Classical and scholarly in its standards and content, it earned the *London Spectator*'s vote as the "most learned, most brilliant, and most attractive" of all American magazines.[122] Perhaps due to Sears's conservatism the periodical had a consistently small circulation, though reportedly large enough to make him a respectable living, and was generally undistinguished in literary criticism.[123] However, it enjoyed a run of twenty years, from 1860 to 1880, and has the distinction of publishing a piece that predates Georg Brandes's seminal study on

Andersen by nine years, laying, or helping to lay, the foundation of Andersen scholarship in the United States.[124] Scudder's article is ostensibly a review of four collections of Andersen's fairy tales and stories as well as his autobiography. However, it is in reality a sixteen-and-a-half-page long essay on Andersen as a writer of fairy tales.

Scudder's remarks touch on a number of subjects. He sees Andersen as a "born," that is, "naive" artist, "one whose art is his nature" and who "exhibits the talent of a first-rate story-teller, combined with the excellencies of a poet and humorist."[125] He underscores Andersen's originality by comparing him with the Grimm Brothers and Shakespeare: "For at first, as he tells us, he sought merely to relate old stories which he had heard as a child, but in his own manner. In this he has not merely done the work of the Brothers Grimm in recovering traditions and legends from the people, and giving them a permanent shape; he has recovered them, and stamped them with his own originality. How far he has followed tradition, and where he has created for himself, we are not prepared to say, but that he does create is plain, and thus an old legend cannot pass through his hands without receiving the impress of his genius. His treatment of legends is parallel to Shakespeare's dramatizing of popular stories. The original power of each of these masters in art is shown in their ability to construct, from common materials, the excellent productions which will always bear their names. Othello is no less Shakespeare's to us because the story is first told by Giraldi Cinthio; and the original presentment of the legends told by Andersen has no particular interest for us except as studies in antiquity, and detracts nothing from our admiration of his genius."[126]

Scudder links the universality of Andersen's stories in part to his original treatment of Danish folk legends but attributes it even more so to the universal nature of legendary lore itself: "It makes a difference . . . in our appreciation of the legends, that we do not look at them from a national point of view. A legend always must carry most interest to the inhabitants of the country that gave it birth, but the interest is not confined there; the most local legends are of universal interest."[127] Scudder deems this circumstance quite fortunate for his countrymen, for, aware of the ongoing discussion concerning the development of a specifically American literature, he is at pains to explain that Americans have no store of national legends, not yet having "grown to our land," and that those imported from other cultures lose much in transit; even less practical and satisfying is the construction of new legends (237). The fairy tale is yet more independent of time and place than the legend: "Fairies owe no nation allegiance: look at the numerous conjectures as to the origin of the word, and it is plain that the very nature of the Fairy is universal. Fairy-land lies within the vision of every one, and its inhabitants are the same in one age as in another. The Indian, the Persian, the Greek, the Scandinavian, all with different eyes have seen the same forms. Fairy-time is the perpetual youth of the world" (238).

To Scudder's mind Andersen attains his greatest universality and at the same time reveals "the delicacy of his fancy" most clearly precisely in his fairy tales and stories: "These dainty people, invisible spirits in their gossamer robes, require the most skilful handling. . . . Successfully to embody these, one must but hint the corporeal character. This faint outline of body, just sufficient to keep within bounds the ethereal nature, and to prevent it from being dissipated into mere airiness, is most exquisitely presented by Andersen. We cannot conceive of spirits without attaching to them some corporeal character, and Andersen gives his fairies just so much as is necessary to satisfy our imagination, while he does not divest them of their essential and preponderating spiritual nature. This we say of his fairies, purely such; in the various modifications of the fairy by which it is made more and more earthly, he retains the same fine perception of its relation to what is human. He uses his invention in the whole range of fairy-land, but his special power is in the treatment not so much of supernatural as in that of preternatural agency. The distinction which we would draw between these two terms is in assigning to supernatural agency all that finds a type but not an abode in nature; to preternatural all that has its abode in nature, but is not limited by the laws of nature. It is in this last sphere that he works most admirably. . . . By an intuitive vision he touches the highest and most subtle characteristic of an object, and furnishes that with the essential element of humanity. . . . These little *dramatis personæ* are not puppets; they are living; and if they are actors, their stage seems that of life. This miniature world is in earnest, and the scale of suffering and enjoyment is as perfect as in our own. The Darning-needle and the Shirt-collar have as much personality as the people to whom they belong, and are of more consequence . . . for this is the secret by which Andersen makes us interested. He invests the object with an individuality which is irresistible" (238–39). Through the subtlety and power of his imagination Andersen is able not only to allow his creations to emerge from aeriform nothingness in varying degrees but also to lend them a personality and character each according to its own nature.

Scudder can refer to Andersen as a poet because he finds his fairy tales and stories lyric rather than dramatic in character (241). At the same time, Andersen displays "wit," in the sense of "intellect," in the structure of his stories, which Scudder demonstrates by analyzing the careful plot construction of "The Red Shoes" (242). In his delineation of character and handling of dialog Andersen is "humorous," in the sense of "improvisational," rather than "witty" (ibid.). This spontaneity resides in the orality of his narrative style: "Some writers of stories would make a difference between their own telling and their writing of them. Andersen's art is so natural, that, with all the elaborateness of his execution, we can easily see how it might be, as he says, that he wrote his narrative upon paper, exactly in the language, and with the expressions, in which he had himself related them by word of mouth to the little ones. . . . Who would not like to hear Andersen tell one of his own stories; yet he only could tell them as they are written; any one else repeating them would strip them of much of their artistic effect" (240–41). Scudder also detects humor in the conventional sense in Andersen's tales, speaking of an amusing and "sly vein of satire" that "streaks many of his works" (248).

Scudder dwells on two aspects of Andersen's fairy tales and stories in particular, one at the very beginning of the article: "If one were to arrange the library of a man who had always been a reader, according to his growth in years, how very few books would be shifted from the child's shelves to the boy's, and thence to the man's; so rarely do our book-companions grow up with us; so commonly do we outgrow them, and use them only as mementoes [sic] of former days. Of the books which remain with us through more than one stage of life, there are very few which we enjoy in each of the stages. . . . [F]airy tales are inseparable from childhood, but in youth action finds its poetry in romance, and it is in the years of riper manhood that these tales recover their enchantment, because it is then that the spirit of childhood within us begins to reässert itself. Childhood has no foreknowledge of the struggle of youth and the reflection of manhood; yet it accompanies each state, and finally regains its ascendancy; not now, however, to be symbolized by the innocence of infancy, but by the white-robed figures with palms in their hands. Now, Andersen's lesser stories belong to that select class of books which please us at every stage of our growth; but since they possess this power of fascination through their responsiveness to the spirit of childhood, we naturally find that this power is exercised most over us when children and when men (235–36). . . ." It is true that "the secret of Andersen's genius lies in the fact that he is essentially and always a child. He is a child in his memory, and in his fancy and feelings. His own time of childhood seems always to be present to his mind, furnishing incidents and characters to his purpose" (250). As suggested in the preceding quotation, however, "for all this we do not think of him as weak or puerile. He appears strong through inherent purity rather than through the overcoming of evil. With most of us singleness of heart is an attribute recovered after long toil and weary conflict; but he is one of the few who seem never to have lost their first childhood" (251). In Andersen, Scudder finds heightened confirmation of his notion of the continuity between childhood and adulthood. That such continuity indeed betokens strength rather than weakness for him is substantiated by his view of Andersen as an embodiment of the early romantics' concept of the poet as visionary: "[T]rue *vates* is Andersen, poet and seer in one. He reads and tells the hidden secrets, not for idle curiosity's sake, but that he may clarify the vision of men" (249).

However, Andersen does not enlighten his fellow men with raised forefinger: "There is a wide difference between this humanizing of lower orders by Andersen and the common fable. A fable is told for one object. The animals talk with a moral purpose; they are mere puppets; we do not believe they really talk, we are sure there is a man behind the scenes. But Andersen uses the moral in such stories, just as he would use it if there were men and women speaking, instead of animals, trees and flowers. They are natural *dramatis personæ* in their own drama. We are merely shown how animals and flowers do talk by themselves without any regard to the effect of their talk upon children. The moral is there, as it is in any drama, but not otherwise. The Pen and the Inkstand is a case in point. This approaches very nearly to a pure fable, yet see how delicately the moral is announced. Blended all the way throughout with the scene, perfectly apparent, yet nothing done for mere effect" (240). Elsewhere in the article Scudder connects the implicit morality of Andersen's tales with their appeal to both children and adults: "As children, we feel without perceiving the noble moral that underlies them. There is a subtle aroma of truth distilling through them which reaches us with winning power. If poison be sometimes stealthily administered through the medium of a delicate perfume, here is a bunch of flowers, each of which, through its fine scent, instils [*sic*] into our souls a virtuous elixir. Childhood cannot analyze or even perceive the elixir any easier than it could detect the poison; but the soul, in the one case, will give evidence of the spiritual food, as the body in the other would testify to the bane. In our older years, we have a rare pleasure in our ability to detect the under-current of moral purpose, and it influences our hearts quite as surely. A child-like nature shall he lead by a filament, and the sweet grace of a moral woven by Andersen may lead one possessing such a spirit in the path of righteousness" (248).

Such a nature may also be led to empathetic insight into the lot of the poor: "[Andersen] represents low life, not like Dickens, by a photograph of this phase of humanity, but by a sketch in which the *differentia* of poverty and low birth is given, that we may understand the common humanity which it shares with better fortune. He excites our interest in it, by showing that it is the same story of life with all, though the actor may be peasant and not kaisar [*sic*]" (249). It is not insignificant that Scudder continues as follows: "Who, that is of generous heart, can read the story of *The Sand Hills of Jutland,* and not see in Jörgen a brother? This story, indeed, for its quiet tone, its sad and yet hopeful spirit, its submission not to mere fate but to a higher Will, and its profound touch of human sorrow, is surely grand. It seems to us to mark a late period in Andersen's life. It is only one who has entered upon the afternoon of his days who sees the world by such a light" (ibid.). Here, Scudder evinces a sense for something new in Andersen's later stories. Coupled with his evocation of Dickens and awareness of the social dimension of the works, it suggests that he apprehended not only increasing maturity but also growing realism in Andersen's writing.

In any case, Scudder devotes most of his attention and some six pages to what was for him at this time the most crucial aspect of Andersen's fairy tales and stories, their religious import. In an inspired few, indeed, Andersen's treatment of related themes attains for him the dignity of tragedy: "But besides all this charm, there is a power of fascination in some of them which is almost fearful. For occasionally this master takes up the lyre, and touches chords that awe us and make us tremble. The tragic terror which so enthrals [*sic*] childhood is, in a few instances, exhibited by Andersen with great power. It must be observed, however, that he is never simply horrifying; he does not *scare* children, but he excites the same sensations within them which a sense of personal guilt affords. With children, the sight of sin and its effects in others produces very much the same emotions of fear and awe which they feel when the sin is committed by themselves. Thus, Andersen, in his two most terrible tales—*The Red Shoes* and *Anne Lisbeth*—has shown the results that follow the yielding to temptation. . . . In *The Red Shoes* . . . there is another element of awe in the individuality which the shoes possess, so that it is as if, from the very beginning, there was a terrible fate impending over Karen through their agency. A far-off terror is foreshadowed by the mysterious gravity which attends each movement, so that we apprehend the gathering storm step by step as we advance in the story" (242–43). Scudder then follows the progress of the storm, quoting generously from the text and observing the "consummate art" with which it is depicted (247).

He then writes, "We have been thus minute in the analysis of this story, because it best presents the very high tragic power which Andersen possesses. . . . It is a fearful story, but it is so because it presents the logic of temptation carried out fully. . . . But it is not wholly fearful, because while the working of sin and final retribution is faithfully followed out, the working of repentance and final forgiveness is as clearly unfolded. It is a most noble attestation of the beauty, and truth, and solemnity of the Christian religion" (ibid.). Scudder finds the same "force and beauty" in "Anne Lisbeth": "In this are seen Andersen's tenderness and his Christian love, that he cannot leave us without hope; if the curtain falls upon death, he gently raises it, and lets us catch a glimpse of that reversal of woe where death is swallowed up in victory, and the light from heaven streams in upon the coffin—the pathway of the escaped soul. In all of his stories, Andersen has touched Death with the hand of a child, and yet of a philosopher" (248).

In November 1875, three months after Andersen's death, Scudder published another article on the Dane under the title "Andersen's Short Stories," which appeared in the *Atlantic Monthly*.[128] The piece covers some of the same ground trod in the earlier essay, but in its four densely printed two-column pages Scudder attempts something fundamentally different.

Scudder reiterates Andersen's ability to impart life to animals and inanimate objects, and he does so more extensively and more cogently than in the article of 1861: "The life which Andersen sets before us is in fact a dramatic representation upon an imaginary stage, with puppets that are not pulled by strings, but have their own muscular and nervous economy. The life which he displays is not a travesty of human life, it is human life repeated in miniature under conditions which give a charming and unexpected variety. By some transmigration, souls have passed into tin-soldiers, balls, tops, beetles, money-pigs, coins, shoes, leap-frogs, matches, and even such attenuated individualities as darning-needles; and when, informing these apparently dead or stupid bodies, they begin to make manifestations, it is always in perfect consistency with the ordinary conditions of the bodies they occupy, though the several objects become by this endowment of souls suddenly expanded in their capacity" (600). He demonstrates this with an extensive reference to "The Jumpers" (Springfyrene), concluding, "[T]he final impression upon the mind is that of a harmonizing of all the characters, and the king, princess, and councilor can scarcely be distinguished in kind from the flea, grasshopper, leap-frog, and house-dog. After that, the marriage of the leap-frog and princess is quite a matter of course" (601). Scudder reckons Andersen's success in this regard among his major contributions to literature: "The likeness that things inanimate have to things animate is constantly forced upon us; it remained for Andersen to pursue the comparison further, and letting types loose from their antitypes, to give them independent existence. The result has been a surprise in literature and a genuine addition to literary forms" (602).

Scudder also returns to the question of whether Andersen's fairy tales and stories are for children or for adults: "It is frequently said that Andersen's stories accomplish their purpose of amusing children by being childish, yet it is impossible for a mature person to read them without detecting repeatedly the marks of experience. There is a subtle undercurrent of wisdom that has nothing to do with childishness, and the child who is entertained returns to the same story afterward to find a deeper significance than it was possible for him to apprehend at the first reading. The forms and the incident are in consonance with childish experience, but the spirit which moves through the story comes from a mind that has seen and felt the analogue of the story in some broader or coarser form" (601).

Scudder again addresses the implicit morality of Andersen's fairy tales and stories: "The use of speaking animals in story was no discovery of Andersen's, and yet in the distinction between his wonder-story and the well-known fable lies an explanation of the charm which attaches to his work. The end of every fable is *hæc fabula docet*, and it was for this palpable end that the fable was created. . . . The lesson is first; the characters, created afterward, are, for purposes of the teacher, disguised as animals; very little of the animal appears, but very much of the lesson. The art which invented the fable was a modest handmaid to morality. In Andersen's stories, however, the spring is not in the didactic but in the imaginative. . . . Is there a lesson in all this? Precisely as there is a lesson in any picture of human life where the same traits are sketched" (ibid.). Using "The Beetle" (Skarnbassen) as an example, Scudder continues, "There is in this and other of Andersen's stories a singular shrewdness, as of a very keen observer of life, singular because at first blush the author seems to be a sentimentalist. The satires, like The Emperor's New Clothes and The Swiftest Runners, mark this characteristic of shrewd observation very cleverly. Perhaps, after all, we are stating most simply the distinction between his story and the fable when we say that humor is a prominent element of the one and absent in the other; and to say that there is humor is to say that there is real life" (ibid.).

It is no accident that Scudder stresses the relationship between morality and imagination in Andersen's fairy tales and stories, for if the Dane's "fancy" claimed his attention in the earlier article, it becomes the focal point of the present study. Scudder devotes almost an entire column to the question of the most appropriate genre designation for Andersen's short narratives, discarding "wonder-story," "history," and "adventure"—as well as "short story," despite the title of the article—before settling on the traditional "fairy tale." He favors this term precisely because of the highly imaginative nature of fairies, whose diminutive size, he writes rather whimsically, represents "an attempted compromise between the imagination and the senses, by which the existence of fairies for certain purposes is conceded on condition they shall be made so small that the senses may be excused from recognizing them" (599). He then sketches the history of the form from its origin to his own time. Since it arose from literal belief in the existence of fairies, the gradual disappearance of this belief has created a certain awkwardness: "These creations of fancy—if we must so dismiss them—had secured a somewhat positive recognition in literature before it was finally discovered that they came out of the unseen and therefore could have no life. Once received into literature they could not well be ignored, but the understanding, which appears to serve as special police in such cases, now has orders to admit no new-comers unless they answer to one of three classes: either they must be direct descendents of the fairies of literature, having certain marks about them to indicate their parentage, or they must be teachers of morality thus disguised, or they may be mere masqueraders; one thing is certain, they must spring from no belief in fairy life, but be one and all referred to some sufficient cause,—a dream, a moral lesson, a chemical experiment" (ibid). Nonetheless, he continues, "[I]t is found that literature has its own sympathies, not always compassed by the mere understanding, and the consequence is that the sham fairies in the sham fairy tales never really get into literature at all, but disappear in limbo; while every now and then a genuine fairy, born of a genuine, poetic belief, secures a place in spite of the vigilance of the guard" (ibid). Scudder exemplifies the vulgarization of the fairy tale with its introduction on the stage: "The effect of producing these scenes upon the stage is to bring them one step nearer to sensuous reality, and one step further from imaginative reality; and since the real life of fairy is in the imagination, a cruel wrong is done when it is dragged from its shadowy hiding-place and made to turn into ashes under the calcium light of the understanding."[129]

As he approaches his own time, Scudder observes that by "tacit agreement" fairy tales have been "consigned to the nursery."[130] Those who write them now do so almost apologetically, creating "that peculiar monstrosity of the times, the scientific fairy tale, which is nothing short of an insult to a whole race of innocent beings."[131] Now that the genuine form has ceased to exist, which Scudder equates with the demise of imagination in general, it is better to retell the authentic fairy tales over and again than to indulge in such reflections of modern skepticism. For, whatever one may do to them, they remain incorruptible: "There they are, the fairy tales without authorship, as imperishable as nursery ditties; scholarly collections of them may be made, but they will have their true preservation, not as specimens in a museum of literary curiosities, but as children's toys. Like the sleeping princess in the wood, the fairy tale may be hedged about with bristling notes and thickets of commentaries, but the child will pass straight to the beauty, and awaken for his own delight the old charmed life."[132]

Scudder devotes so much space to Andersen's imagination and the evolution of the fairy tale in order to fulfill the ultimate purpose of his article: to determine the historical significance of Andersen's work in the genre. He limits himself to the fairy tales and stories both out of personal predilection and because he, as editor of the recent Author's Edition, knows all too well that it is these for which, "though he will be mentioned in the biographical dictionaries as the writer of novels, poems, romances, dramas, sketches of travel, and an autobiography, Andersen will be known and read. . . ," certainly in the English-speaking world.[133] Concerning Andersen's position in the history of the fairy tale, Scudder writes further, "It is worth noting . . . that just when historical criticism, under the impulse of the Grimms, was ordering and accounting for these fragile creations,—a sure mark that they were ceasing to exist as living forms in literature,— Hans Christian Andersen should have come forward as master in a new order of stories, which may be regarded as the true literary successor to the old order of fairy tales, answering the demands of a spirit which rejects the pale ghost of the scientific or moral or jocular or pedantic fairy tale. Andersen, indeed, has invented fairy tales purely such."[134]

Toward the end of the article Scudder writes of Andersen's influence and potential influence on other members of his guild, mindful of genius as a prerequisite: "Now that Andersen has told his stories, it seems an easy thing to do, and we have plenty of stories written for children that attempt the same thing, sometimes also with moderate success; for Andersen's discovery was after all but the simple application to literature of a faculty which has always been exercised. . . . It is possible to follow in his steps, now that he has shown us the way, but it is no less evident that the success which he attained was due not merely to his happy discovery of a latent property, but to the nice feeling and strict obedience to laws of art with which he made use of his discovery."[135] In conclusion, Scudder specifies Andersen's historical locus more precisely: "Especially is it to be noted that these stories, which we regard as giving an opportunity for invention when the series of old-fashioned fairy tales had been closed, show clearly the coming in of that temper in novel-writing which is eager to describe things as they are. Within the narrow limits of his miniature story, Andersen moves us by the same impulse as the modern novelist who depends for his material upon what he has actually seen and heard, and for his inspiration upon the power to penetrate the heart of things; so that the old fairy tale finds its successor in this new realistic wonder-story, just as the old romance gives place to the new novel. In both, as in the corresponding development of poetry and painting, is found a deeper sense of life and a finer perception of the intrinsic value of common forms."[136]

Like his biography of Lowell, Scudder's articles on Andersen not only illuminate their immediate subject but also reflect something of the course of literary history in the United States during the nineteenth century as well. Around 1860, one could still operate matter-of-factly within a romantic-idealist frame of reference, and this was certainly Scudder's point of departure. By the midseventies, however, the literary-cultural climate and, in part, Scudder himself had changed. Now, he felt it necessary to defend, in a sort of rearguard action, not only the fairy tale per se but, through it, imagination itself. He did this by asserting the presence of a realistic temper in Andersen's "new realistic wonder-stories" as a whole, an animus tending in the later works toward more modern formal realization, and by adjudging them legitimate offspring of the romantic-idealist tradition. If the achievement of the New England renaissance lay in substantial part in confronting the "utilitarian, moralistic cast of mainstream culture, which tended to object to the autonomy and even to the legitimacy of art," as Buell contends, then one must respect Scudder's critical and editorial project all the more, whatever its success, undertaken, as it was, in an age even less hospitable to imagination than the antebellum period.[137]

Scudder's article for the *Atlantic Monthly* is in part an objective study, in part the elegiac tribute of a true believer to his departed master. Almost a decade later he published yet another article on Andersen, which appeared under the title "The Home of Hans Christian Andersen" in *Harper's New Monthly Magazine* and was based on impressions gathered during a recent visit to Denmark.[138] Accompanied by ten illustrations depicting scenes in Copenhagen and Odense, only one of which is related specifically to Andersen, the piece is clearly designed to appeal to the public's general interest in foreign lands as well as the Danish writer. For this reason Scudder kept his critical comments to a minimum, and one should not overinterpret them. Nonetheless, there is an unwonted sobriety in his characterization of Andersen the man and the poet, whom he describes as "the first child author. . . . [H]e was the first child who had contributed to literature. The work by which he is best known is nothing more nor less than an artistic creation of precisely the order which is common among children. . . . He was himself . . . a child all his life. The *naïveté* which is so large an element in his stories was an expression of his own artless nature; his was a condition almost of arrested development."[139] It almost goes without saying that there is a considerable rhetorical difference between naïveté per se and naïveté as near arrested development.

Nonetheless, Scudder rehearses what he had written in the earlier articles about Andersen's "peculiar contribution" of creating life in animals and inanimate objects analogous to that of humans.[140] He also takes mild *Schadenfreude* in a thwarted opportunity for Danes to express their smugness toward Andersen. In connection with Saabye's statue of the poet, which was erected in 1880, he writes, "The statue was planned before Andersen's death in 1875, and his countrymen, who had been forced into a pride in his genius, and had adopted a good-natured tone of admiration toward him, somewhat as one might humor a spoiled child, entertained themselves with the thought that Andersen would every day take a walk in the Rosenborg Gardens and admire the bronze effigy of himself. I think they really regretted the loss of this reflected pleasure."[141] Moreover, he concludes the article by relating an episode that occurred during his visit to Odense and which, though possibly objectionable to animal lovers, reflects both his abiding sentimental attachment to Andersen and the unbroken naive delight he took in Andersen's creations: "Best of all, as I strolled along the river down to which the garden used to run from the house where Andersen lived, I saw a number of ducks paddling about, and to my supreme joy they all set upon one forlorn little duck and began to peck at it. I was content with this. It was worth the visit to Odense to see the veritable Ugly Duckling at the foot of Andersen's gooseberry-bush garden."[142]

7

Conclusion and Context

Scudder's articles stand at the forefront of American commentary on Andersen during the nineteenth century. They do so in part because they generally represent as well as expand upon ideas and impressions expressed by Americans as a whole. It is true that Scudder did not discuss the author as a mythical prototype, related to the myth of America. Although he certainly believed in a peculiarly American mission, the concerns he dealt with in his articles on Andersen, as in general, were largely high-cultural rather than sociopolitical or materialist in nature. Many of his countrymen, on the other hand, were taken from early on by the romance of Andersen's life, and, if they allowed themselves to be impressed by his own mythmaking, they were not entirely wrong to do so or to associate his life with their own national experience. Scudder also departed from the majority of his landsmen by characterizing the fairy tales and stories as partly the products of intellect. Most American critics, especially those writing in the seventies, did not consider Andersen a great mind, and even Scudder spoke more in terms of wisdom than of mental power.

However, this clearly did not prevent Scudder from valuing Andersen or his art, and in this he was one with other American critics. Whether they used words such as "sweet," "fresh," "simple," and "childlike" or went into analytical detail to capture the essence of the writer and his work, virtually all who made the effort—and they did so throughout the period in question—expressed appreciation of Andersen's naïveté, in the Schillerian sense. One of the chief reasons they respected his *naturel* is that they perceived a character of high moral caliber in his work. Operating entirely or partially within the Augustan mentality of the preceding century, they held him in high esteem even if they could not condone his "puerility" or vanity. Scudder was only one of many, if the most cogent, who commented approvingly on this aspect of Andersen's work, just as he was foremost

190

among the smaller number of critics who explicitly affirmed the religious spirit they descried in it as late as 1885. Of course, Scudder and others who note the implicit morality of Andersen's writing say something about his artistry as well as his character.

While Andersen's temper and character occupy many critics, indeed, aesthetic considerations naturally play a significant role in most assessments of his work. A few commentators, most of them writing during the seventies, criticize the plot construction of the novels or render a mixed verdict on the handling of character in them. On balance, however, and with emphasis on different elements at different times, the great majority find that the positive features decidedly outweigh the negative. Especially after 1869, a large number of critics praise the descriptive power manifest in both the longer prose and the fairy tales and stories. Although heightened awareness of descriptive detail at this time is not surprising, given the advent of realism, it is worth noting that the later period also witnessed substantial commentary on the poetic nature of the prose, long as well as short. However, critics reserved their greatest accolades for Andersen's preeminence in the one aesthetic category that was almost universally associated with him, imagination. Not all who commented on it were favorably impressed, even in the early, "romantic" years of his reception and especially after 1870. Nonetheless, the large majority, the better part of whom wrote before 1863, affirmed the power of his imagination in tones ranging from simple approbation to wonderment and awe verging on fear. It is likely that the considerable number of early reviewers who referred admiringly to his genius, quaintness, or originality also had his imagination in mind.

Judging by their rarity, certain additional observations presuppose an unusual degree of aesthetic and/or intellectual sophistication on the part of the critics who made them. Collectively, and especially in the case of Stoddard, the author of the article in *Scandinavia*, Boyesen, and most notably Scudder, these comments represent the beginnings of scholarly study of Andersen in the United States, which has been just as sporadic as it remains desirable.

Scudder's position at the head of American Andersen critics derives in important part from the originality of some of his insights and his likely influence on later commentators. He was the first American to recognize the inner life that Andersen breathed into animals and inanimate objects corresponding to their physical characteristics. He was also the first who perceived that these animals and things speak "in character," in accord with their bodies or shapes and essential natures. It is quite probable that those who later remarked on these aspects of Andersen's fairy tales and stories were indebted to him. As an Andersen devotee and associate of Scudder, Bagger surely knew his article of 1861. Boyesen must have been familiar with it as well, for he writes of his personal acquaintance with this "well-known man of letters" in an article devoted to Andersen. In any event, the number of such individuals was small, limited to Bagger, Leland, the *Scandinavia* writer, and Boyesen in the case of the characters' inner life and restricted to Boyesen alone with regard to their language. There were also very few writers, confined to the seventies, who discerned in the tales as well as other works a distinct subject immediately engaging other subjects and thereby extracting their essence. That the narrative style of Andersen's fairy tales is oral rather than literary was lost on most of his early (and many later) translators and remains an uncommon insight to this day.[1] It is therefore all the more remarkable that a substantial number of American critics, most of them writing from 1848 to 1863, discerned this essential feature. Some of them, to be sure, had the good fortune to hear Andersen recite the works as well as to read them from the printed page. Scudder, however, was not so lucky. Before learning to read Danish beginning in the late sixties, he had access to Andersen principally through Mary Howitt's variously faulty work based on a German translation and Charles Boner's overly literary language. Yet, he was the one who pointed to the orality of Andersen's style most forcefully.[2]

Realism is not something one generally associates with Andersen, certainly not with his fairy tales, which most people outside Scandinavia immediately and exclusively connect with his name. For reasons that will become clearer below the Danish expression for these works, which translates as "fairy tales and *stories*," failed to establish itself firmly in English. Nevertheless, thirteen reviews disclose an awareness of realism in Andersen's narrative style, and, while most relate to the longer prose, one concerns the fairy tales and stories as a whole and another the later story "The Ice Maiden" (Isjomfruen). The majority of these reviews appeared from 1870 on, a time when realism became a crucial issue; this number includes the two that criticize Andersen for too little of it. However, at least a handful of earlier reviews recognized his realism, among them those dealing with the tales, and all but one judged it favorably. A similar number of comments ascribe a social dimension to Andersen's work, only two explicitly denying its existence. It is perhaps of some significance that almost all of them fall in the period from 1845 to 1863, which suggests that Andersen's work did not appear so socially relevant to those writing from a specifically realist perspective. Not surprisingly, Scudder numbers among the critics who evince awareness of Andersen's sympathy for the downtrodden, as expressed in the fairy tales and stories rather than in the longer prose, where one might sooner anticipate such discernment. He was the only one who discussed the universality of Andersen's tales, and he did so extensively at that.

Recognition of the humor and satire in Andersen's works ranks among the most perspicacious observations of American reviewers. Especially impressive is the fact that around a third of all comments of this kind were made in connection with the fairy tales and stories. If most came during the late phase of Andersen's reception, it may have been because the realist's eye for the ridiculous or incongruous and reprehensible was generally keener, because more watchful, than the romantic's. Such recognition, like insight into the tacitly moral character of the works, implies a level of maturity in the author that belies the label of "childlike" which was, and is, often attached to him. Considering the current image of Andersen in the English-speaking world, it must therefore count as the Americans' most trenchant judgment that his tales speak to the young and old alike. Scudder expressed this sentiment, as many others, in the greatest breadth and depth, but another twenty of his cloth acknowledged the dual appeal of the works, seven of them from 1848 to 1863, when one might have anticipated relatively less appreciation for experience than for innocence.

With the exception of Leland and Boyesen, who had far less to say on the subject, however, Scudder was alone in his assessment of Andersen's relation to the fairy tale as a genre and his position in its history. Further along in the chapter it will become clear that his notion of Andersen's significance in the contemporary struggle between imagination and utilitarianism, which he shared with John S. Hart [?] and John Esten Cooke, was particularly acute and pertinent.[3]

In our discussion of the first American review of Andersen, Charles A. Dana's commentary on *The Improvisatore* in the *Harbinger* in 1845, we noted a willingness to turn Andersen's work to the reviewer's own ideological purposes, in this instance, to place it in the service of Christian socialism. We observed this willingness elsewhere as well, either as the chief motive for the review or as one among others. Especially early on, American reviewers wrote on Andersen inter alia to express their convictions concerning the Civil War; to foster a positive outlook on life in the United States; to characterize American literature through contrast with other national literatures; to promote writing by Americans; and to uphold morality, either implicitly or explicitly. Related to these reviews is a number of others, mostly late ones, that exhibit a sense of personal fellowship with Andersen or what can only be described as missionary zeal in spreading the "good news" about him. I use this expression advisedly, for Bagger and Griffin speak of Andersen almost as a Christ figure. In these articles moral and religious impulses are particularly strong and relate to Andersen both as an individual and as an artist.

At this juncture it is possible to address the questions raised at the end of the introduction as guides through the numerous writings on Andersen's varied works. The first was why Andersen was received in the United States at all. The answer is threefold, lying first of all quite simply in the fact that Andersen's works came on the American market in English translation, initially from the mid-forties to the early fifties, that is, that they became available to American readers. Secondly, as we saw in the introduction, magazine culture in the United States had by this time reached a sufficiently high level of sophistication that it took notice of the new publications as a matter of course. The final, most important part of the answer is that American critics immediately and overwhelmingly took Andersen seriously as an artist, first as a novelist but quite soon as a distinctive artistic personality who also wrote fairy tales and other short fiction as well as travel books. Their response was not uniformly positive, and there are signs of a lapse in cultural memory between Andersen's crossing of the Atlantic and his "(re)discovery" in the seventies. At the same time, there are other indications that he became a literally timeless figure in the United States. On the whole, American criticism demonstrates that in this country Andersen quickly became and then remained a self-evident feature of the cultural landscape of the West, a figure who was read if not always discussed.

Unfortunately, the reviews provide few if any clues to certain of the questions raised in the introduction, and one is therefore constrained to draw inferences from circumstantial evidence. One of these questions is why certain works were reviewed while others were not. The English translations that began to appear in the mid-1840s were available to Americans almost as soon as to British readers, often in American editions. However, the critical response was indeed unevenly distributed across the genres and works over time. Andersen first gained renown in the United States with *The Improvisatore,* and there is direct and indirect evidence indicating that the novel was widely read in the country. Even toward the end of his life some critics thought of him principally as the author of this work. However, its notoriety produced few reviews. Despite the scrutiny a couple of his other novels received during the seventies his efforts in the genre as a whole failed to attract great attention, and some were virtually or totally ignored. Paradoxically, it is entirely possible that *The Improvisatore* was the motivation for a review of *In Sweden*. In any event, the latter received almost as many early reviews as the former, and, collectively, the travel books approached the novels in the total number of reviews elicited. Before the publication of Nina Baym's *Novels, Readers, and Reviewers* in 1984 one might have attributed the neglect of Andersen's novels to American hostility to fiction stemming from the Puritan tradition and the absence of broad social convention in the United States.[4] While the popularity of travel writing has long been recognized, which would account for the appeal of Andersen's travel books, however, Americans in fact read and reviewed large numbers of novels during the period in question, both domestic and foreign. Precisely the high profile of Frederika Bremer and Scandinavian culture in general at that time only makes the response to Andersen's novels, or the lack of it, more puzzling.

Andersen's autobiography did create something of a stir on its appearance in 1847, and the fairy tales and stories accounted for a large percentage of the reviews. However, none of the eleven individual collections generated more than two, and most of them appeared during the early to middle years of Andersen's critical reception. Now, reviews in American magazines at this time were typically short, which may explain the brevity and even the generality of those devoted to the tales, if not their frequent banality.[5] In view of the great popularity of these works, to which Scudder and other sources attest, however, one cannot help but wonder why not more of them were written. It is tempting to speculate that here, as well as with the novels and other works, the readily available English reviews sufficed to meet most American needs, this despite Americans' growing desire to pair cultural autonomy with their political independence from England. However, evidence presented further along in the chapter suggests that this was in fact not the case, at least with regard to the fairy tales and stories. In chapter 4 we saw that the reviewers who discussed these works during the early phase of Andersen's reception, though competent, were on the whole not distinguished as critics. All the same, the very fact that they chose to review the tales at all may be seen to reflect a certain broad-mindedness that was rare at the time, especially if one suspects that critics' dearth of interest in Andersen's fairy tales stemmed from already deeply engrained Anglo-American reserve toward the fairy tale as a genre, to which we shall return shortly.

It remains unclear why after 1852 there ensued a gap in writing on Andersen of nearly two decades' duration, interrupted only by a modest flourish during the early sixties, most of which is accounted for by reviews of Fanny Fuller's *The Ice Maiden, and Other Tales* and a few general articles. Many of his works continued to be published in new or reprint editions, to be sure. Although most did not go beyond two, *The Improvisatore* appeared in four, and various collections of the fairy tales and stories went through an astonishing forty-five, as many as seven in a single year.[6] Judging by later writing, one surmises that the later editions maintained or increased awareness of these works. However, American reviewers virtually ignored them. So, however, did their counterparts in England, at least relative to the attention they gave them on their initial appearance between 1845 and 1848. Bredsdorff writes that the period from 1848 to 1875—the year of Andersen's death!—brought fewer reviews than the preceding three years and that they had little effect on the image of the poet established during that brief space.[7] According to this scholar, Andersen was dead and buried as a novelist after 1857, and even the new editions of fairy tales and stories that came out during the last decade of his life received scant notice.[8] Whether these developments in the United States and England are related, and, if so, how intimately, is impossible to say, but American review critics also appear to have all but closed the book on Andersen by 1869.

Of course, it is no mystery why the resurgence of critical interest occurred around 1870. Many of the reviews that began to appear in comparatively great numbers that year were written in direct response to individual volumes of Scudder's Author's Edition. Surely, many or most of the other reviews as well as the general articles owe their existence in significant part to the heightened awareness of Andersen and his work created by the edition. Interestingly, this was a purely American phenomenon. Although American books were available in England at this time, it appears that only one review of the Author's Edition was published in an English periodical. Even this notice did not refer to Scudder's work, as it left Hurd and Houghton's Riverside Press. A British publisher had taken over a portion of the run, issuing it under his own imprint, and it was to this edition that the reviewer responded.[9] Curiously, the British Museum possesses neither edition, and English Andersen biographer Robert Nisbet Bain never heard of either of them, writing in 1895 that the final version of the autobiography had never been translated into English.[10]

In any event, perusal of the statistics in chapter 1 reveals that the later American reception of Andersen exceeded the earlier by a margin approaching 100 percent. One contributing factor was the continuing maturation of American magazine culture. Between 1850, by which time three-fourths of the early reviews had already appeared, and 1870, the number of American magazines doubled and continued to rise steeply.[11] Moreover, these years witnessed the founding of quality magazines such as *Appleton's Journal*, the *Atlantic Monthly*, the *Galaxy*, *Harper's New Monthly Magazine*, *Putnam's Magazine*, *Scribner's Monthly*, and the *Overland Monthly; Putnam's* and the *Atlantic* were particularly noted for the excellence of their reviewing.[12] These seven periodicals alone published two-thirds of the late reviews and articles, the *Atlantic* accounting for six, or close to a quarter, of them. Despite the absence of direct evidence one may surely assume that the relationship between Hurd and Houghton and the *Atlantic*, represented by Scudder and Howells, led to this relatively large number of reviews.[13] Certainly, one must also credit Howells's desire to promote the reading of good literature and its discussion in the United States.[14]

It is safe to say that the echo created by the Author's Edition both bespoke and sustained the viability of Andersen's works in the United States. The critical reception of the edition, like sales of the individual volumes, was still selective. Only one of the ten was not reviewed— the one emphasizing "stories" rather than "fairy tales," significantly— but the autobiography alone received more than three, and four of the books received only one or two. All the same, the coverage was broader as well as more extensive than during the earlier period. Especially considering the general articles, moreover, the commentaries were by and large longer and more penetrating. This has to do with the rising expectations of the quality magazines and, of course, with the comparatively higher *niveau* of the reviewers as a group. Both the earlier and later groups of reviewers had their share of what Mott has called "magazinists," often anonymous individuals who were professionally engaged in publishing magazines and were distinct from occasional or regular contributors who either sought simply to earn a living by the pen or aspired to create great art.[15] While the earlier group also included recognized figures such as the Duyckincks and Dana and the major writers Stoddard and Taylor, the later group boasted Stoddard, Stedman, Scudder, and Howells as well as Boyesen and the anonymous but exceptionally articulate author of the article in *Scandinavia*. Furthermore, the study of modern languages and literatures in the United States was entering its early phase as a distinct discipline, the Modern Language Association soon to be founded in 1883, and the last-named men were clearly not only creative writers but critics given to more systematic reflection on their craft.

On the whole, the notions of art evinced by the reviews disclose a development one would expect in view of the age, progressing from an Augustan concern for moral character and a romantic preoccupation with subjectivity and aesthetics to a realist insistence on actuality and social context. However, the reviews were no more monolithic in their assumptions than the movements themselves, displaying various mixtures of interests and even anachronisms such as J. Ross Browne's early realism and Emily F. Wheeler's late moralism. Here, as in so many other respects, Horace Scudder embodies American Andersen criticism in its entirety in his emphasis on morality and religion, art, and lived experience alike. Scudder wrote exclusively on the fairy tales and stories, but, perhaps benefiting from familiarity with the novels, he was able to perceive a realist spirit in them that escaped most other commentators. Of course, he had access to all of the tales.[16] The obliviousness of other critics to Andersen's growing realism may well be attributable in part to the relatively small percentage of "stories" included in the volumes reviewed, as described in chapter 1. The vast majority of reviewers were exposed to far fewer stories than tales and thus had far less opportunity to recognize what Scudder clearly saw.

Even assuming that critics had had access to all of Andersen's stories, however, it might not have had a substantial impact on their general notion of either the "fairy tales" or of Andersen as an author. By this point it should be evident that as late as the 1870s Andersen was by no means thought of exclusively as a writer of fairy tales and that the stories and tales themselves were not at all universally considered to be for children alone. Among the early reviewers only Stoddard anticipated their eventual role in Americans' understanding of Andersen. Beginning in the late sixties, however, an increasing number of reviews—only one of the fairy tales and stories themselves!—indicate that the modern notion of Andersen and "Andersen's fairy tales" was starting to take hold of Americans' thinking about the writer and his work, at least subliminally. This insidious development and the dearth of reviews of the tales probably have as much to do with extraneous factors, for instance the fact that critics of the seventies grew up with Andersen's fairy tales, as with the works themselves.

Of course, the absence of an even remotely sustained critical discussion of the fairy tales and stories may stem from an appreciation similar to that of the poetry of seventeenth-century English poet Robert Herrick. Patrick writes that Herrick's lyrics "aptly expressed and successfully communicated the meanings and emotions which he intended to convey. He thus accomplished the prime task of an artist, providing works of art which were so self-communicative that their appreciation and understanding required no explanation or commentary. . . . Such appreciation is like the appreciation due natural perfection; analysis is possible but extraneous."[17] Less flattering for potential reviewers is the fact that grown men were entirely capable of enjoying fantasy and real or imagined simplicity without being willing to admit to such pleasure in the company of other adults.[18] We have seen that certain critics treated Andersen as "the children's poet" despite revealing their awareness of his mature appeal. Such reluctance is likely a sign of what was probably the root cause of the American response to Andersen and his fairy tales, which requires some explanation.

Many students of children's literature in the United States remark that the American climate has traditionally been inhospitable and even hostile to fantasy in writing for the young. Though unanimous in this regard, these scholars offer widely differing opinions in explanation. One suggests that the promise of America made the fairy tale superfluous, that is, that the bounty of the New World lay within reach of everyone, thereby eliminating the cause of the wishes and fears that lay at the roots of the old oral folktale and its literary successors.[19] Another cites, less sanguinely, a predilection of the American mind to systematize the ineffable, to organize hopes and fears under rubrics such as millenialism—nota bene the American mind formed during the Enlightenment.[20] Yet another traces the attitude of nineteenth-century Americans back to the Puritans' Calvinist concern for the salvation of the soul and fear of pleasures of the senses, which gradually transformed into a generalized moralism and distrust of entertainment.[21]

There is probably truth in all these contentions, but religious conservatism and moralism loom particularly large. Around the turn of the nineteenth century, as MacLeod writes, "Americans still looked on children's books as vehicles for instruction, not entertainment, though they were prepared to accept a moderate flavouring of fictional entertainment for the sake of more successful instruction."[22] As late as the 1830s Congregational minister and teacher Jacob Abbott introduced his widely popular Rollo books as a means of educating children in moral behavior. About the same time, writer, publisher, and bookseller Samuel Griswold Goodrich launched his highly successful series of Peter Parley books as a morally edifying replacement for traditional fairy tales and nursery rhymes, which he and many others found wanting in moral value.[23]

However, the emergence of the modern notion of childhood over the first half of the nineteenth century created an atmosphere that was more conducive to the acceptance and eventual cultivation of fairy tales and other kinds of fantasy literature. As middle- and upper-class children were gradually freed from work and other adult responsibilities, there arose a sentimental view of children as such that lent childhood an inherent value it had never before possessed.[24] After midcentury, children's literature began to introduce elements of fiction already established in writing for adults, such as sentiment and social reality.[25] By around 1870, quality children's magazines such as Scudder's *Riverside* had brought about a shift of emphasis from instruction to the standard fare of prose fiction.[26] However, not all kinds of fiction participated in this change in equal measure. The American fairy tale itself possessed and retained an "innate streak of common sense" that was both its "hallmark and limitation."[27] And even as Scudder published Andersen's fairy tales in the *Riverside Magazine* and the Author's Edition, the genre as a whole was still viewed with some degree of suspicion as a trivial waste of time.[28]

Thus, when Andersen's fairy tales and stories first appeared in the United States in 1846, they entered an unreceptive high culture at a particularly unpropitious time. And they entered under the only guise in which they could be perceived in the country, as a form of children's literature. By 1870, when the tales began to come out in the Author's Edition, they were to all appearances as firmly established in the populace at large as they were in England.[29] While children's literature per se had in the meantime gained widespread acknowledgment in literary circles, however, the genre in which Andersen did his most characteristic and best work still had uncertain footing there—as writing for the nursery, not to mention for adults. Moreover, the advent of realism in literature militated against recognition, a disadvantage compounded by the fact that Americans had little opportunity to experience the more realistic Andersen. As intimated earlier, the wonder is perhaps not so much that Andersen's fairy tales were reviewed so little as that they were reviewed at all. Seen in this light, those numerous American critics who perceived the relevance of Andersen's stories for the mature reader deserve all the more credit.

Yet—and this is perhaps the most remarkable discovery for the present writer—even if the fairy tale had been firmly established in the United States, evidence gleaned from Andersen criticism in other countries indicates that his works would have fared no better among American critics than they in fact did. It is understandable that Andersen's reception in neighboring Sweden began earlier and encompassed more of his lifework, including plays and poetry, than in the distant United States or even insular England. According to Åström, the initial review appeared in 1829, the year after the debut of Andersen's first major prose work in Denmark, though it was followed by few others for several years.[30] Indeed, the flood tide of Andersen's reception reached its high point only in 1840 and had largely ebbed by 1852. At the peak of his presence and popularity in the Swedish press, Andersen was considered principally as a novelist. Though *O. T.* was passed over in silence, *The Improvisatore* and *Only a Fiddler* were warmly received. However, the announcement of *The Two Baronesses* in 1848 already creates the impression of a rediscovery of Andersen as a novelist. While a number of biographical articles point to an interest in Andersen's life, *Das Märchen meines Lebens* (The Fairy Tale of My Life) of 1847 was never translated into Swedish, and only one review of it appears to have been written.[31] By the end of the forties Andersen was viewed primarily as a writer of fairy tales. As his work in the genre came to dominate his writing, he was reviewed less frequently and taken less seriously as an artist, though his popularity in the general public seems to have increased.

If this sounds familiar, there is more. Even during Andersen's heyday in Sweden his fairy tales and stories received few reviews, not all of which were positive. A collection published in 1838 was praised for its lively style but criticized for its naïveté and questionable morality. The scattered notices of the forties bring little that is new.[32] Indeed, only a couple reveal an awareness of the sophistication of works such as *The Nightingale*, about which Åström can only shake his head.[33] The great majority view the tales as—children's literature—denying the form the dignity of art and Andersen that of an artist. Åström is reluctant to attribute Swedish criticism of Andersen to one particular cause or another but notes that much of it proceeded from a realist perspective, particularly among Hegelian critics. Nonetheless, it may strike one as curious that a nation possessing a strong indigenous folk tradition and emerging from a romantic period profoundly influenced by German romanticism, with its heavy commitment to the *Kunstmärchen,* should have had so little, and so little of consequence, to say about Andersen.[34] That is, until one considers the German reception of the tales itself.

If one disregards the earliest Swedish reviews, which were followed by several years of silence, the German reception of Andersen anticipated the Swedish by around three years, beginning with responses to *The Improvisatore* in 1835.[35] Though a large number of editions were not reviewed, indeed, it unfolded over the next fifteen years with much greater continuity and far greater intensity. Möller-Christensen registers a total of 129 reviews and general or biographical articles that appeared during this time, reaching high points in 1838 and then again in 1847. One reason for the difference is surely the fact that the institution of literary criticism had a much broader base in Germany, which by this time boasted one of the leading cultures in Europe. Another is that Andersen took great pains to promote himself and his work through visits to Germany and the establishment of acquaintanceships and friendships among the German cultural and even political elite, in large part to answer the shabby treatment he felt he received at the hands of Danish critics. Möller-Christensen opines, moreover, that Andersen had the good fortune to come on the German literary scene at the right time, when the conservative Biedermeier culture dominant during the thirties was still prepared to embrace the idealistic notion of genius of the recent classical-romantic past as well as the progressive dream of social ascent, both of which Andersen embodied.[36] *The Improvisatore* was given a warm welcome in 1835, and *O. T.* received even greater, if less positive, attention in 1837. However, it was with *Only a Fiddler* the following year that Andersen made his breakthrough in Germany. Möller-Christensen attributes the great success of the novel to the interplay between a biographical sketch included as a preface and the autobiographical features of the work per se, which she feels planted the seed of the Andersen myth in Germany.[37]

As in the case of Sweden, more of Andersen's literary production was accessible to Germans than to English speakers, and German reviewers responded accordingly. Although his plays were either rejected as being undramatic or were totally ignored, his lyric poetry found a generally positive reception throughout the period in question. His *Travel Silhouettes* (*Skyggebilleder af en Reise til Harzen, det sach-siske Schweitz etc. i Sommeren 1831*), an early imitation of Heinrich Heine's *Trip to the Harz* (*Die Harzreise*), was initially panned but then received exceptionally positive comments. *A Poet's Bazaar* (1843) enjoyed considerable favor for the intensity and freshness of its descriptions as well as for the related, early impressionistic features of its style. Judging by the excerpts included in Åström's and Möller-Christensen's studies, the Germans' reviews were generally longer and more penetrating than those of their neighbors to the north, comparable in these respects to the English reviews. Although they gave Andersen substantial space and discussed him with concentrated intensity from 1845 to 1848, however, their general opinion of him and his work was distinctly on the decline during these years. Aspects of the novels that had received praise early on were interpreted as an inability to write organic, seamless prose in connection with *The Two Baronesses* (1848). The number of reviews spiked in 1847 with the appearance of the autobiography in an edition of collected works, but they plainly reveal that the Andersen myth had begun to lose credibility among German critics. Even before German dreams of democracy reached a peak in the events of 1848, the real-world concerns represented by the writers of Young Germany (das Junge Deutschland) and the advent of realism in general had weakened the hold of Biedermeier idealism on the country. Moreover, the Three Years' War, which Prussia and Denmark fought over the Schleswig-Holstein question from 1848 to 1851, tended to diminish the sense of cultural commonality that Germans felt for Danes (and vice versa). By 1850, Andersen was increasingly viewed as anachronistic, and, much as in Sweden, his fairy tales and stories were the only works from his pen that attained almost universal acceptance—with a certain, familiar reservation.

Andersen's *Picture Book Without Pictures* became a major success on its appearance in 1841 and retained its popularity in successive editions throughout the main phase of the author's reception in Germany. The tales themselves, however, had no such luck. The first collection, which came out in 1838, not only received mixed reviews but also encountered a certain lack of interest since some commentators treated the works as—children's literature. Indeed, a couple criticized them for being too sophisticated for children![38] By the mid-forties, subsequent editions were attracting favorable notices, but the overall number of reviews remained quite modest. Only one received as many as six, and a couple got only one or two. Tellingly, the three editions that appeared in 1850, one of which was a collected edition, were entirely ignored. The late fairy tales and stories, which were more realistic in nature and were written more for adults, suffered virtually the same fate. It may be the case, as Möller-Christensen suggests, that the "idyllic" initial notion of Andersen made it difficult for reviewers to discern the problematic sophistication of works such as "The Shadow" and "The Snow Queen." And certain critics in fact uncovered significant truths, such as Andersen's ability to "inspire" animals and inanimate objects with life in accord with the nature of their bodies.[39] However, those who recommend the tales to adults often represent them simply as a means of escaping the tribulations of everyday life.[40] And the one who mentions "The Shadow" specifically sees it "merely" as a "'new, humoristic, and original'" variation on Adelbert Chamisso's *The Wondrous History of Peter Schlemihl* (*Peter Schlemihls wundersame Geschichte*).[41] Despite the march of events and changes of perception around midcentury it strikes this writer as almost inconceivable that the nation which produced not only the Grimm Brothers but also Novalis, Clemens Brentano, Achim von Arnim, Friedrich de la Motte Fouqué, Joseph Freiherr von Eichendorff, and Wilhelm Hauff, not to mention the writers already named, should not have penetrated further into the work of a figure who was related to them by nature and conviction and who learned so much from them.

Bredsdorff based his presentation of the English reception of Andersen on some one hundred reviews, distinctly fewer than the number that appeared in Germany.[42] However, more than half of them came out between 1845 to 1848, when Andersen was a novelty in England, which may well make this brief span of time the most intense period of Andersen criticism to have ever occurred in any country. As mentioned earlier, the some three decades that then elapsed before Andersen's death not only witnessed fewer reviews in far less concentration but also failed to change the already established image of him. Although *The Improvisatore* maintained its early popularity for many years, Andersen was virtually dead as a novelist as early as 1857. At this time, indeed, the English "shoved Andersen into the nursery and shut the door behind him!"[43] During the last decade of his life even new editions of his fairy tales and stories received little notice. We have already seen that the Author's Edition attracted almost no attention in England.

English reviewers had access to Andersen's works in the same order and around the same time as their American counterparts. Given the historical and current ties between the two countries, it is therefore no surprise that the English discussed Andersen under many of the same rubrics and with much the same understanding as the Americans. For example, they, too, see Andersen's work less as the product of intellectual power or profundity than of an original and imaginative, poetic temperament. Some appreciate the moral or religious nature of the works, while others find too little or even too much of it. Despite Bredsdorff's contention that Andersen and *The Improvisatore* arrived in England at just the right time, when taste was shifting from the fashionable, upper-class novel to the poetic realism of Dickens and Thackeray, English reviewers exhibit far less awareness of the social relevance of Andersen's work than the Americans.[44] They also appear far less impressed than the Germans or even the Americans by the mythical proportions of his autobiography with respect to its artistic as well as social aspects, perhaps due to the standing of the literary and political culture of the nation and/or, as Bredsdorff suggests, simply because of their preexisting familiarity with Andersen's life, which had already been portrayed in biographical sketches published in work editions and magazines.[45] Nonetheless, the English have as keen a sense for the Dane's humor and satire as the Americans.

Considering the consignment of the fairy tales and stories to the nursery little over a decade after their appearance in England, it is safe to say that their reception in the country was, on balance and at best, no more notable than that of the other countries discussed in the present chapter. One could hardly expect it to have been otherwise, since the fairy tale and other genres of fantasy literature had as tenuous a position in Victorian England as in the United States, and for similar reasons.[46] The Germanophile endeavors of Carlyle and Coleridge had not created a favorable environment for either the folktale or the *Kunstmärchen*. Dickens and Ruskin came to the defense of the fairy tale, it is true, but only in 1853 and 1868, respectively, after Andersen's heyday in English magazines.[47] And both sought rather to counter the prevalent moralizing tendency of practitioners of the genre, embodied most recently and most notoriously by George Cruikshank, than to recognize the form as a means of mature reflection.[48] While the two wrote in the name of imagination, it is clear that they had the child's imagination foremost in mind.[49] Lewis Carroll's *Alice's Adventures in Wonderland* did not appear until 1865.

Bredsdorff concedes the presence of much chaff among the English reviews, and this is evident in many from which he quotes.[50]

At the same time, he finds no small number of attempts at a real understanding of the literary value and originality of the fairy tales and stories.[51] Among these is surely the perception of a reviewer for the *Atheneum* in 1847 that "Fancy" in Andersen's tales represents a healthy antidote to the "machines of utilitarian inventions."[52] In any case Bredsdorff clearly felt that William Jerdan said "something crucial and accurate about H. C. Andersen's tales and their peculiar character" when he wrote in the *Literary Gazette* in 1848 that the "subjects which to ordinary minds would not suggest a single idea beyond their external form or use, become, in his [Andersen's] alembic, profuse of matter and reflective illustration, and his invention invests them with human vitality and superhuman interest; out of both which result the purest sentiments, the purest morality, and the sagest advice. And to contemplate the charm, the radiant colours of poetry are thrown over the whole with a lavish hand, so that we are at a loss to tell whether we are most benefited by the real, or delighted by the imaginative."[53] Bredsdorff finds similar penetration in a review that appeared in *Blackwood's Edinburgh Magazine* in 1860. Whereas English writers such as Ruskin seek in their tales to establish identity "between the thing meant and the thing spoken," that is, to exploit allegory, in Andersen's works "[m]inute identities are omitted: he carries you on with a delightful story at which children gape as supernatural and impossible, but to which the wise man listens with still more attention; for in this supernatural and impossible he recognises everyday life and experience. Instead of tying himself and his reader down to the close fitting of his tale, he leaves the attentive listener impressed at the end with the double sensation of having been at a theatre and a church. He has laughed at clowns doing the most preposterous actions and speaking the most ludicrous nonsense; and afterwards discovers that he has received a very serious lecture—a reprimand for thoughtless conduct, and encouragement to mend his ways."[54] In this review Bredsdorff discerns "attempts at a real assessment of H. C. Andersen's literary contribution and an understanding that the fairy tales are more than entertaining reading for children."[55]

However, it was a review of Caroline Peachey's *Danish Fairy Tales and Legends,* which appeared in the *Examiner* in 1846, that Bredsdorff finds the most insightful. Questioning why the tales should be called Danish, the reviewer writes, "There is an occasional Northern colouring, but only so far as it could not be helped. All the rest is so free from everything national or exclusive, that we do not remember to have met with any production so given up to a sense of the variety of being that exists in the universe. . . . We need not say that it implies a rare and surprising art to convey such impressions as these. When Johnson laughed at Goldsmith for thinking of writing a story in which 'little fish' should be the actors, the author of *Animated Nature* very properly told him that it was not so easy a matter as he thought it; and that if he (Johnson) were to write such a story, he would make his little fish talk like 'great whales.' There is no such confusion of ideas in Mr. Hans Christian Andersen. His whales and his little fish all talk in character. . . . Nay, his very peg-tops and balls are full of individuality. . . . The fault of the book (if we must find one) is, that all the stories have too much meaning; that they overflow with intention and moral; not always obviously, sometimes obscurely, but still with incessant intelligence. You desire occasionally something more childish and less clever. But the genius and refinement are undeniable."[56] One may object to the reviewer's gentle criticism of the stories' abundance of meaning as well as to his apparent equation of implicitness with obscurity. In a passage not quoted, moreover, he overlooks the irony in the opening sentence of "The Nightingale," and one may wish that he had chosen that quite sophisticated work as an example of Andersen's art rather than "The Emperor's New Clothes." However, one can understand Bredsdorff's respect for the review, which he expresses as follows: "It is doubtful whether there is any single announcement of H. C. Andersen's fairy tales superior to this one, in Denmark, England, or elsewhere, which has hit the mark so surely and precisely as this critique in *The Examiner.*"[57]

Imaginativeness, universality, "variety of being," the vitality and individuality of nonhuman figures speaking in character like human beings, abundance of implicit moral meaning, and appeal to adults as well as to children—these are indeed features of Andersen's fairy tales and stories that are still considered sources of their distinction.[58] They are also features identified by American reviewers, in certain instances by several or many of them. At least in the case of Scudder most are discussed more cogently and in greater depth than in any of the English—or German or Swedish—reviews.[59] This is also true of certain other major characteristics of, or factors related to, the tales. For example, a reviewer for the *Daily News* notes in 1875—the sole English critic to do so—that Andersen is the only writer who "has succeeded in recovering, and reproducing, the kind of imagination which constructed the old world fairy tale," an idea that Scudder expanded upon at some length in 1861 and then again in 1875.[60] While a couple of English reviewers detect what one might term "poetic realism" in *The Two Baronesses* and *In Sweden,* only one, writing in 1870, hints at the realism of Andersen's later tales, which Scudder had sensed as early as his first article and clearly articulated in the second.[61] And none of the English critics appears to have recognized the orality of Andersen's narrative style in the tales, which struck several American commentators, Scudder foremost among them.

There are surely aspects of Scudder's articles that one may consider to be shortcomings, though they appear as such in part due to subsequent discoveries or changes in perception. In his treatment of Andersen, as of all major figures, for example, he tends far more toward apology than toward criticism.[62] Although he is aware of the antiquity and internationality of folktales, he seems to have an ahistorical view of the fairy tale per se, its relatively recent development in, and transmission from, seventeenth-century France.[63] Today, moreover, one would likely place less emphasis than he on religion and "The Red Shoes," which appears neither in Dal's survey of favorite fairy tales nor in Conroy's and Rossel's collection of tales mentioned in chapter 1, note 16. Although he observes a spirit of realism in the tales as a whole, he fails either to discern or to discuss it with specific regard to the more realistic, later stories. Nevertheless, Scudder's grasp of the Anglo-American context in which Andersen's tales became so significant and the breadth and depth of his understanding of Andersen's peculiar achievement are both remarkable and unique in the English-language discussion of the poet during the period under scrutiny. One suspects that, had Scudder been an Englishman, Bredsdorff would, at the very least, have numbered him among the most prominent commentators on Andersen in English.

On April 24, 1862, a review of the article Scudder published in the *National Quarterly Review* appeared in the Danish newspaper *Dagbladet* (*The Daily Paper*).[64] The writer devotes considerable space to the piece but has nothing good to say about it. First of all, he states that Danish readers will "naturally" (naturligviis) find nothing new in it, adding that it contains on the whole the same observations that have led European criticism to rank Andersen so highly in his peculiar genre. Indeed, he later opines that Scudder's comments about Andersen's power over "unsophisticated" (umiddelbare) and "childlike" (barnlige) minds are often taken from European sources. After summarizing points that Scudder makes, he pokes poorly concealed fun at the American's analysis of "The Red Shoes," which, he suggests, must be longer than the tale itself. He concludes by translating from the final paragraph of Scudder's article: "[H]e [Andersen] is one of the few who seem never to have lost their first childhood. He creates for himself a pure world, in which he lives. Whatsoever he touches is transmuted to the same simple beauty; he touches our hearts, and whatever within us is child-like, lovingly responds. The children of his creation are immortal—immortal childhood itself is the symbol of Andersen's genius."[65] What the reviewer thinks of the passage one can only surmise based on the general tenor and tone of his comments.

The review is problematic in several respects. It is not at all clear why Danish readers should have automatically discounted the possibility of increasing their understanding of Andersen by reading the article. The explanation may well have less to do with an underappreciation of critical acumen in "uncivilized" and "materialistic" America—after all, the article appeared in the "distinguished" (ansete) *National Quarterly Review*—though this certainly may have played a role, than with an overestimation of analytical ability in the Old World.[66] In this connection one notes that the reviewer specifies European, rather than Danish, criticism, perhaps aware, as Bredsdorff tells us, that the English reception, at least that of the fairy tales and stories, was more profound than contemporary Danish criticism.[67] In any event, he was simply unaware that some of Andersen's early tales were indeed adaptations of Danish folktales, which Scudder affirms and the reviewer denies. Moreover, his summary of Scudder's observations is far from complete.

The author of the review was C. St. A. Bille (1828–98), who was also the founder and current editor of *Dagbladet*.[68] Owing to his varied writing as well as to his activity as Member of Parliament, Bille became known as the most eloquent (if rather pedantic) Dane of his time. Especially after his trip to England in 1856 he assumed a liberal, metropolitan, and anticlerical, that is, "English," posture in the paper. As a Dane and a personal friend of Andersen, Bille had a certain vested interest in promoting and defending a man who had already become Denmark's national treasure. However, his was an entirely different turn of mind, which may explain both his mockery of Scudder's extensive discourse on the religious dimension of "The Red Shoes" and his tacit frown at the American's emphasis on the role of childhood in Andersen and his fairy tales and stories.

In any case, Bille omits several of Scudder's insights which, as we have just seen, are developed far beyond similar or identical perceptions in the English reviews and at least one of which the English entirely overlooked. To say the very least, Scudder's articles bear comparison with any of the English reviews or, for that matter, any written in Germany or Sweden. He read the same works as his colleagues in England and did so within a similar historical and cultural context, but he saw them more clearly and saw more in them than most, which makes Bille's accusation of plagiarism particularly egregious.

Indeed, not all the observations of another young critic, writing at the end of the sixties and destined for preeminence in his field, were original. Georg Brandes's lengthy essay "H. C. Andersen som Eventyrdigter" (H. C. Andersen as a Fairy Tale Poet, also translated simply as Hans Christian Andersen) goes well beyond any previous writing on Andersen's fairy tales and stories, but it also covers much of the same ground trod in the best of the reviews and the work of Scudder.[69] With regard to this common ground, Brandes's distinction lies in the truly incomparable richness of historical, anthropological, and psychological perspective as well as the relative wealth of formal detail with which he scrutinizes Andersen and his tales. I would contend that Scudder bears much the same relation to his American and English peers and is therefore a worthy predecessor to Brandes as an Andersen critic. Unfortunately, neither his understanding of the tales nor the work of his compatriots was able to prevent a limited and distorted view of the Dane from becoming prevalent in the United States.[70] Even in this lack of success, however, he stands with the best of contemporary commentators on Andersen.

Notes

PREFACE

1. Steffen Auring et al., *Borgerlig enhedskultur 1807–48,* vol. 5 of *Dansk litteraturhistorie* (Copenhagen: Gyldendal, 2000), 124–56; Lise Busk-Jensen et al., *Dannelse, folkelighed, individualisme 1848–1901,* vol. 6 of the same title, 56–73.

INTRODUCTION

1. *The Andersen-Scudder Letters: Hans Christian Andersen's Correspondence with Horace Elisha Scudder,* ed. Jean Hersholt and Waldemar Westergaard (Berkeley and Los Angeles: University of California Press, 1949), 3. For more information on Scudder's later, quite varied professional activity see chapters 6 and 7.

2. See Elias Bredsdorff, *Danish Literature in English Translation, with a Special Hans Christian Andersen Supplement: A Bibliography* (Copenhagen: Ejnar Munksgaard, 1950). Howitt translated Andersen's autobiography from the German translation, *Das Märchen meines Lebens ohne Dichtung* [*The Fairy Tale of My Life without Poetry*].

3. Viggo Hjørnager Pedersen, "Hans Andersen as an English Writer," in *Essays on Translation,* by Hjørnager Pedersen (Copenhagen: Nyt Nordisk Forlag Arnold Busck, 1988), 95.

4. Ibid.

5. See Sven Hakon Rossel, "Hans Christian Andersen Research in the United States," in *Andersen og Verden: Indlæg fra den Første Internationale H. C. Andersen-Konference 25–31. August 1991,* ed. H. C. Andersen-Centret, Odense Universitet, 518 (Odense: Odense Universitetsforlag, 1993). Between 1950 and 1980 alone forty-nine editions of the fairy tales and stories appeared in the United States; see Carol L. Schroeder, *A Bibliography of Danish Literature in English Translation, 1950–1980* (Copenhagen: Det danske Selskab, 1982).

6. See Rossel, "Hans Christian Andersen Research in the United States," 518, and Erik Dal, "Hans Christian Andersen's Tales and America," *Scandinavian Studies* 40 (1968): 11–13.

7. See chapter 6, 155.

8. See Dal, "Hans Christian Andersen's Tales and America," and Rossel, "Hans Christian Andersen Research in the United States."

9. See my "The Image of H. C. Andersen in American Magazines During the Author's Lifetime," in *H. C. Andersen: Old Problems and New Readings,* ed. Steven Son-

drup (Odense: University of Southern Denmark Press, 2004), 175–98, and "The Author's Edition of H. C. Andersen's Works: An American-Danish Collaboration," *Orbis Litterarum* 60 (2005): 449–76.

10. We shall see that some of the reviewers dealt with the quality of translations of Andersen's works, the direct means by which he gained such access, and reference will be made to formal studies of these renderings.

11. John Tebbel and Mary Ellen Zuckerman, *The Magazine in America, 1741–1990* (New York: Oxford University Press, 1991), 8; Frank Luther Mott, *A History of American Magazines, 1741–1850* (New York: Appleton, 1930), 341–42; and Mott, *A History of American Magazines, 1865–1885* (Cambridge: Harvard University Press, 1938), 5.

12. Tebbel and Zuckerman, *The Magazine in America, 1741–1990*, 57.

13. See *American Periodicals, 1741–1900: An Index to the Microfilm Collections,* ed. Jean Hoornstra and Trudy Heath (Ann Arbor, Mich.: University Microfilms International, 1979). The series encompasses around 1,100 periodicals.

14. William Frederick Poole and William I. Fletcher, *Poole's Index to Periodical Literature,* revised edition (New York: Peter Smith, 1938). Poole is vague regarding his principles of selection. Whatever they may have been, he includes only 145 American magazines for the period from 1802 to 1881 (he also indexes British periodicals) and overlooks some of the titles on Andersen listed in other, older media.

15. *Index to Early American Periodicals to 1850,* vol. 5 (New York: Readex Microprint, 1964).

16. See <http://moa.umdl.umich.edu> and <http://memory.loc.gov/ammem/ndlpcoop/moahtml/snchome.html>.

17. "Making of America" and "The Nineteenth Century in Print," for example, contain only thirty-four magazines combined.

18. See Mott, *A History of American Magazines, 1741–1850,* 392; *A History of American Magazines, 1850–1865* (Cambridge: Harvard University Press, 1938), 129–30; and *A History of American Magazines, 1865–1885,* 249. Elias Bredsdorff located around one hundred British reviews of Andersen's work for his study *H. C. Andersen og England* (Copenhagen: Rosenkilde og Baggers Forlag, 1954), 484. It is unclear precisely which and how many of these, that is, which and how many of the magazines in which they were published, were available in the United States, but the number was surely much higher than that listed by Poole; *Poole's Index to Periodical Literature,* 37.

19. Mott, *A History of American Magazines, 1850–1865,* 129.

20. The same problems that confound empirical study of reader response to literature obtain in the relationship between critic and reader and critic and critic. See, for example, James L. Machor, "Introduction: Readers, Texts, Contexts," in *Readers in History: Nineteenth-Century American Literature and the Contexts of Response,* ed. Machor (Baltimore: Johns Hopkins University Press, 1993), especially xxi–xxvi.

21. See chapter 15 of Bredsdorff's *H. C. Andersen og England,* 428–88.

22. Before leaving this subject it is worth noting that English magazines plundered their American counterparts as well as vice versa and that some American magazines also had English editions; see Clarence Gohdes, *American Literature in Nineteenth-Century England* (New York: Columbia University Press, 1944), especially chapter 2. To the extent that American magazinists' work was read in England they returned the earlier favor, even though, or perhaps precisely because, English reviewers had long since ceased to devote more than occasional attention to Andersen. See the discussion of the English critical reception of Andersen in chapter 7, beginning on 204.

23. I succeeded in identifying 54 percent of the authors either by signature or based on the current editorial circumstances of the periodicals, as reflected in various sources. I was able to ascertain the identity of an additional 13 percent with reasonable certainty, though their names are followed by a question mark in the bibliography of primary sources. Little if any information is available about some of the writers.

24. In response to William Charvat's admonition against accepting reviewer opinion as being representative of public opinion in general, Nina Baym writes, "But novel reviewing . . . was directed toward readers, was conducted in constant awareness of what people were reading, and was always trying to understand the reasons for public preferences. The reviews offer guidance and correction in a way that enables us to see what they thought they were guiding and correcting"; Nina Baym, *Novels, Readers, and Reviewers: Responses to Fiction in Antebellum America* (Ithaca: Cornell University Press, 1984), 19. Charvat expresses his caveat in *The Profession of Authorship in America, 1800–1870: The Papers of William Charvat*, ed. Matthew J. Bruccoli (Columbus: Ohio State University Press, 1968), 291–92.

25. See note 18.

26. Harald Åström, *H. C. Andersens genombrott i Sverige: Översättningarne och kritikken, 1828–1852* (Odense: Andelsbogtrykkeri, 1972). Bredsdorff and Åström make general observations from synchronic and diachronic points of view, respectively, but their basic approaches are as described above. Surprisingly, a comprehensive study of Andersen's critical reception in his native Denmark does not exist. Erling Nielsen deals with that of the fairy tales and stories in "Eventyrenes modtagelseskritik," in *H. C. Andersens Eventyr*, ed. Erik Dal, Nielsen, and Flemming Hovmann, 6: 121–230 (Copenhagen: C. A. Reitzels Forlag, 1963–1990).

27. Ivy York Möller-Christensen, *Den gyldne trekant: H. C. Andersens gennembrud i Tyskland, 1831–1850* (Odense: Odense Universitetsforlag, 1992).

28. Möller-Christensen makes a nod toward the early reception theory of Hans Robert Jauß, but her study is essentially historical and analytic in nature.

29. *The Complete Andersen: All of the 168 Stories by Hans Christian Andersen*, trans. and ed. Jean Hersholt (New York: Heritage Press, 1942). In his biography of Andersen, Bredsdorff writes, "Discounting adaptors and translators of single tales there have been about thirty English and American translators of collections of the *Fairy Tales and Stories* between 1846 and 1974, and in my opinion by far the best and most loyal are R. P. Keigwin, Paul Leyssac, Reginald Spink, L. W. Kingsland, and Jean Hersholt"; *Hans Christian Andersen: The Story of His Life and Work, 1805–1875* (London: Phaidon Press, 1975), 336.

30. See the "Værkregister til bind I–VII, in *H. C. Andersens Eventyr*, 7:395–404.

CHAPTER 1. AMERICAN ANDERSEN CRITICISM

1. This total does not include the seminal study published by Horace Scudder in the *National Quarterly Review*. Although it presents itself as a review, it is in fact a broad examination of Andersen as a writer of fairy tales and is therefore counted as a general article. Some of the collections listed here include works other than fairy tales and stories. Where the emphasis is clearly on the fairy tales and stories, however, inclusion would appear to be justified. I should add that I was unable to gain access

to some of the volumes reviewed. In some instances I therefore had to content myself with the information in the reviews themselves and/or in Bredsdorff's bibliography, *Danish Literature in English Translation*.

2. Bredsdorff does not list any British collections entitled *Little Ellie, and other Tales* or *The Story Teller* in his *Danish Literature in English Translation*. His first entry of the former refers to an American edition published in 1856 (124), which is probably a later printing of the volume reviewed in 1850. His only entry of the latter also pertains to an American edition, first published in 1850 and reissued in 1856 (123; Bredsdorff indicates the place of publication but not the publisher, who, as the reviews of the books indicate, was C. S. Francis of New York [see chapter 4, 84–87]). It appears that these books were the first original American collections, if not translations, of Andersen's fairy tales and stories. Neither Bredsdorff nor the reviews name the translator(s).

3. This number embraces both reviews devoted specifically to the novel and significant commentary in discussions of other works or groups of works.

4. This figure does not reflect a substantial number of articles that appeared primarily in the *New York Times* and do not contain significant commentary on Andersen's life, personality, or work.

5. The small number of reviews per volume is problematic not least of all because it means that reviewers were often discussing different individual texts. For this reason one must seek to determine the overall contours of the reviewers' response to the works in general and any development within that response.

6. For the reference to *Mother Elderberry* see *International Magazine*, July 1851, 553.

7. Englishwoman Anne S. Bushby included renderings of forty of his poems in a volume of her own work, *Poems by the Late Anne S. Bushby* (London: Bentley, 1876). See Bredsdorff, *Danish Literature in English Translation*, 176–77. More recently, R. P. Keigwin has published *Syv Digte/Seven Poems* (Odense: H. C. Andersen House, 1955).

8. Bredsdorff lists these poems; *Danish Literature* in *English Translation*, 175–77. The *Living Age*, for example, published Andersen's "Consolation" [Fortrøstning] in the issue for March 26, 1864 (578), and included his "The Poet's Last Song" [Psalme] in the number for November 6, 1875 (322), clearly in recognition of the author's recent death (My thanks go to Johan de Mylius for tracing the original of the second translation; e-mail to the author, July 1, 2003). As an eclectic magazine, that is, one that gleaned its contents from foreign publications, the *Living Age* reprinted these translations from English sources.

9. Hersholt's edition does not contain this piece. The translation is my own.

10. The total number of Andersen's fairy tales and stories varies from one edition and study to the next depending on factors such as whether those that were originally part of longer works are included in the count. The historical-critical edition published by the Danish Society for Language and Literature contains 176 titles, while Hersholt's volume comprises 168. Bredsdorff uses the number 156, restricting himself to the pieces published in Denmark during Andersen's lifetime; *Hans Christian Andersen*, 308.

11. Dal, "Hans Christian Andersen's Tales and America," 11–13.

12. *The Andersen-Scudder Letters*, 142.

13. Bredsdorff, *Danish Literature in English Translation*, 121–29.

14. The *Kunstmärchen*, which reached its high point in German romanticism, reveals a self-conscious usage of the narrative techniques and motifs of the folktale,

including elements of the supernatural, to reflect on important concerns of the time.

15. Scudder used similar criteria to determine how to divide works between the two volumes of "fairy tales" in the Author's Edition, *Wonder Stories told for Children* and *Stories and Tales* (my emphasis). See, for example, "Advertisement," in *Wonder Stories told for Children,* by Hans Christian Andersen, ed. by Scudder, Author's Edition (Boston and New York: Hurd and Houghton, 1870), v.

16. Of course, what constitutes a literary classic is a matter of consensus rather than of rigor. Nevertheless, it is significant that all seven of these works were included in one or more of three lists of best or favorite tales compiled by knowledgeable readers. See Bredsdorff, *Hans Christian Andersen,* 308; Patricia L. Conroy and Sven H. Rossel, trans. and eds., *Tales and Stories by Hans Christian Andersen* (Seattle: University of Washington Press, 1980), vii–viii; and Erik Dal, "Our Own Twenty Plus Fifteen Favourite Tales," in *Hans Christian Andersen: A Poet in Time; Papers from the Second International Hans Christian Andersen Conference, 29 July to 2 August 1996,* ed. Johan de Mylius, Aage Jørgensen, and Viggo Hjørnager Pedersen, 48 (Odense: Odense University Press, 1999).

17. See Friedrich Schiller, *On the Naive and Sentimental in Literature,* trans. Helen Watanabe O'Kelly (Manchester: Carcanet New Press, 1981). For information about Heiberg, Andersen's sometime supporter and critic, see, for example, P. M. Mitchell, *A History of Danish Literature,* 2nd ed. (New York: Kraus-Thomsen, 1971), 135–40.

18. I have been unable to locate this magazine. I have therefore listed it here and included the article it contains in the total count of writings but not in the figures related to the works discussed.

CHAPTER 2. THE LONGER PROSE

1. Elias Bredsdorff, *H.C. Andersen og England,* 428.

2. See *Living Age,* April 19, 1847, 106, and *Southern Literary Messenger,* May 1847, 328.

3. See, for example, James Harrison Wilson, *The Life of Charles A. Dana* (New York: Harper & Brothers, 1907).

4. Ibid., especially 30–60. Also see Frank Luther Mott, *A History of American Magazines, 1741–1850,* 763–65. Mott offers no information about circulation, but it must have been quite limited. An issue of volume 1 reports that the number of subscribers had already reached one thousand by that point, but Lindsay Swift surmises that it never attained two thousand; *Brook Farm: Its Members, Scholars, and Visitors* (New York: Macmillan, 1900), 267. Mott provides a rough estimate of the average circulation of American periodicals in 1860: quarterlies 3,370; monthlies 12,000; and weeklies, including newspapers, 2,400; *A History of American Magazines, 1850–1865,* 10. During the 1840s the numbers must have been markedly lower.

5. See, for example, Barbara L. Packer, "The Transcendentalists," in *The Cambridge History of American Literature,* ed. Sacvan Bercovitch and Cyrus R. K. Patell, 2:329–604, esp. 463–68 (New York: Cambridge University Press, 1995), and Stanley M. Vogel, *German Literary Influences on the American Transcendentalists* (New Haven: Yale University Press, 1955).

6. See, for example, Carl J. Guarneri, *The Utopian Alternative: Fourierism in Nineteenth-Century America* (Ithaca: Cornell University Press, 1991), especially 51–59.

7. Charles A. Dana, review of *The Improvisatore, Harbinger,* October 4, 1845, 263.

8. At the time the review was written "Teuton" did not have the largely pejorative connotations from which it suffers today. While the word has somewhat negative overtones as used here, it is clear from the context that Dana, a decided Germanophile at the time who taught German in the Brook Farm school and translated part of Goethe's autobiography, employed the expression with respect. Indeed, the influence of German idealism in the United States was currently at its height. See Henry A. Pochmann, *German Culture in America: Philosophical and Literary Influences, 1600–1900* (Madison: University of Wisconsin Press, 1961), 768n338 and 59–151.

9. Review of *The Improvisatore, Ladies' Repository,* November 1869, 397. The review may have been written by Emily F. Wheeler, who penned another review of Andersen's works and possibly a third for the *Ladies' Repository.* See chapter 3, 73, below.

10. Mott, *A History of American Magazines, 1850–1865,* 301–5. While conservative, midcentury Cincinnati was the magazine center of the West, indeed, the fourth largest such center in the country; Mott, *A History of American Magazines, 1741–1850* and *1850–1865,* 386 and 114, respectively.

11. Mott, *A History of American Magazines, 1850–1865,* 301. Elsewhere, to be sure, Mott speaks more highly of the magazine, for example, as the forum in which Sara Josepha Hale continued the work in women's education that she had begun in *The Ladies' Magazine; A History of American Magazines, 1741–1850,* 349–50.

12. Mott, *A History of American Magazines, 1850–1865,* 303–4.

13. Quoted according to Helge Topsöe-Jensen, "The Background of the Letters," in *The Andersen-Scudder Letters,* xix.

14. It is especially curious that William Dean Howells did not review the Author's Edition of the novel later in the *Atlantic Monthly.* As former American consul in Venice and the author of *Venetian Life* (1866) and *Italian Journeys* (1867), he was singularly qualified to do so. As we shall see, moreover, he in fact reviewed three of Andersen's other works in the *Atlantic.* See [Horace E. Scudder], *The Atlantic Index, 1857–1888* (Boston: Houghton Mifflin, 1889), 105.

15. "Sketches of Life in Sweden," *International Magazine,* July 1851, 450. For a sketch of this magazine, see 43 below.

16. "Literature" [*The Improvisatore*], *Putnam's Magazine,* November 1869, 626. A sketch of this magazine is found on 39 below.

17. Quoted according to Gordon Milne, *George William Curtis and the Genteel Tradition* (Bloomington: Indiana University Press, 1956), 6.

18. Ibid., 75 and passim.

19. Mott, *A History of American Magazines, 1850–1865,* 383–405.

20. Ibid., 11; Eugene Exman, *The House of Harper: One Hundred and Fifty Years of Publishing* (New York: Harper and Row, 1967), 79. *Harper's* was thus one of very few American magazines that were national, not to mention international, in reach. Most, including the *Atlantic Monthly,* remained regional for decades to come; see Mott, *A History of American Magazines, 1850–1865,* 102 and 495–98.

21. J. Henry Harper opined that the short essays Curtis wrote for the Easy Chair for over forty years were "generally considered the most delightful monthly feature in an American periodical"; quoted according to Milne, *George William Curtis and the Genteel Tradition,* 75.

22. George William Curtis, "The Editor's Easy Chair," *Harper's New Monthly Magazine*, October 1875, 748.

23. Ibid.

24. The story is "The Great Carbuncle," which appeared in *Twice-Told Tales* in 1837.

25. *Harper's New Monthly Magazine*, 748.

26. "Reminiscences," *Appleton's Journal*, October 1876, 355–59.

27. See Mott, *A History of American Magazines, 1865–1885*, 417–21. As the following pages show, Stoddard became one of Andersen's more significant American commentators.

28. No information on the periodical's circulation was available.

29. Mott, *A History of American Magazines, 1865–1885*, 417.

30. See *The National Cyclopaedia of American Biography*, s.v. "Freeman, James Edward." One might have discussed Freeman's reminiscences among the general articles in chapter 5. Since they are most pertinent to *The Improvisatore*, however, I have included them here.

31. Freeman, "Reminiscences," *Appleton's Journal*, 359.

32. Ibid.

33. Ibid.

34. Review of *O. T.*, *Atlantic Monthly*, September 1870, 383–84.

35. See Mott, *A History of American Magazines, 1850–1865*, 493–515.

36. Van Wyck Brooks uses this expression in *The Times of Melville and Whitman* (New York: E. P. Dutton, 1947), 233.

37. See Mott, *A History of American Magazines, 1850–1865*, 507. Also see Sedgwick, *The Atlantic Monthly, 1857–1909: Yankee Humanism at High Tide and Ebb* (Amherst: University of Massachusetts Press, 1994), 87–88.

38. *The Atlantic Index*, 105.

39. Howells, review of *O. T.*, 383.

40. Ibid.

41. Ibid.

42. Ibid. See note 14.

43. Ibid.

44. Ibid.

45. Ibid., 383–84.

46. Ibid., 384.

47. Review of *Only a Fiddler*, *Galaxy*, November 1870, 713. See Mott, *A History of American Magazines, 1865–1885*, 361.

48. Review of *Only a Fiddler*, *Putnam's Magazine*, October 1870, 461.

49. Mott, *A History of American Magazines, 1850–1865*, 423–24, 426, and 32. In his biography of James Russell Lowell, Horace Scudder devotes considerable space to *Putnam's*, which, he writes, was seen by many as the fulfillment of the ideal of an American literary magazine; *James Russell Lowell: A Biography*, 2 vols. (Boston: Houghton Mifflin, 1901), 1:349.

50. Mott, *A History of American Magazines, 1850–1865*, 426, 429–30. The magazine was revived under different editorship in 1906 but then ran only to 1910.

51. See Harriet F. Bergmann, "Richard Henry Stoddard," in *Antebellum Writers in New York and the South*, ed. Joel Myerson, 321–23, vol. 3 of *Dictionary of Literary Biography* (Detroit: Gale Group, 1979), and Robert D. Harvey, "Richard Henry Stod-

dard," in *American Literary Critics and Scholars, 1850–1880,* ed. John W. Rathbun and Monica M. Grecu, 230–35, vol. 64 of *Dictionary of Literary Biography* (Detroit: Gale Group, 1988). Also see the discussion of Stoddard in chapter 5.

52. Mary Elizabeth Braddon, Charles Reade, and Wilkie Collins were all popular British novelists of the day.

53. The *Newgate Calendar* began publication around 1774; a later series dates from about 1826. It dealt with crimes and criminals associated with Newgate, a prison in London.

54. Benjamin T. Spencer, for example, treats the eddies of resistance and pessimism within the attempt to develop a specifically American literature in *The Quest for Nationality: An American Literary Campaign* (Syracuse, N.Y.: Syracuse University Press, 1957), especially 297–308.

55. See, for example, Vernon Louis Parrington, *The Romantic Revolution in America, 1800–1860,* vol. 2 of *Main Currents in American Thought: An Interpretation of American Literature from the Beginnings to 1920,* by Parrington (New York: Harcourt-Brace, 1927), especially 379–85; Vogel, *German Literary Influences on the American Transcendentalists;* Pochmann, *German Culture in America;* and Sigrid Bauschinger, *The Trumpet of Reform: German Literature in Nineteenth-Century New England,* trans. Thomas Hansen (Rochester, N.Y.: Camden House, 1999).

56. William Dean Howells, review of *Only a Fiddler, Atlantic Monthly,* November 1870, 632–34. See *The Atlantic Index,* 105.

57. Ibid., 632.

58. Ibid.

59. Ibid., 634.

60. Ibid.

61. Ibid.

62. Ibid., 632.

63. Ibid.

64. Ibid., 634.

65. Ibid. See Sedgwick, *Atlantic Monthly, 1857–1909,* 72.

66. Howells, review of *Only a Fiddler,* 632. "Pre-Raphaelite" refers to a movement in English art and, to a lesser extent, literature that emerged from the establishment of the Pre-Raphaelite Brotherhood in 1848 by Dante Gabriel Rossetti and John Everett Millais, among others, and that enjoyed the support of art critic John Ruskin. While varying widely in style and purpose, the Pre-Raphaelites generally reacted against what they perceived to be the artificial conventions of contemporary painting and sought to restore the faithfulness to nature that they saw in Italian religious art prior to Raphael. See Timothy Hilton, *The Pre-Raphaelites* (London: Thames and Hudson, 1970).

67. Howells, review of *Only a Fiddler,* 633.

68. Howells, review of *O. T.,* 383.

69. Henry Mills Alden [?], "Editor's Literary Record," *Harper's New Monthly Magazine,* December 1869, 144.

70. *Ladies' Repository,* January 1870, 78.

71. Review of *To Be or Not to Be, Putnam's Magazine,* September 1857, 411–12.

72. Bredsdorff, *Danish Literature in English Translation,* 175.

73. Review of *A Picture-Book Without Pictures, Daguerreotype,* September 4, 1847, 141–42. No information on the magazine's circulation was available.

74. See *American Periodicals, 1741–1900,* 73.

75. Review of *A Picture-Book Without Pictures,* 141.

76. Ibid. For more on this work see chapter 4, 88.

77. "Sketches of Life in Sweden," *International Magazine,* July 1851, 450–52; "Swedish Landscapes," August 1851, 20–22.

78. Mott, *A History of American Magazines, 1850–1865,* 406–8. Mott provides no information on the magazine's circulation, but its fate suggests that the number must have been small.

79. Ibid., 407, 31, and 158.

80. See Joy Bayless, *Rufus Wilmot Griswold: Poe's Literary Executor* (Nashville, Tenn.: Vanderbilt University Press, 1943), 206, and Elizabeth Robins Pennell, *George Godfrey Leland: A Biography,* 2 vols. (Boston: Houghton Mifflin, 1906). Also see 46.

81. Leland, "Sketches of Life in Sweden," 450.

82. Ibid.

83. Leland, "Swedish Landscapes," 20.

84. Van Wyck Brooks describes the Yankee, or New England, character as follows: "A clear distinct mentality, a strong distaste for nonsense, steady composure . . . intelligence, a habit of under-statement, a slow and cautious way of reasoning, contempt for extravagance, vanity and affectation . . ."; *The Flowering of New England* (New York: E. P. Dutton, 1937), 34. This is not to minimize, only to relativize, the prominence of sentimentality in American fiction of the nineteenth century. Despite Hawthorne's laments about (the success of) women's domestic sentimental fiction, Bell cautions that even major writers had their "humanities"; Michael Davitt Bell, "Conditions of Literary Vocation: Women's Fiction and the Literary Marketplace in the 1850s," in *The Cambridge History of American Literature,* 121–23. Even though sentimental fiction survived the Civil War, it may well be the case that Andersen's novels would have fared better among critics had they been reviewed more extensively earlier.

85. Ibid., 22.

86. Ibid.

87. "Pictures from the North," *Continental Monthly,* April 1863, 398–403.

88. Mott, *A History of American Magazines, 1850–1865,* 540–43.

89. It is unclear why Leland should have written reviews of the work at different times. It may be that the work gained renewed relevance for him in view of the current conflict, especially given his experience in Paris in 1848. One cannot state with absolute certainty that he was in fact the author of the review, but the *Continental* would appear to be one of the many magazines—with a low overhead—in which chief editor and reviewer were one and the same individual; see Baym, *Novels, Readers, and Reviewers,* 20. Leland claimed that earnings from the magazine barely covered the cost of publication, which suggests the nature of its circulation; Mott, *A History of American Magazines, 1850–1865,* 542.

90. Leland , "Pictures from the North," 398.

91. Ibid.

92. Ibid.

93. Ibid., 399–400.

94. Ibid., 403.

95. Ibid.

96. Ibid.

220 NOTES

97. Ibid.
98. Review of *In Spain and a Visit to Portugal, Punchinello,* May 14, 1870, 110.
99. Mott, *A History of American Magazines, 1865–1885,* 440–42. No information on the—probably quite limited—circulation of the magazine was available.
100. Ibid., 440.
101. Henry Mills Alden [?], "Editor's Literary Record," *Harper's New Monthly Magazine,* August 1870, 462.
102. According to Van Wyck Brooks, for example, the first editors and writers of the *North American Review* "were greatly obliged to Scott, the first of living writers, in their opinion"; *The Flowering of New England,* 113. Also see Kenneth S. Lynn, *William Dean Howells: An American Life* (New York: Harcourt Brace Jovanovich, 1970), 180–83.
103. Brooks writes amusingly of historian, orator, and statesman George Bancroft's return from study in Göttingen in 1822 as a dandy: "He had half forgotten the English language. French, German, soft Italian phrases blossomed on his lips, a flaunting of the dulcet strain that was much too much for Brattle Street"; *The Flowering of New England,* 129.
104. William Dean Howells, review of *In Spain and a Visit to Portugal, Atlantic Monthly,* September 1870, 377–79. See *The Atlantic Index,* 105.
105. Ibid., 377.
106. Ibid., 379.
107. Ibid.
108. Ibid.
109. Ibid., 378.
110. See, for example, Dal, "Hans Christian Andersen's Tales and America," 13–24, and Pedersen, "Hans Andersen as an English Writer," 95–108. Also see W. Glyn Jones, "H. C. Andersen in English—A Feasibility Study I" and "Andersen in English—A Feasibility Study II," in *Andersen og Verden,* 85–99 and 210–16, respectively.
111. Howells, review of *In Spain and a Visit to Portugal,* 377.
112. H. C. Andersen, *Samlede Skrifter,* 2nd ed. (Copenhagen: C. A. Reitzels Forlag, 1878), 8:328.
113. Howells, review of *In Spain and a Visit to Portugal,* 378.
114. In German romanticism the self-conscious and widespread mixing of verse and prose was legitimated as a means of overcoming the alleged compartmentalization of life during the eighteenth century and regaining the putative dynamic wholeness of primitive existence captured in Friedrich Schlegel's notion of romantic poetry as a "progressive universal poetry" [eine progressive Universalpoesie]. See August Wilhelm and Friedrich Schlegel, *Athenaeum: Eine Zeitschrift* (1798; repr., Berlin: Rütten and Loening, 1960), 1:204. Of course, the practice was not unknown in American writing, from Longfellow's *Hyperion* to Horace Scudder's Bodley books for children (see chapter 6).
115. Howells, review of *In Spain and a Visit to Portugal,* 379.
116. Review of *A Poet's Bazaar, Atlantic Monthly,* October 1871, 512.
117. Sedgwick, *The Atlantic Monthly, 1857–1909,* 152–53.
118. See Virginia Harlow, *Thomas Sergeant Perry: A Biography, and Letters to Perry from William, Henry, and Garth Wilkinson James* (Durham, N.C.: Duke University Press, 1950).
119. *The Atlantic Index,* 29. For more information on Boyesen, who also wrote four general articles on Andersen and was one of his major American critics, see chapter 5, 131.

120. See, for example, Perry D. Westbrook, *Acres of Flint: Sarah Orne Jewett and Her Contemporaries*, revised ed. (Metuchen, N.J.: Scarecrow Press, 1981), 1–10.

121. Review of *A Poet's Bazaar, Overland Monthly*, January 1872, 102–3.

122. Mott, *A History of American Magazines, 1865–1885*, 403.

123. Ibid., 406–9. The magazine resumed publication five years later under different management and then ran until 1935.

124. Review of *A Poet's Bazaar, Overland Monthly*, 102.

125. Ibid.

126. Ibid.

127. This, of course, is not to imply that similar "anachronisms" have not occurred in other literatures. In Danish letters, to mention only one notable example, Steen Steensen Blicher may have had a romantic sensibility, but his short stories of the 1820s, for which he is best known, are written in a style that Howells would have appreciated.

128. Andrew Hilen, *Longfellow and Scandinavia: A Study of the Poet's Relationship with the Northern Languages and Literatures* (New Haven: Yale University Press, 1947), especially 106–12; here, 106–7.

CHAPTER 3. THE AUTOBIOGRAPHY

1. The German titles of the two autobiographies are *Das Märchen meines Lebens ohne Dichtung* and *Dichtung und Wahrheit*, respectively. See W. Glyn Jones, "H. C. Andersen in English—A Feasibility Study I," 86.

2. Bredsdorff, *Hans Christian Andersen*, 367.

3. Ibid., 176.

4. Andersen to Scudder, 21 April 1868, *The Andersen-Scudder Letters*, 10–12.

5. Bredsdorff, *H. C. Andersen og England*, 451.

6. Mott, *A History of American Magazines, 1741–1850*, 766. This, however, did not result in a large circulation or financial success; ibid., 768.

7. Ibid., 766–67.

8. Ibid.

9. See, for example, Kendall B. Taft, preface and "Minor Knickerbockers" [Introduction], in *Minor Knickerbockers* (New York: American Book Company, 1947), v–vi and xiii–xxvii, respectively.

10. See Homer F. Barnes, *Charles Fenno Hoffman* (New York: Columbia University Press, 1930), especially 87–112.

11. See Taft, *Minor Knickerbockers*, lxxxiv. *Literary World*, February 19, 1848, 41. Quoted according to Barnes, *Charles Fenno Hoffman*, 90–91.

12. Hoffman [?], review of *The True Story of My Life*, 53.

13. Ibid.

14. Ibid.

15. Ibid.

16. Ibid.

17. Ibid.

18. Ibid.

19. Ibid., 55.

20. Review of *The True Story of My Life, Godey's Magazine and Lady's Book*, October 1847, 215.

21. Mott, *A History of American Magazines, 1741–1850*, 581.

22. See, for example, Ruth E. Finley, *The Lady of Godey's: Sara Josepha Hale* (Philadelphia: Lippincott, 1931), and Sherbrooke Rogers, *Sarah Josepha Hale: A New England Pioneer, 1788–1879* (Grantham, N.H.: Thompson and Rutter, 1985).

23. Mott, *A History of American Magazines, 1741–1850*, 82, 588.

24. Isabelle Webb Entrikin writes, for example, that Hale "appeared *as usual* at *her* 'Editors' Table'" (my emphasis); *Sarah Josepha Hale and Godey's Lady's Book* (Philadelphia: n.p., 1946), 81. Entrikin also relates that Hale corresponded with Mary Howitt in 1847, which may have led to the review of Andersen's autobiography (89).

25. Review of *The True Story of My Life, Christian Examiner and Religious Miscellany*, November 1847, 461.

26. See Mott, *A History of American Magazines, 1741–1850*, 284–92. Mott includes no information concerning the circulation of the magazine.

27. Ibid., 292.

28. See, for example, *Appleton's Cyclopaedia of American Biography*, s.v. "Lamson, Alvan," and *American National Biography*, s.v. "Gannett, Ezra Stiles."

29. Based on their surnames, three individuals appearing on an (incomplete) list of the *Examiner*'s authors come into question as the writer of the review: historian and statesman George Bancroft, poet William Cullen Bryant, and Unitarian minister Samuel Barrett. See Kenneth Walter Cameron, *Research Keys to the American Renaissance: Scarce Indexes of* The Christian Examiner, The North American Review, *and* The New Jerusalem Magazine (Hartford, Conn.: Transcendental Books, 1967).

30. Hoffman also alludes to Andersen's religious faith: "This is the spirit which carried Andersen through every vicissitude of life. In grief or in joy he has that never-failing resource of a pure heart, prayer"; review of *The True Story of My Life, Literary World*, 19 February 1848, 54.

31. Review of *The True Story of My Life, Massachusetts Quarterly Review*, December 1847, 127.

32. See Mott, *A History of American Magazines, 1741–1850*, 775–79, and Henry Steele Commager, *Theodore Parker* (Boston: Little, Brown, 1936), 130–34.

33. Commager, *Theodore Parker*, 134.

34. Mott, *A History of American Magazines, 1741–1850*, 777.

35. Commager writes, "His [Parker's] criticism was subjective, as became an intuitionalist; he interpreted himself rather than his material." *Theodore Parker*, 135.

36. Commager discusses the clash between Parker's spiritualist (Schleiermacherian) views and conservative Unitarian institutionalism; ibid., 80–100.

37. Review of *The True Story of My Life, United States Magazine and Democratic Review*, December 1847, 525–37. No circulation information was available.

38. Mott, *A History of American Magazines, 1741–1850*, 683.

39. Ibid., 679–80.

40. See Jonathan Arac, "Narrative Forms: Establishing National Narrative," in *The Cambridge History of American Literature*, 2:623–24. Also see *The National Cyclopaedia of American Biography*, s.v. "O'Sullivan, John Louis."

41. Review of *The True Story of My Life, United States Magazine and Democratic Review*, 525.

42. Ibid.

43. Ibid; my emphasis.

44. Well over half of the passages quoted deal with the span of time in question, while only about a fourth of the autobiography itself does so (as published in volume 1 of the *Samlede Skrifter*).

45. Review of *The True Story of My Life, United States Magazine and Democratic Review*, 525.

46. Ibid., 536–37.

47. Ibid., 537. The expression "moon calf" referred in antiquity to an abortion supposedly caused by the influence of the moon. In more recent times it has denoted a deformed baby or a congenital idiot. Carlyle used the expression in his pamphlet *Occasional Discourse on the Nigger Question* (1853) to characterize current justifications for the emancipation of slaves in the West Indies. In the present context the metaphor thus represents a strong condemnation of those who speak ill of American literature.

48. General Winfield Scott had entered Mexico City in September, though the war did not end formally until February 1848. In 1846, Representative David Wilmot, a Democrat from Pennsylvania, had proposed an amendment to an appropriation bill drafted to settle the uncertain border with Mexico, which stated that slavery would not exist in any territory acquired from that country. The so-called Wilmot Proviso failed but was brought up again in 1847 and later.

49. Review of *The Story of My Life, Galaxy*, May 1871, 745.

50. Mott, *A History of American Magazines, 1865–1885*, 360–62.

51. Ibid., 375.

52. Ibid.

53. "Literature," *Putnam's Magazine*, November 1869, 625–26. See 39 of the present study. For more on Stedman, see 111–13, 116, and especially 96–97 of this study.

54. See Mott, *A History of American Magazines, 1865–1885*, 363 and 375, and *The National Cyclopaedia of American Biography*, s.v. "Meline, James Florant."

55. See Elmer Davis, *History of the* New York Times, *1851–1921* (New York: New York Times, 1921), 3–47, especially 19–20, and 118.

56. Both book-length histories of the *Times* give very short shrift to its treatment of the arts: Davis, *History of the* New York Times, and Meyer Berger, *The Story of the* New York Times, *1851–1951* (New York: Simon and Schuster, 1951).

57. Davis, *History of the* New York Times, *1851–1921*, 38. Review of *The Story of My Life, New York Times*, May 17, 1871, 2.

58. Hans Christian Andersen, *The Story of My Life*, Author's Edition (Boston and New York: Hurd and Houghton, 1871).

59. Ibid., iii.

60. Review of *The Story of My Life, Scribner's Monthly*, June 1871, 222–23.

61. Mott, *A History of American Magazines, 1865–1885*, 467.

62. Ibid., 480.

63. Ibid., 459.

64. Ibid., 457–58. See Dal, "Hans Christian Andersen's Tales and America," 10.

65. Dal, "Hans Christian Andersen's Tales and America," 10.

66. Review of *The Story of My Life, Scribner's Monthly*, 222.

67. Ibid.

68. Ibid.

69. Ibid.

70. Ibid., 222–23.

71. Review of *The Story of My Life, Harper's New Monthly Magazine,* July 1871, 299.

72. Review of *The Story of My Life, Atlantic Monthly,* September 1871, 379–80.

73. *The Atlantic Index,* 106.

74. Howells, review of *The Story of My Life,* 380.

75. Dal, "Hans Christian Andersen and America," 3.

76. Westergaard describes Scudder's procedure as follows: "Scudder used Mary Howitt's translation where the text ran parallel with *Mit Livs Eventyr* [The Fairy Tale of My Life], but throughout he made the insertions and additions that Andersen had used in 1855 in revising his autobiography"; Waldemar Westergaard, "Notes," *The Andersen-Scudder Letters,* 165n12. For Scudder's writings, see chapter 6 below and Peter A. Brier, "Horace Elisha Scudder," in *American Literary Critics and Scholars, 1880–1900,* ed. John W. Rathbun and Monica M. Grecu, 243–49, esp. 243–45, vol. 71 of *Dictionary of Literary Biography* (Detroit: Gale Group, 1988).

77. Howells, review of *The Story of My Life, Atlantic Monthly,* 380.

78. Ibid.

79. Ibid.

80. Ibid.

81. Ibid.

82. Ibid.

83. Ibid.

84. Ibid.

85. Emily F. Wheeler, review of *The Story of My Life, Ladies' Repository,* January 1873, 55–59. I have been unable to find any substantive information about Wheeler, but happenstance led to my discovery that she was at one time associated with Northwestern University and became Chair of French and Belles Lettres at Cincinnati Wesleyan College in 1879; "Notes," *Nation,* July 31, 1879, 78.

86. Ibid., 55.

87. Ibid.

88. Ibid., 58.

89. Ibid., 57.

90. Ibid., 59.

91. See Harry W. Baehr, Jr., *The* New York Tribune *Since the Civil War* (New York: Dodd, Mead, 1936), 2. This figure apparently includes both the daily and weekly American editions of the paper as well as the sizeable British edition.

92. Ibid., 3–174.

93. Ibid., 10.

94. Ibid., 83; Royal Cortissoz, *The Life of Whitelaw Reid,* 2 vols. (New York: Charles Scribner's Sons, 1921), 1:20–29, and Bingham Duncan, *Whitelaw Reid: Journalist, Politician, Diplomat* (Athens: University of Georgia Press, 1975), 1–10.

95. Baehr, *The* New York Tribune *Since the Civil War,* 130.

96. Ibid., 137.

97. Whitelaw Reid, "Obituary: Hans Christian Andersen," *New York Tribune,* 5 August 1875, 5.

98. Andersen's letter is dated April 17, 1875. For a discussion of his—initially negative—reaction to these and other gifts from American children see Bredsdorff, *Hans Christian Andersen,* 269–71.

99. *New York Times,* 5 August 1875, 4, cols. 2 and 6–7.

100. No title, *New York Times,* 5 August 1875, 4, col. 2.

101. "Obituary: Hans Christian Andersen," *New York Times,* 5 August 1875, 4, cols. 6–7.

102. "Hans Christian Andersen," *Potter's American Monthly,* November 1875, 835–36.

103. Mott, *A History of American Magazines, 1865–1885,* 260–61.

104. Ibid., 261. Also see *Dictionary of American Biography,* s.v. "Lossing, Benson John."

105. Ibid.

106. *Potter's American Monthly,* 836.

107. Ibid., 835–36. The wording, of course, suggests familiarity with the article in the *Times.*

108. Ibid., 836.

109. Ibid.

110. See W. Glyn Jones, "H. C. Andersen in English—A Feasibility Study I," especially 85–88, and Ivy York Möller-Christensen, *Den gyldne trekant,* 268–79.

111. See Horatio Alger, Jr., *Bound to Rise; or, Up the Ladder* (Boston: Loring, 1873), and *Struggling Upward; or, Luke Larkin's Luck* (Philadelphia: Porter and Coates, 1890). Today, most critics agree both that Alger's books are bad and that they do *not* embody the rags-to-riches myth. See "Horatio Alger, Jr.," in *Nineteenth-Century Literature Criticism,* ed. Laurie Lanzen Harris and Emily B. Tennyson, 8: 13–49, especially 13–14. (Detroit: Gale Research, 1985). Nonetheless, Alger's stories remain synonymous with the myth.

112. What Van Wyck Brooks writes about the United States applies to Andersen as well: "If, on the individual plane, the Cinderella story became and remained the favourite American myth, if the typical American life-pattern was 'up' from something,—from slavery, from the streets, from the slums, from ignorance and darkness, how could the Americans *not* have believed, as a nation, as a race, in perfectibility, in equality, the pursuit of happiness, improvement, progress?" *The Confident Years, 1885–1915* (New York: E. P. Dutton, 1952), 586.

Chapter 4. The Fairy Tales and Stories

1. George William Curtis, "The Editor's Easy Chair," *Harper's New Monthly Magazine,* October 1875, 749.

2. See, for example, the discussion of "The New Literature" in the *Southern Literary Messenger* beginning on 89 below.

3. Henry Mills Alden, review of *Seven Little People and their Friends,* by Horace E. Scudder, *Atlantic Monthly,* January 1863, 143–44 (Alden is identified as the reviewer in *The Atlantic Index,* 11); Charles Eliot Norton, review of *Dream Children,* by Scudder, *North American Review,* January 1864, 304 (Cameron identifies Norton as the reviewer in *Research Keys to the American Renaissance,* 132).

4. See Bredsdorff, *H. C. Andersen og England,* 439.

5. See Bredsdorff, *Danish Literature in English Translation,* 121.

6. *A Christmas Greeting to My English Friends* (London, 1847).

7. Charles S. Francis can be considered Andersen's earliest American publisher, issuing every translation of the tales reviewed in American magazines up to 1860, eight in all. It may have been through his agency in London that he gained the opportunity to publish Beckwith-Lohmeyer's collection. See John Tebbel, *A History of Book Publishing in the United States* (New York and London: R. R. Bowker, 1972), 1:522–23.

8. Review of *A Christmas Greeting: Thirteen Stories from the Danish of Hans Christian Andersen*, trans. Charles Beckwith-Lohmeyer, *Union Magazine*, April 1848, 192.

9. Mott, *A History of American Magazines, 1741–1850,* 769.

10. Ibid.

11. Ibid., 772.

12. See William S. Osborne, *Caroline M. Kirkland* (New York: Twayne, 1972), 15–86.

13. *American National Biography*, s.v. "Kirkland, Caroline Matilda."

14. Beginning in the spring of 1848 Kirkland spent approximately six months in Europe recording impressions for contributions to the *Union*. It is therefore not certain, if nonetheless likely, that she wrote the review of Andersen's tales. During her absence her friend Bayard Taylor assumed editorial responsibility for the magazine. See Osborne, *Caroline M. Kirkland*, 108–12 and 88–94, and the discussion of Taylor in chapter 5.

15. See Osborne, *Caroline M. Kirkland*, 88–89.

16. See Jones, "*H. C. Andersen in English—A Feasibility Study I*," 93–94.

17. *Living Age*, May 1848, 383, and *Southern Literary Messenger,* July 1848, 454; my emphasis. *A Danish Story-Book* first appeared in London in 1846.

18. Review of *Hans Andersen's Story-Book*, *Sartain's Union Magazine*, February 1849, 156.

19. See Mott, *A History of American Magazines, 1741–1850,* 769n1, 771, and *The Oxford Companion to American Literature*, 6th ed., s.v. "Hart, John S[eely]."

20. See Osborne, *Caroline M. Kirkland*, 92.

21. Osborne speaks of Kirkland's lack of "critical acumen," which she herself readily acknowledged; ibid., 108.

22. Mary Howitt was very well known inter alia for numerous volumes of fiction and poetry as well as for her work as translator.

23. See, for example, Finn Barlby, ed., *Det dæmoniske spejl: Analyser af H. C. Andersens "Skyggen"* (Copenhagen: Forlaget Dråben, 1998), and Barlby, ed., *Det hvide spejl: Analyser af H. C. Andersens "Sneedronningen"* (Copenhagen: Forlaget Dråben, 2000).

24. Review of *The Ugly Duck and other Tales, Little Ellie, and other Tales*, and *The Story Teller, Literary World*, November 16, 1850, 389.

25. Mott, *A History of American Magazines, 1741–1850,* 766.

26. Ibid., 711.

27. See Osborne, *Caroline M. Kirkland*, 94.

28. Review of *Hans Andersen's Wonderful Tales*, *Sartain's Union Magazine*, February 1851, 140.

29. Only "The Little Match Girl" appears in both volumes. "The Traveling Companion" is the only tale of the lot that approaches "The Shadow" and "The Snow Queen" in occultness of tone, but it remains more transparent and positive in its thematic center than they.

30. Andersen is noted for his interest and faith in scientific and technological progress, which manifests itself in fairy tales and stories such as "The Great Sea Serpent" of 1871, which revealed his enthusiasm for the transatlantic cable; see *H. C. Andersens Eventyr,* 7:362–64. However, Erik Dal points out that Andersen at times felt "the danger or menace of the big impersonal machines, when facing them in the mine at Motala in Sweden in 1851 or in the printing office of *The Times* in London in 1857. He would call them 'Master Bloodless,' an expression . . . used quite a few times"; "Hans Christian Andersen's Tales and America," 8.

31. "A Handful of Autumn Leaves," *Southern Literary Messenger,* December 1852, 715. See Bredsdorff, *Danish Literature in English Translation,* 123.

32. See Mott, *A History of American Magazines, 1741–1850,* 629–57, here 631.

33. Ibid., 655.

34. See John O. Beaty, *John Esten Cooke, Virginian* (New York: Columbia University Press, 1922), especially 1–72.

35. Gerald M. Garmon, *John Reuben Thompson* (Boston: Twayne, 1979), 50.

36. *Picture Book Without Pictures* appeared as an independent work in two parts in 1839 and 1840. Andersen did not wish to have it included in collections of the fairy tales and stories, but the similarity of the individual "evenings" to these texts, among other reasons, led many contemporary editors to do so nonetheless, and the practice continues to this day. For this reason, and since the review discussed in chapter 2, 43, sheds little light on the work, the portion of the present review that deals with it is considered here.

37. See, for example, Henry A. Pochmann, *German Culture in America,* 332–33, and Stanley M. Vogel, *German Literary Influences on the American Transcendentalists,* 10.

38. For a detailed history of the ut pictura poesis doctrine through the eighteenth century see Niklaus Rudolf Schweizer, *The Ut pictura poesis Controversy in Eighteenth-Century England and Germany* (Bern: Herbert Lang, Peter Lang, 1972).

39. "The New Literature," *Southern Literary Messenger,* April 1854, 214–16, here 214.

40. Garmon writes that Cooke edited the *Messenger* during the entire year beginning in 1854 which John Reuben Thompson spent abroad recording impressions for the magazine; Garmon, *John Reuben Thompson,* 50.

41. "The New Literature," 215 and 214.

42. Ibid.

43. Ibid., 215. See Van Wyck Brooks, *The Flowering of New England,* 172.

44. "The New Literature," 214. Cooke's statement was precipitous in 1854, but, as will become clear in chapters 6 and 7, it anticipated what has been called a golden age of children's literature, which prevailed from 1870 to 1914.

45. Review of *The Sand-Hills of Jutland, Southern Literary Messenger,* August 1860, 159.

46. See Joseph Leonard King, Jr., *Dr. George William Bagby: A Study of Virginian Literature, 1850–1880* (New York: Columbia University Press, 1927), 114.

47. Ibid., 84.

48. Bagby, "A Witch in the Nursery," *Southern Literary Messenger,* July–August 1862, 488–500. The article is unsigned, and at one point the author speaks of a number of English writers as "our own," suggesting, of course, a British author. However, Benjamin Blake Minor, sometime publisher and editor of the *Messenger,* attests to the fact that Bagby was indeed not only a humorist, but could write "seriously, vigorously and

argumentatively"; *The Southern Literary Messenger, 1834–1864* (New York: Neale Publishing, 1905). Moreover, the *Messenger* was not an eclectic, that is, it published original material, and many Americans still retained proprietary sentiments toward everything written in English, especially prior to their own generation. For these reasons I have proceeded on the assumption that Bagby was indeed the author (the tenor of the review calls John Esten Cooke to mind, but Beaty's bibliography of his writings does not include this title; *John Esten Cooke, Virginian*, 167).

49. Ibid., 498.

50. Review of *The Sand-Hills of Jutland, New Englander*, November 1860, 1105.

51. See Mott, *A History of American Magazines, 1850–1865*, 312–15. In later years the magazine was called the *New Englander and Yale Review*.

52. Ibid., 312.

53. See Sven H. Rossel, "Introduction: Hans Christian Andersen's Life and Authorship," in *Tales and Stories by Hans Christian Andersen*, xxvi. Indeed, Rossel writes that "only a third of the 156 tales and stories represent him [Andersen] at his best, and most of these date from the 1840s"; xxv.

54. *The Ice-Maiden, and Other Tales*, trans. Fanny Fuller (Philadelphia: F. Leypoldt; New York: C. T. Evans, 1863).

55. See Sven H. Rossel, "Hans Christian Andersen Research in the United States," 518.

56. Review of *The Ice-Maiden, and Other Tales, Peterson's Magazine*, April 1863, 321. See Mott, *A History of American Magazines, 1850–1865*, 306–11.

57. Review of *The Ice-Maiden and Other Tales, Continental Monthly*, April 1863, 500. See p. 46.

58. Mott states that this issue was Leland's last; *A History of American Magazines, 1850–1865*, 542.

59. See, for example, Jack Zipes, *When Dreams Came True: Classical Fairy Tales and Their Tradition* (New York: Routledge, 1999), 69–75. Also see Bredsdorff, *Hans Christian Andersen*, 308–12.

60. Neither Leland's memoirs nor his biography intimate anything to this effect; see Charles Godfrey Leland, *Memoirs* (London: William Heinemann, 1894) and Elizabeth Robins Pennell, *Charles Godfrey Leland*, 2 vols. (Boston: Houghton Mifflin, 1906). Leland relates little about his editorship of the *Continental* other than its role in the debate over abolition; *Memoirs*, 249. Leland was, however, accomplished in the acquisition of foreign languages. Over the course of his education in Philadelphia and at Princeton he gained proficiency in Latin, Greek, Spanish, Italian, and French as well as German, reviewing books in the latter three languages. Having studied in Heidelberg and Munich in addition to Paris and become, in his words, an intimate friend of the internationally acclaimed Norwegian violinist Ole Bull, it is entirely possible that he gained at least a reading command of Danish. It may be that he began his study of Icelandic prior to writing the present review; see Brooks, *The Times of Melville and Whitman*, 46.

61. Anker Jensen, *Studier over H. C. Andersens Sprog* (Haderslev: Carl Nielsen, 1929), 11. W. Glyn Jones refers to Jensen's study in "H. C. Andersen in English—A Feasibility Study I," 95–96.

62. See the introduction, p. 13.

63. See pp. 80–81 above.

64. Henry Mills Alden, review of *Seven Little People and their Friends*, by Horace E. Scudder, *Atlantic Monthly*, January 1863, 144.

65. "Table Talk," *Appleton's Journal*, April 3, 1869, 27.

66. Review of *Wonder-Stories Told for Children*, *Putnam's Magazine*, April 1870, 508.

67. See Mott, *A History of American Magazines, 1850–1865*, 429.

68. Ibid., 430.

69. See *American National Biography*, s.v. "Godwin, Parke."

70. Edmund Clarence Stedman, "Literature—at Home," *Putnam's Magazine*, November 1869, 626.

71. See *American National Biography*, s.v. "Stedman, Edmund Clarence." The author of the article asserts that under the influence of Hippolyte Taine, Stedman brought scientific rigor to American criticism and was the foremost contemporary critic of American poetry. Brooks calls him the best since Poe and Lowell; *The Times of Melville and Whitman*, 321. More recently, Tomsich offers a balanced treatment in *A Genteel Endeavor: American Culture and Politics in the Gilded Age* (Stanford, Calif.: Stanford University Press, 1971), 113–35.

72. *American National Biography*, s.v. "Stedman, Edmund Clarence." Aldrich (1836–1907), in addition to varied editorial activity, wrote poetry, novels, and short stories. Extremely popular during his own time, his verse and short prose, in which he did his best work, are now generally considered polished but superficial and derivative. See *American National Biography*, s.v. "Aldrich, Thomas Bailey," and Charles E. Samuels, *Thomas Bailey Aldrich* (New York: Twayne, 1965), 119–37, especially 129–37.

73. Much like Aldrich, Stedman was an elegant, if not profound, poet. Had Godwin been a creative writer, his turn of mind and interests would likely have made a realist of him in time.

74. Emily F. Wheeler, review of *The Story of My Life*, 57. Wheeler speaks here of the tales in general. Given the date of the review and the possibility that she had already discussed two other volumes of the Author's Edition, however, it is probable that she has Scudder's collection in mind.

75. Among other literary pursuits Wheeler herself wrote stories for children.

76. Wheeler, review of *The Story of My Life*, 58.

77. Review of *Wonder-Stories Told for Children*, *Ladies' Repository*, July 1870, 78.

78. William Dean Howells, review of *O. T.*, 383.

79. Ibid.

80. *Fairy Tales and Sketches*, trans. Caroline Peachey et al. (London: Bell & Daldy, 1870).

81. Review of *Fairy Tales and Sketches*, *Overland Monthly*, June 1871, 580. See p. 53 above and Mott, *A History of American Magazines, 1865–1885*, 406.

82. "Editor's Table," *Appleton's Journal*, August 21, 1875, 245–46. *Appleton's* became a monthly in July 1876; see Mott, *A History of American Magazines, 1865–1885*, 417.

83. See Mott, *A History of American Magazines, 1865–1885*, 231, 419.

84. "Editor's Table," 245.

85. Ibid.

86. Ibid.

87. Ibid.

88. Ibid., 246.

89. Ibid.

90. "The Month," *Penn Monthly,* September 1875, 630–31. See Mott, *A History of American Magazines, 1865–1885,* 34–35. Mott offers no information concerning the magazine's circulation.
91. "The Month," 630–31.
92. George William Curtis, "The Editor's Easy Chair," 748–49. See p. 34 above.
93. Ibid., 748.
94. Ibid., 749.
95. Ibid.

CHAPTER 5. THE GENERAL INTEREST ARTICLES

1. *Saturday Evening Gazette,* July 4, 1857, 4. See Mott, *A History of American Magazines, 1850–1865,* 176–77.
2. Ibid. Mott contends that "magazines throughout the nineteenth century gave travel an attention second only to that devoted to fiction" and speaks of a "flood of travel books" that came out after the Civil War"; *A History of American Magazines, 1865–1885,* 257–58. Gillian Avery et al. confirm this, maintaining that the travelogue book was "always a particularly American genre," reaching the peak of its popularity in the 1880s and 1890s. "Children's Literature in America: 1870–1945," in *Children's Literature: An Illustrated History,* ed. Peter Hunt, 227 (Oxford: Oxford University Press, 1995).
3. Q. [Charles G. Rosenberg], "Hans Christian Andersen, the Poet and Novelist," in *You Have Heard of Them* (New York: Redfield, 1854), 73–81. See Natalie Spassky, *American Paintings in the Metropolitan Museum of Art* (New York: Metropolitan Museum of Art, 1985), 2:92-93.
4. The currently best-known figures include Felix Mendelssohn-Bartholdy, Hector Berlioz, Lola Montez, Lady Bulwer, Walter Savage Landor, and Thomas Moore. Rosenberg also offers chapters on the statesmen Benjamin D'Israeli and Henry Clay.
5. H. C. Andersen, *Samlede Skrifter,* 2nd ed., 1:298; Hans Christian Andersen, *The Story of My Life,* Author's Edition, 216.
6. See my "Confluence and Crosscurrents: Schiller's 'Das Lied von der Glocke' and Hans Christian Andersen's 'Die alte Kirchenglocke,'" *Anderseniana* (1996): 79–95.
7. *H. C. Andersens Dagbøger, 1825–1875,* 12 vols., ed. Det Danske Sprog- og Litteraturselskab (Copenhagen: G • E • C Gads Forlag, 1974), 3:66.
8. Rosenberg relates that he visited the Serres on a Tuesday. Considering this fact and Andersen's entries during the times he was in Maxen, where the Serres lived, or in nearby Dresden, February 24, 1846 is the only plausible date for the visit.
9. *You Have Heard of Them,* 78.
10. Ibid.
11. Ibid.
12. Ibid.
13. Ibid., 79.
14. Ibid., 79–80.
15. Ibid., 80.

16. Mott relates that in 1852 Rosenberg was the chief illustrator of a short-lived New York humor magazine called *Young Sam; A History of American Magazines, 1850–1865*, 182.

17. *You Have Heard of Them*, 81.

18. See, for example, Rossel, "Hans Christian Andersen Research in the United States," 518.

19. Richard Henry Stoddard, "Hans Christian Andersen," *National Magazine*, November 1855, 428–33.

20. Mott, *A History of American Magazines, 1850–1865*, 31.

21. See *American National Biography*, s.v. "Stevens, Abel."

22. This is indicated by a writer for the *Nation* in 1866 who grouped Stoddard together with Bayard Taylor, Edmund Clarence Stedman, and other "genteel" poets on a level below Longfellow et al., "who fill the highest places." In 1884, to be sure, respondents to a poll taken by the *Critic* of New York did not include Stoddard among their fifteen most highly esteemed living American writers. See Mott, *A History of American Magazines, 1865–1885*, 237–38.

23. Edmund Clarence Stedman, introduction in *Recollections Personal and Literary*, by Richard Henry Stoddard (New York: A. S. Barnes, 1903), ix.

24. Ibid., xi.

25. See the bibliography in Robert D. Harvey, "Richard Henry Stoddard," in *American Literary Critics and Scholars, 1850–1880*, 230–35.

26. Stedman, introduction, xii.

27. See Tomsich, *A Genteel Endeavor*, especially 113–66.

28. Richard Henry Stoddard, *Recollections Personal and Literary*, 97. In view of this definition it is quite understandable that his memoirs take virtually no note of Howells or Whitman and none at all of Mark Twain.

29. Ibid., 203.

30. Ibid., 101.

31. Stedman, introduction, xiii.

32. Stoddard, *Recollections Personal and Literary*, 163, 274–75. In this regard I concur with William Charvat, who writes, "Nothing better demonstrates the dilemma of literary history than its uncertainty about what to do with popular writers in general, and with the fireside poets—Bryant, Longfellow, Lowell, Holmes—in particular. In every new history the space devoted to them shrinks. The shrinkage *may* be justified on critical, but hardly on historical, grounds, for the importance of these poets in their own century cannot decrease [my emphasis]. We err, as historians, in allowing the taste of the modern reader to nullify the taste of the nineteenth-century reader"; William Charvat, *The Profession of Authorship in America, 1800–1870: The Papers of William Charvat*, ed. Matthew J. Bruccoli (Columbus: Ohio State University Press, 1968), 290.

33. Stoddard, *Recollections Personal and Literary*, 123.

34. "Hans Christian Andersen," 428.

35. Ibid.

36. Stedman, introduction, x.

37. See Stoddard, *Recollections Personal and Literary*, 182 and 120.

38. Ibid., 238.

39. The poem indeed appeared in a sketch of Andersen's life that preceded the text of the novel; Hans Christian Andersen, *The Improvisatore: Life in Italy*, trans. Mary

Howitt (New York: Harper & Brothers, 1845), 8. Entitled "The Miller's Journeyman" in Howitt's English, the poem originated as a song (sung by Hemming) in Andersen's operetta *Agnete og Havmanden* [Agnete and the Merman] and later appeared separately as "Møllerens Datter" [The Miller's Daughter] in *Digte, kjendte og glemte* [Poems Known and Forgotten] in 1867. My thanks to Johan de Mylius for tracking down the origin of the poem; Johan de Mylius, e-mail to the author, August 28, 2000.

40. "Hans Christian Andersen," 431.

41. Ibid., 433.

42. Ibid., 432.

43. Ibid., 433.

44. Ibid.

45. See p. 89. Richard Henry Stoddard, *Adventures in Fairy Land* (Boston: Ticknor, Reed, and Fields, 1853).

46. Ibid., 432.

47. Stoddard, *Recollections Personal and Literary*, 50–67 and passim.

48. For an overview, see, for example, *American National Biography*, s.v. "Taylor, Bayard." Also see James L. Gray, "Bayard Taylor," in *American Travel Writers, 1850–1915*, ed. Donald Ross and James J. Schramer, 321–35, vol. 189 of *Dictionary of Literary Biography* (Detroit: Gale Group, 1998); Paul C. Wermuth, "Bayard Taylor," in *Antebellum Writers in New York and the South*, 326–30; and Paul C. Wermuth, *Bayard Taylor* (New York: Twayne, 1973).

49. *Northern Travel: Summer and Winter Pictures[;] Sweden, Denmark, and Lapland* (London: Sampson Low & Son, 1858 [1857]; New York: G. P. Putnam, 1858 [1857]).

50. Ibid., 222–34.

51. Ibid., 232 (I have used the edition of 1862).

52. Ibid. Andersen turned 52 in April 1857.

53. Ibid., 233.

54. Even the generally sympathetic Richard Croom Beatty, writing in 1936, finds that Taylor largely failed to fulfill the main obligation of the travel writer, namely, to understand the people he visits and to communicate this understanding to his readers; *Bayard Taylor: Laureate of the Gilded Age* (Norman: University of Oklahoma Press, 1936), 206.

55. Marie Hansen-Taylor and Horace E. Scudder, *Life and Letters of Bayard Taylor*, 2 vols. (London: Elliot Stock, 1884), 1:335.

56. Russell H. Conwell, *The Life, Travels, and Literary Career of Bayard Taylor* (Boston: B. B. Russell, 1879), 261.

57. J. Ross Browne, "A Californian in Iceland," *Harper's New Monthly Magazine*, January 1863, 145–62; February, 289–311; and March, 448–67.

58. See Joseph Csicsila, "J. Ross Browne," in *Nineteenth-Century American Fiction Writers*, ed. Kent P. Ljungquist, 57–64, vol. 202 of *Dictionary of Literary Biography* (Detroit: Gale Group, 1999).

59. Ibid., 58.

60. Browne, "A Californian in Iceland," 146.

61. Ibid., 147.

62. Ibid.

63. Ibid.

64. Ibid., 148.

65. Ibid.

66. Browne worked for a time for the *Congressional Globe*, the predecessor of the *Congressional Record*, but eventually quit, sickened by the corruption and demagoguery he saw in Washington; Csicsila, "J. Ross Browne," 60.

67. Browne, "A Californian in Iceland," 148.

68. Ibid.

69. Ibid., 149.

70. Ibid.

71. Theodore Johnson, "The Story-Teller of Copenhagen," *Putnam's Magazine*, January 1869, 92–97.

72. Ibid., 94.

73. Johnson writes "O. Z.," which suggests at least partial reliance on a German source: O[dense] T[ugthus] = O[dense] Z[uchthaus].

74. "The Story-Teller of Copenhagen," 94.

75. Ibid., 95.

76. Ibid. Interestingly, all four of the plays Johnson mentions explicitly were among the five included in the German edition of Andersen's collected works published in 1847 and 1848 (H. C. Andersen, *Gesammelte Werke*, 38 vols. [Leipzig: Carl B. Lorck]), another indication that Johnson read Andersen at least in part in German.

77. Ibid.

78. Ibid.

79. Ibid., 97.

80. "Hans Christian Andersen," *Appleton's Journal*, July 8, 1871, 45–46.

81. See Scudder's letter to Andersen October 11, 1872, *The Andersen-Scudder Letters*, 128.

82. Ibid., 171n85. In his diary entry for January 14, 1871, Andersen notes receipt of a letter from his "landsman" Bagger, who apparently thanked him for advising him many years earlier not to become a poet "naar han ikke aldeles kunde lade det være" [unless he could absolutely not help himself], which Bagger had taken to heart, subsequently emigrating to America; *H. C. Andersens Dagbøger, 1825–1875*, 9:9. Bagger seems to have lived in the United States long enough to lose complete fluency in Danish, for he writes, somewhat unclearly, that he understood "*sufficient* of the Danish tongue to *fully* appreciate [Andersen's] readings" (my emphasis); "Hans Christian Andersen," 45.

83. Ibid. Also see Scudder to Andersen, January 23, 1872, *The Andersen-Scudder Letters*, 116.

84. "Hans Christian Andersen," 45.

85. Ibid.

86. Ibid. Andersen did not record these meetings in his diary.

87. Ibid., 45.

88. Schläft ein Lied in allen Dingen,
    Die da träumen fort und fort,
    Und die Welt hebt an zu singen,
    Triffst du nur das Zauberwort.

Quoted according to Joseph von Eichendorff, *Werke*, 5 vols. (Munich: Winkler, 1981), 1:132. My translation.

89. "Hans Christian Andersen," 46.

90. Ibid.

91. G. W. (Gilderoy Wells) Griffin, *My Danish Days: With a Glance at the History, Traditions, and Literature of the Old Northern Country* (Philadelphia: Claxton, Remsen and Haffelfinger, 1875).

92. *Appleton's Cyclopaedia of American Biography*, s.v. "Griffin, Gilderoy Wells."

93. Andersen's diary also records failed visits among other interactions; *H. C. Andersens Dagbøger, 1825–1875*, 9:191–94, 196, 203, 225, 317–18, and 10:177.

94. Griffin, *My Danish Days*, 189–223.

95. Peder Tordenskjold (born Wessel) was a Danish naval hero in the Great Northern War of 1700–1721.

96. Griffin, *My Danish Days*, 209.

97. Ibid.

98. Ibid., 206.

99. Ibid.

100. Ibid., 208.

101. Andersen spoke to Griffin about Jenny Lind as follows: "She exerted the noblest influence over me. She made me forget myself, and first made me acquainted with the command which God has given to genius. On the stage, she is a great artist; at home, a sensitive child"; *My Danish Days*, 191.

102. D. G. Hubbard, "The Last Days of Hans Christian Andersen," *Potter's American Monthly*, July 1878, 194–97. It is unclear where Hubbard obtained his information, but a couple of unidiomatic expressions suggest a German source.

103. Ibid., 197.

104. "Reminiscences of Hans Christian Andersen," *Scandinavia*, February 1885, 38–43.

105. Mott, *A History of American Magazines, 1885–1905*, 231.

106. Frederick Hale, ed., *Danes in North America* (Seattle: University of Washington Press, 1984), 139. Although the writer apparently thinks of the periodical as a newspaper, its format clearly identifies it as a magazine.

107. The Danish immigrant quoted above writes that his countrymen "occupy a modest position in Scandinavian society here"; ibid.

108. See, for example, *Den Danske Bank*, <http://www2.jp.dk/erhvervsbogklub/dendanskebankkapt1.html>. Vilhelm Andersen writes, "Frederiksen, who was a member of an active-minded family . . . was a man of ideas in the style of the sixties, in his politics as Member of Parliament (1866–77) and leader of the 'moderate party' as well as in his great business activity. Like his father-in-law . . . he also had his '64' [a reference to Denmark's defeat at the hands of Prussia and Austria in 1864], and twice at that, first in Sweden and after the collapse over in America"; Vilhelm Andersen, *Det nittende aarhundredes anden halvdel*, vol. 4 of Carl S. Petersen and Vilhelm Andersen, *Illustreret dansk litteraturhistorie*, 4 vols. (Copenhagen: Gyldendalske Boghandel - Nordisk Forlag, 1925), 331.

109. On p. 41 of the article the author mentions having seen a painting of Peter Stuyvesant marching at the head of a procession in New York and rebuffs a comment made in another Chicago magazine, the *Dial*.

110. Andersen's diaries reveal that he met Frederiksen in 1863, but little more; *H. C. Andersens Dagbøger, 1825–1875*, 5:355 and 393, 10:1.

111. "Reminiscences of H. C. Andersen," 38.

112. Ibid., 38–39.

113. Ibid., 39.

114. Also see 41.

115. Ibid.

116. Ibid., 39–40.

117. Ibid., 40.

118. Ibid. For additional comments on Andersen's imagination, see 42.

119. Ibid., 40.

120. Ibid. Also see the final paragraph of the article, 43.

121. Ibid., 40–41.

122. Ibid., 42.

123. See 38.

124. Ibid., 42.

125. Ibid.

126. Ibid., 43.

127. Ibid., 42.

128. "Hans Christian Andersen," *Dial*, November 1884, 159–62.

129. See Mott, *A History of American Magazines, 1865–1885*, 543.

130. Ibid.

131. Ibid., 540.

132. "An Acquaintance with Hans Christian Andersen," *Century*, March 1892, 785–89.

133. For a brief introduction to the magazine, see chapter 3, p. 69 of the present study.

134. Hjalmar Hjorth Boyesen, "Hans Christian Andersen," in *Essays on Scandinavian Literature* (New York: Charles Scribner's Sons, 1895), 155–78.

135. See Robert S. Frederickson, "Hjalmar Hjorth Boyesen," in *American Realists and Naturalists*, ed. Donald Pizer and Earl N. Harbert, 38, vol. 12 of *Dictionary of Literary Biography* (Detroit: Gale Group, 1982).

136. Ibid., 37–38.

137. Ibid., 40.

138. Mott, *A History of American Magazines, 1865–1885*, 540.

139. Boyesen writes, "I confess, until I had the pleasure of making Andersen's acquaintance, 'The Story of My Life' impressed me most unpleasantly. After I had by personal intercourse possessed myself of the clue to the man's character, I judged differently"; "Hans Christian Andersen," 160.

140. Boyesen, "An Acquaintance with Hans Christian Andersen," 785.

141. Ibid.

142. Boyesen, "Hans Christian Andersen," 159.

143. Boyesen, *Essays on Scandinavian Literature*, 167–68.

144. Boyesen, "An Acquaintance with Hans Christian Andersen," 786.

145. Ibid., 787.

146. Ibid., 786.

147. Ibid., 788.

148. Boyesen, "Hans Christian Andersen," 160. Also see *Essays on Scandinavian Literature*, 168–69.

149. Boyesen, "Hans Christian Andersen," 161.

150. Ibid.

151. Ibid.

152. Ibid.

153. Boyesen, *Essays on Scandinavian Literature,* 171.
154. Ibid., 173.
155. Boyesen, "Hans Christian Andersen," 159.
156. Ibid., 159–60.
157. Ibid., 160.
158. Ibid.
159. Boyesen, *Essays on Scandinavian Literature,* 173–74.
160. Ibid., 174.
161. Boyesen, "An Acquaintance with Hans Christian Andersen," 785.
162. Boyesen, "Hans Christian Andersen," 160.
163. Ibid.
164. Ibid.
165. Boyesen, *Essays on Scandinavian Literature,* 174.
166. Ibid., 176.
167. Ibid., 176–77.
168. Ibid., 175.
169. Ibid., 178.
170. See Tomsich, *A Genteel Endeavor,* 15–16.
171. "Hans Christian Andersen," 162, and "An Acquaintance with Hans Christian Andersen," 785.
172. "Hans Christian Andersen," 160.
173. One might assume that Boyesen omitted the poetry due to the fact that he was using, and thus perhaps thinking in terms of, the Author's Edition, but this edition contains neither the poetry nor the plays.
174. See Per Seyersted, *Hjalmar Hjorth Boyesen: From Norwegian Romantic to American Realist* (Oslo: Solum Forlag; Atlantic Highlands, N.J.: Humanities Press, 1984), 16.
175. Boyesen, "An Acquaintance with Hans Christian Andersen," 789.
176. Griffin, for example, who was born in 1840, writes, "I had been an admirer of the genius of Andersen from my earliest recollection, and I looked forward to the time when I should see him with no ordinary pleasure"; *My Danish Days,* 190.

CHAPTER 6. HORACE E. SCUDDER

1. *Merriam Webster's Collegiate Dictionary,* 11th ed., s.v. "anonymous."
2. Ibid.
3. See Brier, "Horace Elisha Scudder," 246.
4. See "The Rich Man's Place," in *American Fairy Tales from Rip Van Winkle to the Rootabaga Stories,* ed. Neil Philip (New York: Hyperion, 1996). While this story is significant in its own right, as indicated below, one might have chosen any of a large number of yet more important and better pieces.
5. Boyesen, "Hans Christian Andersen," 786.
6. As stated earlier, no full-scale study of Scudder's life or work exists. For information on the former I have relied heavily on the following: Alexander V. G. Allen, "Horace E. Scudder: An Appreciation," *Atlantic Monthly,* April 1903, 549–60; Ellen B. Ballou, "Horace Elisha Scudder and the *Riverside Magazine,*" *Harvard Library Bul-*

letin 14 (1960): 426–52; Ballou, *The Building of the House: Houghton Mifflin's Formative Years* (Boston: Houghton Mifflin, 1970); and Ellery Sedgwick, *The Atlantic Monthly, 1857–1909.* In order to facilitate reading I have referred to these writings only when citing specific passages or where I thought the information was important enough that the reader might want to consult the work. Unless otherwise indicated, the comments on Scudder's creative writing and thought are my own.

7. See, for example, F. E. Mayer, *The Religious Bodies of America*, 4th ed. (Saint Louis, Mo.: Concordia Publishing House, 1961), 359–61.

8. *Doings of the Bodley Family in Town and Country* (New York: Hurd and Houghton, 1875).

9. Quoted according to Ballou, *The Building of the House*, 105.

10. Ibid., 104.

11. See Ballou, "Horace Elisha Scudder and the *Riverside Magazine*," 431–32.

12. Henry Mills Alden, review of *Seven Little People and Their Friends*, by Horace E. Scudder, *Atlantic Monthly*, January 1863, 143–44.

13. To be sure, Allen writes that it was difficult for anyone to escape Dickens's influence at that time; "Horace E. Scudder," 553.

14. Review of *Seven Little People and Their Friends*, 144.

15. *Life and Letters of David Coit Scudder* (New York: Hurd and Houghton, 1864).

16. "The Life of William Blake," *North American Review*, October 1864, 465–82.

17. Scudder, *Dream Children* (Cambridge, Mass.: Sever & Francis, 1864).

18. Ibid., viii. The text by Lamb is one of the *Essays of Elia*.

19. Ibid., viii–ix.

20. "The children seem to have found their Dickens at last." Henry Mills Alden, review of *Dream Children*, *Atlantic Monthly*, February 1864, 256.

21. The story concludes as follows: "'O, I remember!' said she. 'When I was a little girl, I put this doll away among the books so carefully that I never could find it again. It was my groceryman. Don't you remember, father?' He smiled; no, he had forgotten it. But John had slept so long that he did not know her. 'Don't disturb me,' said he; 'I was told to sleep.'" Ibid., 74.

22. See Topsøe-Jensen, "The Background of the Letters," Dal, "Hans Christian Andersen's Tales and America." Also see note 25 below.

23. In the November issue of 1868 Scudder writes, "When it was announced that the great Dane was to write for us, all the newspapers in the country took up the word, and rejoiced at the prospect"; "Patchwork," *Riverside Magazine*, November 1868, 527.

24. Mott, *A History of American Magazines, 1865–1885*, 176. See, for example, Gillian Avery, Louisa Smith, C. W. Sullivan III, Zena Sutherland, "Children's Literature in America: 1870–1945," in *Children's Literature: An Illustrated History*, 230–31.

25. See my "The Author's Edition of H. C. Andersen's Works: An American-Danish Collaboration," *Orbis Litterarum*, 60 (2005): 449–76.

26. *Men and Letters: Essays in Characterization and Criticism* (Boston: Houghton Mifflin, 1887), iii.

27. *Stories From My Attic* (New York: Hurd and Houghton, 1869).

28. On April 23, 1870, *The Andersen-Scudder Letters*, 75.

29. *Stories From My Attic*, 251.

30. Ibid., 127.

31. In these two pieces one detects the influence of historian and diplomat John

Lathrop Motley (1814–77), whose *Rise of the Dutch Republic* (1856) and other works on Dutch history celebrate the emergence of modern man and the American type.

32. Mark Irwin West, "Horace E. Scudder," in *American Writers for Children Before 1900*, ed. Perry J. Ashley, 320, vol. 42 of *Dictionary of Literary Biography* (Detroit: Gale Research, 1986).

33. Scudder to Andersen, April 23, 1870, *The Andersen-Scudder Letters*, 75.

34. *Stories From My Attic*, 6. Scudder did not marry until 1873.

35. Lawrence Buell, *New England Literary Culture: From Revolution Through Renaissance* (Cambridge: Cambridge University Press, 1986), 64.

36. William Dean Howells, review of *Stories From My Attic*, *Atlantic Monthly*, December 1869, 766–67 (see *The Atlantic Index*, 198).

37. Andersen to Scudder, November 1, 1870, *The Andersen-Scudder Letters*, 84.

38. *Stories From My Attic*, 65.

39. See Brier, "Horace Elisha Scudder," 243–45.

40. *Childhood in Literature and Art* (Boston and New York: Houghton Mifflin, 1894), 173.

41. *The Bodleys Telling Stories* (New York: Hurd and Houghton, 1878).

42. Ibid., 214.

43. *The Bodleys on Wheels* (Boston: Houghton Osgood 1879); *The Bodleys Afoot* (Boston: Houghton Osgood, 1880).

44. *Mr. Bodley Abroad* (Boston: Houghton Mifflin, 1881).

45. *The Bodley Grandchildren and their Journey in Holland* (Boston: Houghton Mifflin, 1882).

46. *The English Bodley Family* (Boston: Houghton Mifflin, 1884).

47. Ibid., 111.

48. Ibid., 28–29.

49. Ibid., 29.

50. Ibid., 106–7. Instances of positive English response to American cultural figures are interspersed throughout the five volumes comprising Van Wyck Brooks's *Makers and Finders: A History of the Writer in America, 1800–1915* (New York: E. P. Dutton, 1937–52). These examples are anecdotal, of course, but Gohdes provides more systematic verification of their thrust in *American Literature in Nineteenth-Century England*, especially chapters 1, 2, and 5.

51. *The Viking Bodleys: An Excursion into Norway and Denmark* (Boston: Houghton Mifflin, 1885).

52. Ibid., 147.

53. Ibid., 156.

54. Ibid., 189.

55. It is instructive to note that even the liberal *United States Magazine and Democratic Review* could write in 1852, in the midst of a smaller wave of immigration, that "[s]ince the Gothic invasion of southern Europe, no migration of men has occurred in the world at all similar to that which is pouring itself upon the shores of the United States." Quoted according to Mott, *A History of American Magazines, 1850–1865*, 122–23. Of course, the immediate consequences of mass immigration united with other factors to create a pessimism toward the future of American culture that led Bret Harte, Henry James, Charles Godfrey Leland, and many others to leave the country.

56. *Childhood in Literature and Art*, 178, 241.

57. Ibid., 225.

58. Z. F. Peirce, review of *Doings of the Bodley Family in Town and Country* and *The Bodleys Telling Stories, Atlantic Monthly,* December 1877, 761–62.

59. William Dean Howells, review of *The Bodleys on Wheels, Atlantic Monthly,* January 1879, 123.

60. Peirce, review of *Doings of the Bodley Family in Town and Country* and *The Bodleys Telling Stories,* 762. In this connection one is reminded of the series "Freedom: A History of US" recently televised by the Public Broadcasting System. Scudder's *Boston Town* (Boston: Houghton Mifflin, 1881) closely resembles the Bodley series.

61. Ballou, "Horace Elisha Scudder and the *Riverside Magazine,*" 445.

62. *The Dwellers in Five-Sisters Court* (New York: Hurd and Houghton, 1876). See "Five-Sisters Court at Christmas-Tide," *Atlantic Monthly,* January 1865, 22–39.

63. Allen identifies the location of the court in Boston; "Horace E. Scudder: An Appreciation," 553.

64. G[eorge] P[arsons] Lathrop, review of *The Dwellers in Five-Sisters Court, Atlantic Monthly,* October 1876, 509.

65. Allen, "Horace E. Scudder: An Appreciation," 553.

66. See Buell, *New England Literary Culture,* 335–70. Manlius himself has strongly caricatured features, but the term "regional comic grotesque" applies more appropriately to a figure whom Nicholas encounters during a return visit to his hometown.

67. The presence of elements of the detective novel is not at all uninteresting per se, but the Manlius plotline no more seeks to go beyond itself than the subsequent love story.

68. *Stories and Romances* (Boston: Houghton Mifflin, 1880).

69. Nina Baym, "Concepts of the Romance in Hawthorne's America," *Nineteenth-Century Fiction* 38 (1984): 438.

70. On the romance as love story see Baym, "Concepts of the Romance in Hawthorne's America," 435.

71. The allusiveness of the character's name itself qualifies his seriousness as an individual. Antipas was a Christian martyr referred to in Revelation 2:13, while Michael Wigglesworth (1631–1705) was the author of the long theological poem "The Day of Doom."

72. *Stories and Romances,* 56. Scudder does not overtly link the son's informality with his vitality, but an implicit connection is certainly present. This is not at all insignificant, for manners and their reform were a major concern of the age and a recurrent topic in magazines. See Mott, *A History of American Magazines, 1865–1885,* 307.

73. Buell, *New England Literary Culture,* 368. Wigglesworth reveals features of the pedant whose erudition proves an obstacle in everyday life as well as of the suitor who is thwarted by his own awkwardness and passivity. While both types derive in American letters from the comic grotesque, they received more serious treatment by Hawthorne, Dickinson, and later in the century especially by Sarah Orne Jewett. Scudder clearly participated in the deepening of these character types, if in a different manner than his more noteworthy contemporaries. See Buell, *New England Literary Culture,* 340, 345.

74. In Wigglesworth and Holcroft, Scudder indeed appears to be settling accounts with his own past. Particularly the effete, somewhat daimonic Wigglesworth, while embodying a recognizable New England type, must have presented himself to Scud-

der's imagination much like a hologram of his earlier self. In a mixed review of *Stories and Romances* S. Kirk writes of the character, "It is a Hawthornish type,—bloodless and silent and shy. . . . The type has not died out in New England, nor is it rare here . . ."; "Recent Volumes of Short Stories," *Atlantic Monthly*, February 1881, 283.

75. *Stories and Romances*, 278.

76. Ibid., 298.

77. Jackson's *Mercy Philbrick's Choice* was the first number published in the series and was followed in 1877 by *Hetty's Strange History*. See, for example, Kate Phillips, *Helen Hunt Jackson: A Literary Life* (Berkeley and Los Angeles: University of California Press, 2003), 203–12. In his review of *Stories and Romances* in the *Atlantic Monthly* Kirk associates Scudder's story with the Roberts series, asserting that the author "redeems" himself for a couple of sermonic pieces "in an amusing representation of the trial of a man who wrote one of the No Name novels"; S. Kirk, "Recent Volumes of Short Stories," 283.

78. *Stories and Romances*, 279, 298. Carol E. Schmudde discusses this problematic with regard to Jackson's No Name novels, writing, "In these novels, even well-intentioned lies and secrets can harm deceiver, deceived, and their social communities"; "Sincerity, Secrecy, and Lies: Helen Hunt Jackson's No Name Novels," *Studies in American Fiction* 21 (1993): 51–66. According to Schmudde, Jackson nonetheless "gleefully manipulated" her anonymity, which enhanced the marketability of her works and heightened the public's desire to penetrate the mystery surrounding her romans—and contes—à clef, this despite the fact that she avowedly wrote anonymously to protect her privacy and that of her friends; ibid., 56–57. It is impossible to determine whether Scudder, when writing "Nobody's Business," was thinking of Jackson or any other specific writer. Considering his elevated view of literature and sense of public as well as private morality, it seems more likely that he had the whole genre of anonymous fiction in mind, especially given its great vogue for around a decade— the Roberts series had imitators—and the mixed artistic success of the individual works. In any event, while Jackson's tone in her contributions to the series is straightforwardly serious, Scudder takes an ironic approach to the subject.

79. Lawrence Buell discusses the "incipient metaliterary character" of both major and minor works written during approximately the first half of the nineteenth century; *New England Literary Culture*, 372.

80. Sedgwick, *The Atlantic Monthly, 1857–1909*, 203.

81. See Wendy Steiner, *The Colors of Rhetoric: Problems in the Relation between Modern Literature and Painting* (Chicago: University of Chicago Press, 1982), 143–44.

82. Allen, "Horace E. Scudder: An Appreciation," 553.

83. For Scudder's editorial work, see Brier, "Horace Elisha Scudder," 243–44.

84. See chapter 2, n. 49.

85. Sedgwick, *The Atlantic Monthly, 1857–1909*, 204.

86. The unsigned first tribute to appear in the *Atlantic Monthly* on Scudder's death states in general, "He preferred to write anonymously, for the most part, and very few of the many admirers of his skillful literary workmanship are aware that he has contributed more pages to the Atlantic than any other writer"; "Mr. Scudder and the Atlantic," *Atlantic Monthly*, March 1902, 433.

87. Thomas Wentworth Higginson, "Horace Elisha Scudder," *Proceedings: American Academy of Arts and Science* 37 (1902): 657. See "A Modern Prophet," in *Men and Letters*, 70–94, here 93.

88. Allen, "Horace E. Scudder: An Appreciation," 550–51. Certainly, the general tenor of "A Modern Prophet" supports Allen's assertion. White and Hopkins characterize the social gospel as "basically an indigenous movement growing within the matrix of American Protestantism. Interacting with the changing realities and problems of an increasingly industrialized and urbanized nation, the social gospel viewed itself as a crusade for justice and righteousness in all areas of the common life. The crusade recruited articulate ministers and lay persons who publicized their new points of view as pastors, educators, editors, and directors of reform organizations"; Ronald C. White, Jr. and C. Howard Hopkins, *The Social Gospel: Religion and Reform in Changing America* (Philadelphia: Temple University Press, 1976), xi–xii. White and Hopkins include a chapter on Christian socialism, focusing on Maurice and writing, "The social gospel was basically an indigenous American movement, but at the same time it was part of a larger interest in social Christianity"; ibid., 26.

89. *Stories and Romances*, 228.

90. *Men and Letters*, 171–94.

91. *James Russell Lowell*, 2:40–41.

92. *Men and Letters*, 187.

93. Ibid., 188.

94. Ibid., 184. While not all of these historians addressed themselves principally to American history, Prescott and Motley focusing on the Spanish empire and the Dutch Republic, respectively, the four shared with varying emphases a vision of America as the culmination of a historical development dominated increasingly by Anglo-Saxon Protestant culture.

95. Ibid., 147–70, here 169. I have found no indication of Scudder's party affiliation, but his background, associations, and thought suggest that he was a Republican with liberal leanings and a lineage reaching back through the reformist branch of the Whig Party to its Federalist predecessors. See Buell, *New England Literary Culture*, 95.

96. See Spencer, *The Quest for Nationality*.

97. *James Russell Lowell*, 1:102. Also see Spencer, *The Quest for Nationality*, 197–99.

98. *James Russell Lowell*, 1:137–38.

99. Ibid., 1:115.

100. Ibid., 1:167. Sedgwick comments on Scudder's attitude toward didacticism in literature; *The Atlantic Monthly, 1857–1909*, 225.

101. *James Russell Lowell*, 1:88.

102. Brier writes expressly of Scudder's formalism: "In literary matters he wanted to encourage an early version of modern formalism, criticism that would focus analytically on texts"; "Horace Elisha Scudder," 248.

103. "Longfellow and His Art," in *Men and Letters*, 23–69.

104. Ibid., 148–49.

105. *Men and Letters*, 217.

106. Ibid., 227.

107. *James Russell Lowell*, 1:73.

108. See Sedgwick, *The Atlantic Monthly, 1857–1909*, 219. Scudder nonetheless had great respect for James and published him in the *Atlantic Monthly*, though Sedgwick claims he did not support the novelist to the extent he should have; ibid.

109. Ibid.

110. Ibid., 221.

111. Quoted according to Brier, "Horace Elisha Scudder," 247.

112. *Childhood in Literature and Art,* 241; 201–16.

113. Higginson, "Horace Elisha Scudder," 657.

114. Ibid., 660.

115. Ibid., 660–61.

116. Ibid., 657.

117. "Mr. Scudder and the Atlantic," 434.

118. Allen, "Horace E. Scudder: An Appreciation," 549.

119. One of these exceptions is Leonard Lutwack, who gives Scudder and his work for Houghton Mifflin proper credit, albeit in the process of debunking what he considers the abdication of criticism in favor of mythmaking during the genteel era. See Leonard Lutwack, "The New England Hierarchy," *New England Quarterly* 28 (1955): 164–85, especially 165–66 and 170–71. Another is Ellery Sedgwick, who expresses no qualifications; *A History of the Atlantic Monthly, 1857–1909,* 213, 218–19.

120. "Hans Christian Andersen and His Fairy Legends," *National Quarterly Review,* September 1861, 235–51.

121. Mott, *A History of American Magazines, 1850–1865,* 530.

122. Ibid., 533.

123. Ibid.

124. See Rossel, "Hans Christian Andersen Research in the United States," 518. Also see the comment on Stoddard's claim to precedence in chapter 5, p. 109.

125. "Hans Christian Andersen and His Fairy Legends," 242, 240.

126. Ibid., 236. In his notion of originality Scudder reveals a neoclassical, rather than a romantic, sensibility. Within the American context, however, this does not reflect an inconsistency, as Buell demonstrates in a chapter entitled in part "Neoclassical Continuities" and passim; *New England Literary Culture,* 84–102.

127. "Hans Christian Andersen and His Fairy Legends," 236. Further references will be given by page number in the text.

128. "Andersen's Short Stories," *Atlantic Monthly,* November 1875, 598–602. Further references will be given by page number in the text.

129. Ibid. Roger Sale speaks of the ballet as *the* form of the fairy tale in the nineteenth century; *Fairy Tales and After: From Snow White to E. B. White* (Cambridge: Harvard University Press, 1978), 59. Zipes writes, "By the beginning of the twentieth century the fairy tale as institution had expanded to include drama, poetry, ballet, music, and opera"; *When Dreams Came True,* 22.

130. "Andersen's Short Stories," 599.

131. Ibid. In the introduction to a selection of "Italian Fairy Tales" published in a long-lived successor to Scudder's *Riverside Magazine* in 1879, we find a similar critique: "I fear some of the readers of *St. Nicholas* will exclaim, on reading the title of this article, 'What, more fairy tales?' and will instantly suspect the writer of designing to pass off on them some moral lesson under the thin disguise of a story, or to puzzle their heads with some of the genuine marvels of science in masks of hobgoblins, kobolds and magicians." Quoted according to Brian Attebery, *The Fantasy Tradition in American Literature: From Irving to Le Guin* (Bloomington: Indiana University Press, 1980), 65.

132. "Andersen's Short Stories," 599–600.

133. Ibid., 600.

134. Ibid.

135. Ibid., 602.
136. Ibid.
137. *New England Literary Culture*, 56–57.
138. "The Home of Hans Christian Andersen," *Harper's New Monthly Magazine*, October 1884, 651–62.
139. Ibid., 651.
140. Ibid.
141. Ibid., 652.
142. Ibid., 662.

Chapter 7. Conclusion and Context

1. See W. Glyn Jones, "H. C. Andersen in English—a Feasibility Study I," 92–94.
2. Bredsdorff discusses Victorian translators of Andersen's fairy tales and stories in *H. C. Andersen og England*, 489–522.
3. See chapter 4, pp. 85 and 90.
4. See Baym, *Novels, Readers, and Reviewers*, 13.
5. Ibid., 19–20.
6. Based on Bredsdorff, *Danish Literature in English Translation*.
7. Bredsdorff, *H. C. Andersen og England*, 467–68.
8. Ibid., 475, 479.
9. Ibid., 482.
10. Ibid.
11. See the introduction, p. 12.
12. Mott, *A History of American Magazines, 1850–1868*, 158. Mott also notes the quality of reviewing in several magazines in which earlier reviews of Andersen's work appeared: the *Harbinger*, the *Christian Examiner*, the *New Englander*, and the *United States Magazine and Democratic Review*, as well as the *Literary World*, the *International Magazine*, and the *National Quarterly Review*; *A History of American Magazines, 1850–1868*, 158, and *A History of American Magazines, 1741–1850*, 408, respectively.
13. At this time Howells was second-in-command at James R. Osgood's *Atlantic*. His early writings were published by Hurd and Houghton, with which, of course, Scudder had already been associated for a couple of years.
14. See Sedgwick, *The Atlantic Monthly, 1857–1909*, 119.
15. See Mott, *A History of American Magazines, 1741–1850*, 494–502, and Baym, *Novels, Readers, and Reviewers*, 20.
16. Judging by the works Scudder discusses in his two articles, he would appear to have detected realism in tales as well as stories, but his mere familiarity with the latter may have influenced his reading of the former.
17. J. Max Patrick, introduction, in *The Complete Poetry of Robert Herrick* (New York: Norton, 1968), vii.
18. See Attebery, *The Fantasy Tradition in American Literature*, 59–60.
19. See Selma G. Lanes, *Down the Rabbit Hole: Adventures and Misadventures in the Realm of Children's Literature* (New York: Atheneum, 1972), 91.

20. Attebery, *The Fantasy Tradition in American Literature*, 25.

21. Anne Scott MacLeod, "Children's Literature in America from the Puritan Beginnings to 1870," in *Children's Literature: An Illustrated History*, 102–6.

22. Ibid., 106.

23. See Lanes, *Down the Rabbit Hole*, 92–93.

24. See MacLeod, "Children's Literature in America from the Puritan Beginnings to 1870," 128.

25. Ibid., 114–15.

26. Ibid., 128–29. Avery et al. write that the period between 1870 and 1914 was a golden age of children's books, when the very best writers of adult fiction also wrote for children—a development that Scudder surely welcomed; Avery et al., "Children's Literature in America: 1870–1945," 225.

27. Lanes, *Down the Rabbit Hole*, 99.

28. Avery et al., "Children's Literature in America: 1870–1945," 230.

29. See Lance Salway, ed., *A Peculiar Gift: Nineteenth Century Writings on Books for Children* (Harmondsworth, U.K.: Kestral Books, 1976), 110.

30. Harald Åström, *H. C. Andersens genombrott i Sverige*, 61, 150. The author provides a summary of his findings on 150–53, from which most of the information in the present segment of the chapter is drawn.

31. Ibid., 144–45.

32. Ibid., 129–31.

33. Ibid., 131.

34. Swedish romantics did in fact collect and imitate the folklore of their country, including the folktale. The fact that they failed to cultivate the literary fairy tale may have to do with the circumstance that the major Swedish romantics were principally poets and that prose fiction in general received little attention during the period. See, for example, Alrik Gustafson, *A History of Swedish Literature* (Minneapolis: University of Minnesota Press, 1961), 155, 158–59.

35. See Möller-Christensen, *Den gyldne trekant*, especially the concluding chapter, 268–79, from which much of the following is drawn.

36. Ibid., 269–70.

37. Ibid., 269.

38. Ibid., 122 and 124.

39. Ibid., 263.

40. Ibid., 256 and 259.

41. Ibid., 263.

42. Bredsdorff, *H. C. Andersen og England*, 428–88, here, 484. Also see Jacki Wullschlager, *Hans Christian Andersen: The Life of a Storyteller* (New York: Knopf, 2001), 295–322 and 351–60.

43. Bredsdorff, *H. C. Andersen og England*, 475.

44. Ibid., 431.

45. Ibid., 450–51.

46. See Dennis Butts, "The Beginnings of Victorianism (c. 1820–1850)," and Julia Briggs and Dennis Butts, "The Emergence of Form (1850–1890)," in *Children's Literature: An Illustrated History*, 77–101 and 130–65, respectively. For a recent dissenting opinion see Nicola Bown, "Introduction: Small Enchantments," in *Fairies in Nineteenth-Century Art and Literature* (Cambridge: Cambridge University Press, 2001), 1.

47. Dickens's "Frauds on the Fairies" was first published in the periodical *Household Words* on 1 October 1853; Ruskin's "Fairy Stories" first appeared as the introduction to an edition of Grimms' fairy tales, *German Popular Stories*, ed. Edgar Taylor (London: John Camden Hotten, 1868).

48. Dickens's own illustrator, Cruikshank had rewritten and published traditional tales in support of issues such as the prohibition of alcohol and slavery. See, for example, Salway, ed., *A Peculiar Gift*, 109–10.

49. Dickens, for example, writes of the fairy tale as a "precious old escape" from the world, which has "greatly helped to keep us, in some sense, ever young"; quoted according to Salway, *A Peculiar Gift*, 118, 111. Ruskin sees the "proper function" of fairy tales in relation to children; ibid., 127–28.

50. Bredsdorff, *H. C. Andersen og England*, 484.

51. Ibid.

52. Ibid., 441.

53. Ibid., 440, 99.

54. Ibid., 477.

55. Ibid.

56. Ibid., 443.

57. Ibid., 444.

58. Some of these features are mentioned in more than one of the reviews which Bredsdorff considers the most insightful; others, such as the appeal to young and old, appear in other reviews as well.

59. I refer here to the reviews available to me through the work of Bredsdorff, Möller-Christensen, and Åström.

60. Bredsdorff, *H. C. Andersen og England*, 483.

61. Ibid., 481. Bredsdorff remarks that the majority of the English reviews dealt with the "fantastic" tales, whereas the more realistic ones went almost unnoticed; ibid., 447.

62. Scudder's treatment of Andersen is indeed sanguine, but he was prepared to exercise criticism where he thought it appropriate. Duberman overstates the case when in his biography of James Russell Lowell he writes that Scudder's earlier biography "suffers fatally from being a tribute"; Martin Duberman, *James Russell Lowell* (Boston: Houghton Mifflin, 1966), 379. Scudder's several critical comments are expressed respectfully, but they are critical nonetheless.

63. See, for example, Zipes, "Spells of Enchantment: An Overview of the History of Fairy Tales," in *When Dreams Came True*, 1–29.

64. *Dagbladet*, April 24, 1862, 2.

65. "Hans Christian Andersen and His Fairy Legends," 251.

66. We recall Andersen's concern for the treatment of the Indians, which Boyesen relates in "An Acquaintance with Hans Christian Andersen," 787. He expressed what must have also been a widespread notion when he asked Boyesen whether Americans were not "very hard and unfeeling, having regard for money and for nothing else?"; ibid., 786.

67. *H. C. Andersen og England*, 447. With regard to the American critics' response to Andersen, particularly Scudder's, it is important to remember that English criticism after 1848 did not change the already established image of Andersen (467–68).

68. For information on Bille, see Vilhelm Andersen, *Den danske Litteratur i det Nittende Aarhundredes anden Halvdel,* 32–33.

69. Brandes was on the whole less an original thinker than an inspirational mediator of others' ideas.

70. It should perhaps be noted that the image of Andersen as a writer of fairy tales for children is not at all unknown even in present-day Denmark.

Chronological List of Primary Sources

1845

Charles A. Dana. Review of *The Improvisatore*. Trans. Mary Howitt. *Harbinger,* 4 October 1845, 263.

1847

Charles Fenno Hoffman [?]. Review of *The True Story of My Life*. Trans. Mary Howitt. *Literary World,* 21 August 1847, 53–55.

Review of *A Picture Book Without Pictures*. Trans. Meta Taylor. *Daguerreotype,* 4 September 1847, 141–42.

Sara Josepha Hale [?]. Review of *The True Story of My Life*. Trans. Mary Howitt. *Godey's Magazine and Lady's Book,* October 1847, 215.

Review of *The True Story of My Life*. Trans. Mary Howitt. *Christian Examiner and Religious Miscellany,* November 1847, 461.

Review of *The True Story of My Life*. Trans. Mary Howitt. *United States Magazine and Democratic Review,* December 1847, 525–37.

Theodore Parker. Review of *The True Story of My Life*. Trans. Mary Howitt. *Massachusetts Quarterly Review,* December 1847, 127.

1848

Caroline M. Kirkland. Review of *A Christmas Greeting: Thirteen Stories from the Danish of Hans Christian Andersen*. Trans. Charles Beckwith-Lohmeyer. *Union Magazine,* April 1848, 192.

Review of *Danish Story-Book*. Trans. Charles Boner. *Southern Literary Messenger,* July 1848, 454.

1849

John S. Hart [?]. Review of *Hans Andersen's Story-Book—with a Memoir by Mary Howitt*. Trans. Mary Howitt. *Sartain's Union Magazine,* February 1849, 156.

1850

Review of *The Ugly Duck, and other Tales. Little Ellie, and other Tales. The Story Teller. Literary World,* November 16, 1850, 389.

1851

John S. Hart [?]. *Hans Andersen's Wonderful Tales. Sartain's Union Magazine,* February 1851, 140.

Charles Godfrey Leland. "Sketches of Life in Sweden" [*Pictures of Sweden.* Trans. Charles Beckwith-Lohmeyer]. *International Magazine,* July 1851, 450-52.

———. "Swedish Landscapes." [*Pictures of Sweden.* Trans. Charles Beckwith-Lohmeyer]. *International Magazine,* August 1851, 20–22.

1852

John Esten Cooke. "A Handful of Autumn Leaves" [*Picture Book Without Pictures*]. *Southern Literary Messenger,* December 1852, 715.

———. "A Handful of Autumn Leaves" [*Hans Andersen's Story-Book*]. *Southern Literary Messenger,* December 1852, 715.

1854

John Esten Cooke. "The New Literature" [General]. *Southern Literary Messenger,* April 1854, 214.

Q. [Charles G. Rosenberg]. "Hans Christian Andersen, the Poet and Novelist." In *You Have Heard of Them,* 73–81. New York: Redfield, 1854.

1855

Richard Henry Stoddard. "Hans Christian Andersen." *National Magazine,* November 1855, 428–33.

1857

Bayard Taylor. "Journey to Gottenburg and Copenhagen." In *Northern Travel: Summer and Winter Pictures[;] Sweden, Denmark, and Lapland,* 222–34. London: Sampson Low and Son, 1858 [1857]; New York: G. P. Putnam, 1858 [1857]).

1860

George William Bagby. Review of *The Sand-Hills of Jutland.* Trans. Anne S. Bushby. *Southern Literary Messenger,* August 1860, 159.

Review of *The Sand-Hills of Jutland. New Englander,* November 1860, 1105.

1861

Horace E. Scudder. "Hans Christian Andersen and his Fairy Legends." *National Quarterly Review,* September 1861, 235–51.

1862

George William Bagby. "A Witch in the Nursery." *Southern Literary Messenger,* August 1862, 488–500.

1863

J. Ross Browne. "A Californian in Iceland" [General]. *Harper's New Monthly Magazine,* January 1863, 145–62; February, 289–311; and March, 448–67.

Charles Godfrey Leland. "Pictures from the North" [*In Sweden*]. *Continental Monthly,* April 1863, 398–403.

———. Review of *The Ice-Maiden, and Other Tales.* Trans. Fanny Fuller. *Continental Monthly,* April 1863, 500.

Review of *The Ice-Maiden, and Other Tales. Peterson's Monthly,* April 1863, 321.

1869

Theodore Johnson. "The Story-Teller of Copenhagen." *Putnam's Magazine,* January 1869, 92–97.

Horace E. Scudder. "Hans Christian Andersen: The Danish Story-Teller." *Riverside Magazine for Young People,* January 1869, 42–46.

"Literary Notes" [Brief comment on Andersen as a writer of fairy tales]. *Appleton's Journal,* April 3, 1869, 27.

Review of *The Improvisatore.* Trans. Mary Howitt. *Ladies' Repository,* November 1869, 397.

Edmund Clarence Stedman. "Literature" [*The Improvisatore.* Trans. Mary Howitt]. *Putnam's Magazine,* November 1869, 625–26.

Henry Mills Alden [?]. "Editor's Literary Record" [*The Two Baronesses*]. *Harper's New Monthly Magazine,* December 1869, 144.

1870

Edmund Clarence Stedman [?]. "Literature—At Home" [*Wonder-Stories Told for Children.* Trans. Mary Howitt]. *Putnam's Magazine,* April 1870, 508.

Review of *In Spain and a Visit to Portugal.* Trans. Anne S. Bushby [?]. *Punchinello,* May 14, 1870, 110.

Review of *Wonder-Stories Told for Children. Ladies' Repository,* July 1870, 78.

Henry Mills Alden [?]. "Editor's Literary Record" [*In Spain and A Visit to Portugal*]. *Harper's New Monthly Magazine,* August 1870, 462.

William Dean Howells. Review of *In Spain and a Visit to Portugal.* Trans. Anne S. Bushby [?]. *Atlantic Monthly,* September 1870, 377–79.

————. Review of *O. T.* Trans. Mary Howitt. *Atlantic Monthly*, September 1870, 383–84.

R. H. Stoddard. Review of *Only a Fiddler.* Trans. Mary Howitt. *Putnam's Magazine*, October 1870, 461.

Review of *Only a Fiddler.* Trans. Mary Howitt. *Galaxy*, November 1870, 713.

William Dean Howells. Review of *Only a Fiddler.* Trans. Mary Howitt. *Atlantic Monthly*, November 1870, 632–34.

1871

Review of *The Story of My Life.* Trans. Mary Howitt and Horace E. Scudder. *Galaxy*, May 1871, 745.

Review of *The Story of My Life.* Trans. Mary Howitt and Horace E. Scudder. *New York Times*, 17 May 1871, 2.

Review of *Fairy Tales and Sketches.* Trans. Caroline Peachey et al. *Overland Monthly*, June 1871, 380.

Review of *The Story of My Life.* Trans. Mary Howitt and Horace E. Scudder. *Scribner's Monthly*, June 1871, 222–23.

Louis Bagger. "Hans Christian Andersen." *Appleton's Journal*, July 8, 1871, 45–46.

Review of *The Story of My Life.* Trans. Mary Howitt and Horace E. Scudder. *Harper's New Monthly Magazine*, July 1871, 299.

William Dean Howells. Review of *The Story of My Life.* Trans. Mary Howitt and Horace E. Scudder. *Atlantic Monthly*, September 1871, 379–80.

Hjalmar Hjorth Boyesen. Review of *A Poet's Bazaar.* Trans. Charles Beckwith-Lohmeyer [?]. *Atlantic Monthly*, October 1871, 512.

1872

Review of *A Poet's Bazaar.* Trans. Charles Beckwith-Lohmeyer [?]. *Overland Monthly*, January 1872, 102–3.

1873

Emily F. Wheeler. Review of *The Story of My Life.* Trans. Mary Howitt and Horace E. Scudder. *Ladies' Repository*, January 1873, 55–59.

1874

E. D. T. "Hans Christian Andersen." *What's Next?* [Chicago], January 1874 [?].

1875

New York Times [Eulogy], August 5, 1875, 4, col. 2.

"Obituary: Hans Christian Andersen." *New York Times,* August 5, 1875, 4, cols. 6–7.

Whitelaw Reid. "Obituary: Hans Christian Andersen." *New York Tribune,* 5 August 1875, 5.

Oliver Bell Bunce. "Editor's Table" [On Andersen principally as a writer of fairy tales]. *Appleton's Journal,* August 21, 1875, 245–46.

"The Month." *Penn Monthly,* September 1875, 630–31.

George William Curtis. "Editor's Easy Chair" [General]. *Harper's New Monthly Magazine,* October 1875, 748–49.

Horace E. Scudder. "Andersen's Short Stories." *Atlantic Monthly,* November 1875, 598–602.

"Hans Christian Andersen." *Potter's American Monthly,* November 1875, 835–36.

G[ilderoy] W[ells] Griffin. *My Danish Days: With a Glance at the History, Traditions, and Literature of the Old Northern Country,* 189–223. Philadelphia: Claxton, Remsen, and Haffelfinger, 1875.

1876

Lucy H. Hooper. "From Abroad: Our Paris Letters" [General]. *Appleton's Journal,* January 15, 1876, 354–56.

James E. Freeman. "Reminiscences" [General]. *Appleton's Journal,* October 1876, 358–59.

1878

D. G. Hubbard. "The Last Days of Hans Christian Andersen." *Potter's American Monthly,* July 1878, 194–97.

1884

Horace Scudder. "The Home of Hans Christian Andersen." *Harper's New Monthly Magazine,* October 1884, 651–62.

Hjalmar H(jorth) Boyesen. "Hans Christian Andersen." *Dial,* November 1884, 159–62.

1885

"Reminiscences of Hans Christian Andersen." *Scandinavia,* February 1885, 38–43.

1892

Hjalmar H(jorth) Boyesen. "An Acquaintance with Hans Christian Andersen." *Century,* 1892, 785–89.

1893

Hjalmar Hjorth Boyesen. "Hans Christian Andersen, the Celebrated Writer of Fairy Tales." *Chicago World's Fair,* 1893.

1895

Hjalmar H(jorth) Boyesen. "Hans Christian Andersen." In *Essays on Scandinavian Literature,* 155–78. New York: Charles Scribner's Sons, 1895.

Works Cited

Alden, Henry Mills. Review of *Seven Little People and their Friends,* by Horace E. Scudder. *Atlantic Monthly,* January 1863, 143–44.

———. Review of *Dream Children,* by Horace E. Scudder. *Atlantic Monthly,* February 1864, 256.

Alger, Horatio, Jr. *Bound to Rise; or, Up the Ladder.* Boston: Loring, 1873.

———. *Struggling Upward; or, Luke Larkin's Luck.* Philadelphia: Porter and Coates, 1890.

Allen, Alexander V. G. "Horace E. Scudder: An Appreciation." *Atlantic Monthly,* April 1903, 549–60.

American Periodicals, 1741–1900: An Index to the Microfilm Collections. Ed. Jean Hoornstra and Trudy Heath. Ann Arbor, Mich.: University Microfilms International, 1979.

Andersen, Hans Christian. *Life in Italy: The Improvisatore.* Trans. Mary Howitt. New York: Harper & Brothers, 1845.

———. *The Story of My Life.* Author's Edition. Boston and New York: Hurd and Houghton, 1871.

———. *Samlede Skrifter,* 2nd ed. Copenhagen: C. A. Reitzels Forlag, 1878.

———. *The Complete Andersen: All of the 168 Stories by Hans Christian Andersen.* Trans. and ed. Jean Hersholt. New York: Heritage Press, 1942.

———. *Eventyr og Historier.* Ed. Bo Grønbech. 4 vols. Odense: Arnkrone, 1958.

———. *Hans Christian Andersen: The Complete Fairy Tales and Stories.* Trans. Erik Christian Haugaard. Garden City, N.Y.: Doubleday, 1974.

———. *H. C. Andersens Dagbøger, 1825–1875.* Ed. Det Danske Sprog- og Litteraturselskab. 12 vols. Copenhagen: G • E • C Gads Forlag, 1974.

———. *Tales and Stories by Hans Christian Andersen.* Trans. and ed. by Patricia L. Conroy and Sven H. Rossel. Seattle: University of Washington Press, 1980.

The Andersen-Scudder Letters: Hans Christian Andersen's Correspondence with Horace Elisha Scudder. Ed. Jean Hersholt and Waldemar Westergaard. Berkeley and Los Angeles: University of California Press, 1949.

Andersen, Vilhelm. *Det nittende aarhundredes første halvdel.* Vol. 3 of *Illustreret dansk litteraturhistorie,* by Carl S. Petersen and Andersen. 4 vols. Copenhagen: Gyldendalske Boghandel-Nordisk Forlag, 1924.

———. *Det nittende aarhundredes anden halvdel.* Vol. 4 of *Illustreret dansk litteraturhistorie,* by Carl S. Petersen and Andersen. 4 vols. Copenhagen: Gyldendalske Boghandel-Nordisk Forlag, 1925.

Arac, Jonathan. "Narrative Forms: Establishing National Narrative." In *The Cambridge History of American Literature*, ed. Sacvan Bercovitch and Cyrus R. K. Patell, 607–28. New York: Cambridge University Press, 1995.

Åström, Harald. *H. C. Andersens genombrott i Sverige: Översättningarne och kritikken, 1828–1852*. Odense: Andelsbogtrykkeri, 1972.

Attebery, Brian. *The Fantasy Tradition in American Literature: From Irving to Le Guin*. Bloomington: Indiana University Press, 1980.

Auring, Steffen, et al. *Borgerlig enhedskultur, 1807–48*. Vol. 5 of *Dansk litteraturhistorie* Copenhagen: Gyldendal, 2000.

Avery, Gillian, et al. "Children's Literature in America: 1870-1945." In *Children's Literature: An Illustrated History*, ed. Peter Hunt, 225–51. Oxford: Oxford University Press, 1995.

Baehr, Jr., Harry W. *The* New York Tribune *Since the Civil War*. New York: Dodd, Mead, 1936.

Ballou, Ellen B. "Horace Elisha Scudder and the *Riverside Magazine*." *Harvard Library Bulletin* 14 (1960): 426–52.

———. *The Building of the House: Houghton Mifflin's Formative Years*. Boston: Houghton Mifflin, 1970.

Barlby, Finn, ed. *Det dæmoniske spejl: Analyser af H. C. Andersens "Skyggen."* Copenhagen: Forlaget Dråben, 1998.

———. *Det hvide spejl: Analyser af H. C. Andersens "Sneedronningen."* Copenhagen: Forlaget Dråben, 2000.

Barnes, Homer F. *Charles Fenno Hoffman*. New York: Columbia University Press, 1930.

Bauschinger, Sigrid. *The Trumpet of Reform: German Literature in Nineteenth-Century New England*. Trans. Thomas Hansen. Rochester, N.Y.: Camden House, 1999.

Bayless, Joy. *Rufus Wilmot Griswold: Poe's Literary Executor*. Nashville, Tenn.: Vanderbilt University Press, 1943.

Baym, Nina. "Concepts of the Romance in Hawthorne's America." *Nineteenth-Century Fiction* 38 (1984): 426–43.

———. *Novels, Readers, and Reviewers: Responses to Fiction in Antebellum America*. Ithaca: Cornell University Press, 1984.

Beatty, Richard Croom. *Bayard Taylor: Laureate of the Gilded Age*. Norman: University of Oklahoma Press, 1936.

Beaty, John O. *John Esten Cooke, Virginian*. New York: Columbia University Press, 1922.

Bell, Michael Davitt. "Conditions of Literary Vocation: Women's Fiction and the Literary Marketplace in the 1850s." In *The Cambridge History of American Literature*, ed. Sacvan Bercovitch and Cyrus R. K. Patell, 2: 74–123. New York: Cambridge University Press, 1995.

Berger, Meyer. *The Story of the* New York Times, *1851–1951*. New York: Simon and Schuster, 1951.

Bergmann, Harriet F. "Richard Henry Stoddard." In *Antebellum Writers in New York and the South*, ed. Joel Myerson, 21–23. Vol. 3 of *Dictionary of Literary Biography*. Detroit: Gale Group, 1979.

Bille, C. St. A. "H. C. Andersen" [Review of "Hans Christian Andersen and His Fairy Legends," by Horace E. Scudder]. *Dagbladet*, April 24, 1862, 2.

Bown, Nicola. *Fairies in Nineteenth-Century Art and Literature*. Cambridge: Cambridge University Press, 2001.

Brandes, Georg. "H. C. Andersen som Æventyrdigter." In *Samlede Skrifter*, 2:91–132. Copenhagen: Gyldendalske Boghandels Forlag [F. Hegel & Søn], 1899.

———. "Hans Christian Andersen." In *Creative Spirits of the Nineteenth Century*, trans. Rasmus B. Anderson, 1–53. New York: Thomas Y. Crowell, 1923.

Bredsdorff, Elias. *Danish Literature in English Translation, with a Special Hans Christian Andersen Supplement: A Bibliography*. Copenhagen: Ejnar Munksgaard, 1950.

———. *H. C. Andersen og England*. Copenhagen: Rosenkilde og Baggers Forlag, 1954.

———. *Hans Christian Andersen: The Story of His Life and Work, 1805–1875*. London: Phaidon Press, 1975.

Brier, Peter A. "Horace Elisha Scudder." In *American Literary Critics and Scholars, 1880–1900*, ed. John W. Rathbun and Monica M. Grecu, 243–49. Vol. 71 of *Dictionary of Literary Biography*. Detroit: Gale Research, 1988.

Briggs, Julia, and Dennis Butts. "The Emergence of Form (1850–1890)." In *Children's Literature: An Illustrated History*, ed. Peter Hunt, 130–65. Oxford: Oxford University Press, 1995.

Brooks, Van Wyck. *The Flowering of New England*. New York: E. P. Dutton, 1937.

———. *New England: Indian Summer, 1865–1915*. New York: E. P. Dutton, 1940.

———. *The World of Washington Irving*. New York: E. P. Dutton, 1944.

———. *The Times of Melville and Whitman*. New York: E. P. Dutton, 1947.

———. *The Confident Years, 1885–1915*. New York: E. P. Dutton, 1952.

Buell, Lawrence. *New England Literary Culture: From Revolution Through Renaissance*. Cambridge: Cambridge University Press, 1986.

Bushby, Anne S. *Poems by the Late Anne S. Bushby*. London: Bentley, 1876.

Busk-Jensen, Lise, et al. *Dannelse, folkelighed, individualisme, 1848–1901*. Vol. 6 of *Dansk litteraturhistorie*. Copenhagen: Gyldendal, 2000.

Butts, Dennis. "The Beginnings of Victorianism (c. 1820–1850)." In *Children's Literature: An Illustrated History*, ed. Peter Hunt, 77–101. Oxford: Oxford University Press, 1995.

Cameron, Kenneth Walter. *Research Keys to the American Renaissance: Scarce Indexes of* The Christian Examiner, The North American Review, *and* The New Jerusalem Magazine. Hartford, Conn.: Transcendental Books, 1967.

Charvat, William. *The Profession of Authorship in America, 1800–1870: The Papers of William Charvat*. Ed. Matthew J. Bruccoli. Columbus: Ohio State University Press, 1968.

Commager, Henry Steele. *Theodore Parker*. Boston: Little, Brown, 1936.

Conroy, Patricia L., and Sven H. Rossel, eds. and trans. *Tales and Stories by Hans Christian Andersen*. Seattle: University of Washington Press, 1980.

Conwell, Russell H. *The Life, Travels, and Literary Career of Bayard Taylor*. Boston: B. B. Russell, 1879.

Cortissoz, Royal. *The Life of Whitelaw Reid*. 2 vols. New York: Charles Scribner's Sons, 1921.

Csicsila, Joseph. "J. Ross Browne." In *Nineteenth-Century American Fiction Writers*, ed. Kent P. Ljungquist, 57–64. Vol. 202 of *Dictionary of Literary Biography*. Detroit: Gale Research, 1999.

Curran, Eileen M. *Biographies of Some Obscure Contributors to 19th-Century Periodicals*. <http://www.indiana.edu/victoria/Obscure_contributors/htm. 2002>.

Cushing, William. *Index to the Christian Examiner*. Boston: J. S. Cushing, 1879.

Dal, Erik. "Hans Christian Andersen's Tales and America." *Scandinavian Studies* 40 (1968): 1–25.

———. "Our Own Twenty Plus Fifteen Favourite Tales." In *Hans Christian Andersen: A Poet in Time; Papers from the Second International Hans Christian Andersen Conference, 29 July to 2 August 1996*, ed. Johan de Mylius, Aage Jørgensen, and Viggo Hjørnager Pedersen, 39–50. Odense: Odense University Press, 1999.

Davis, Elmer. *History of the New York Times, 1851–1921*. New York: New York Times, 1921.

Den Danske Bank. <http://www2.jp.dk/erhvervsbogklub/dendanskebankkapt1.html>.

Duberman, Martin. *James Russell Lowell*. Boston: Houghton Mifflin, 1966.

Duncan, Bingham. *Whitelaw Reid: Journalist, Politician, Diplomat*. Athens: University of Georgia Press, 1975.

Eichendorff, Joseph von. *Werke*. Vol. 1 of 5 vols. Munich: Winkler, 1981.

Entrikin, Isabelle Webb. *Sarah Josepha Hale and Godey's Lady's Book*. Philadelphia: n.p., 1946.

Exman, Eugene. *The House of Harper: One Hundred and Fifty Years of Publishing*. New York: Harper and Row, 1967.

Finley, Ruth E. *The Lady of Godey's: Sara Josepha Hale*. Philadelphia: Lippincott, 1931.

Frederickson, Robert S. "Hjalmar Hjorth Boyesen." In *American Realists and Naturalists*, ed. Donald Pizer and Earl N. Harbert, 37–42. Vol. 12 of *Dictionary of Literary Biography*. Detroit: Gale Research, 1982.

Freedom: A History of US. Public Broadcasting System. 2002.

Garmon, Gerald M. *John Reuben Thompson*. Boston: Twayne, 1979.

Gohdes, Clarence. *American Literature in Nineteenth-Century England*. New York: Columbia University Press, 1944.

Gray, James L. "Bayard Taylor." In *American Travel Writers, 1850–1915*, ed. Donald Ross and James J. Schramer, 321–35. Vol. 189 of *Dictionary of Literary Biography*. Detroit: Gale Research, 1998.

Guarneri, Carl J. *The Utopian Alternative: Fourierism in Nineteenth-Century America*. Ithaca: Cornell University Press, 1991.

Gustafson, Alrik. *A History of Swedish Literature*. Minneapolis: University of Minnesota Press, 1961.

Hale, Frederick, ed. *Danes in North America*. Seattle: University of Washington Press, 1984.

Hansen-Taylor, Marie, and Horace E. Scudder. *Life and Letters of Bayard Taylor*. 2 vols. London: Elliot Stock, 1884.

Harlow, Virginia. *Thomas Sergeant Perry: A Biography, and Letters to Perry from William, Henry, and Garth Wilkinson James*. Durham, N.C.: Duke University Press, 1950.

Harris, Laurie Lanzen, and Emily B. Tennyson, eds. "Horatio Alger, Jr." In *Nineteenth-Century Literary Criticism*. 8:13–49. Detroit: Gale Research, 1985.

Harvey, Robert D. "Richard Henry Stoddard." In *American Literary Critics and Scholars, 1850–1880*, ed. John W. Rathbun and Monica M. Grecu, 230–35. Vol. 64 of *Dictionary of Literary Biography*. Detroit: Gale Group, 1988.

Herscholt, Jean, and Waldemar Westergaard, eds. *Andersen-Scudder Letters: Hans Christian Andersen's Correspondence with Horace Elisha Scudder*. Berkeley and Los Angeles: University of California Press, 1949.

Higginson, Thomas Wentworth. "Horace Elisha Scudder." *Proceedings: American Academy of Arts and Science* 37 (1902): 657.

Hilen, Andrew. *Longfellow and Scandinavia: A Study of the Poet's Relationship with the Northern Languages and Literatures*. New Haven: Yale University Press, 1947.

Hilton, Timothy. *The Pre-Raphaelites*. London: Thames and Hudson, 1970.

"Horatio Alger, Jr." In *Nineteenth-Century Literature Criticism*, ed. Laurie Lanzen Harris and Emily B. Tennyson, 8:13–49. Detroit: Gale Research, 1985.

Howells, William Dean. Review of *Stories From My Attic*, by Horace E. Scudder. *Atlantic Monthly*, December 1869, 766–67.

———. Review of *The Bodleys on Wheels*, by Horace E. Scudder. *Atlantic Monthly*, January 1879, 123.

Howitt, Mary. "The Life of Hans Christian Andersen." In *The Improvisatore: Life in Italy*, by Andersen. Trans. Howitt, 3–9. New York: Harper & Brothers, 1845.

Index to Early American Periodicals to 1850. Vol. 5. New York: Readex Microprint, 1964.

Jensen, Anker. *Studier over H. C. Andersens Sprog*. Haderslev: Carl Nielsen, 1929.

Jones, W. Glyn. "H. C. Andersen in English—A Feasibility Study I" and "Andersen in English—A Feasibility Study II." In *Andersen og Verden: Indlæg fra den Første Internationale H. C. Andersen-Konference 25–31. August 1991*, ed. H. C. Andersen-Centret, Odense Universitet, 85–99 and 210–16, respectively. Odense: Odense Universitetsforlag, 1993.

Keigwin, R. P., trans. *Syv Digte/Seven Poems*. Odense: H. C. Andersen House, 1955.

King, Jr., Joseph Leonard. *Dr. George William Bagby: A Study of Virginian Literature, 1850–1880*. New York: Columbia University Press, 1927.

Kirk, S. "Recent Volumes of Short Stories." *Atlantic Monthly*, February 1881, 280–84 (281–83).

Lanes, Selma G. *Down the Rabbit Hole: Adventures and Misadventures in the Realm of Children's Literature*. New York: Atheneum, 1972.

Lathrop, G. P. Review of *The Dwellers in Five-Sisters Court*. *Atlantic Monthly*, October 1876, 509.

Leland, Charles Godfrey. *Memoirs*. London: William Heinemann, 1894.

Lutwack, Leonard. "The New England Hierarchy." *New England Quarterly* 28 (1955): 164–85.

Lynn, Kenneth S. *William Dean Howells: An American Life*. New York: Harcourt Brace Jovanovich, 1970.

Machor, James L. "Introduction: Readers, Texts, Contexts." In *Readers in History: Nineteenth-Century American Literature and the Contexts of Response*, ed. Machor, vii–xxix. Baltimore: Johns Hopkins University Press, 1993.

MacLeod, Anne Scott. "Children's Literature in America from the Puritan Beginnings to 1870." In *Children's Literature: An Illustrated History*, ed. Peter Hunt, 102–29. Oxford: Oxford University Press, 1995.

Making of America. <http://moa.umdl.umich.edu>.

Mayer, F. E. *The Religious Bodies of America*. 4th ed. Saint Louis, Mo.: Concordia Publishing House, 1961.

Milne, Gordon. *George William Curtis and the Genteel Tradition*. Bloomington: Indiana University Press, 1956.

Minor, Benjamin Blake. *Southern Literary Messenger, 1834–1864*. New York: Neale Publishing, 1905.

Mitchell, P. M. *A History of Danish Literature*. 2nd ed. New York: Kraus-Thomsen, 1971.

Möller-Christensen, Ivy York. *Den gyldne trekant: H. C. Andersens gennembrud i Tyskland, 1831–1850*. Odense: Odense Universitetsforlag, 1992.

Mott, Frank Luther. *A History of American Magazines, 1741–1850*. New York: Appleton, 1930.

———. *A History of American Magazines, 1850–1865*. Cambridge: Harvard University Press, 1938.

———. *A History of American Magazines, 1865–1885*. Cambridge: Harvard University Press, 1938.

———. *A History of American Magazines, 1885–1905*. Cambridge: Harvard University Press, 1957.

"Mr. Scudder and the Atlantic." *Atlantic Monthly*, March 1902, 433.

Nielsen, Erling. "Eventyrenes modtagelseskritik." In *H. C. Andersens Eventyr*, ed. Erik Dal, Nielsen, and Flemming Hovmann, 6:121–230. Copenhagen: C. A. Reitzels Forlag, 1990.

The Nineteenth Century in Print. <http://memory.loc.gov/ammem/ndlpcoop/moahtml/snchome.html>.

Norton, Charles Eliot. Review of *Dream Children*, by Horace E. Scudder. *North American Review*, January 1864, 304.

Osborne, William S. *Caroline M. Kirkland*, 15–86. New York: Twayne, 1972.

Packer, Barbara L. "The Transcendentalists." In *The Cambridge History of American Literature*, ed. Sacvan Bercovitch and Cyrus R. K. Patell, 2:329–604. New York: Cambridge University Press, 1995.

Parrington, Vernon Louis. *The Romantic Revolution in America, 1800–1860*. Vol. 2 of *Main Currents in American Thought: An Interpretation of American Literature from the Beginnings to 1920*, by Parrington. New York: Harcourt-Brace, 1927.

Patrick, Max. Introduction. In *The Complete Poetry of Robert Herrick*. New York: Norton, 1968.

Pedersen, Viggo Hjørnager. "Hans Andersen as an English Writer." In *Essays on Translation*, by Hjørnager Pedersen. Copenhagen: Nyt Nordisk Forlag Arnold Busck, 1988.

Peirce, Z. F. Review of *Doings of the Bodley Family in Town and Country* and *The Bodleys Telling Stories*. *Atlantic Monthly*, December 1877, 761–62.

Pennell, Elizabeth Robins. *George Godfrey Leland: A Biography*. 2 vols. Boston: Houghton Mifflin, 1906.

Philip, Neil, ed. *American Fairy Tales from Rip Van Winkle to the Rootabaga Stories.* New York: Hyperion, 1996.

Phillips, Kate. *Helen Hunt Jackson: A Literary Life.* Berkeley and Los Angeles: University of California Press, 2003.

Pochmann, Henry A. *German Culture in America: Philosophical and Literary Influences, 1600–1900.* Madison: University of Wisconsin Press, 1961.

Poole, William Frederick, and William I. Fletcher. *Poole's Index to Periodical Literature.* Revised edition. New York: Peter Smith, 1938.

Rogers, Sherbrooke. *Sarah Josepha Hale: A New England Pioneer, 1788–1879.* Grantham, N.H.: Tompson and Rutter, 1985.

Rossel, Sven Hakon. "Introduction: Hans Christian Andersen's Life and Authorship." In *Tales and Stories by Hans Christian Andersen,* trans. and ed. Patricia L. Conroy and Rossel. Seattle: University of Washington Press, 1980.

———. "Hans Christian Andersen Research in the United States." In *Andersen og Verden: Indlæg fra den Første Internationale H. C. Andersen-Konference 25.–31. August 1991,* ed. H. C. Andersen-Centret, Odense Universitet, 517–30. Odense: Odense Universitetsforlag, 1993.

Rowland, Herbert. "Confluence and Crosscurrents: Schiller's 'Das Lied von der Glocke' and Hans Christian Andersen's 'Die alte Kirchenglocke.'" *Anderseniana* (1996): 79–95.

———. "The Image of H. C. Andersen in American Magazines During the Author's Lifetime." In *H. C. Andersen: Old Problems and New Readings,* ed. Steven Sondrup, 175–98. Odense: University of Southern Denmark Press, 2004.

———. "The Author's Edition of H. C. Andersen's Works: An American-Danish Collaboration." *Orbis Litterarum,* 60 (2005): 449–76.

Sale, Roger. *Fairy Tales and After: From Snow White to E. B. White.* Cambridge: Harvard University Press, 1978.

Salway, Lance, ed. *A Peculiar Gift: Nineteenth Century Writings on Books for Children.* Harmondsworth, U.K.: Kestral Books, 1976.

Samuels, Charles E. *Thomas Bailey Aldrich.* New York: Twayne, 1965.

Schiller, Friedrich. *On the Naive and Sentimental in Literature.* Trans. Helen Watanabe O'Kelly. Manchester: Carcanet New Press, 1981.

Schlegel, August Wilhelm, and Friedrich. *Athenaeum: Eine Zeitschrift* (1798). Reprint, Berlin: Rütten and Loening, 1960.

Schmudde, Carol E. "Sincerity, Secrecy, and Lies: Helen Hunt Jackson's No Name Novels." *Studies in American Fiction* 21 (1993): 51–66.

Schroeder, Carol L. *A Bibliography of Danish Literature in English Translation, 1950–1980.* Copenhagen: Det danske Selskab, 1982.

Schweizer, Niklaus Rudolf. *The Ut pictura poesis Controversy in Eighteenth-Century England and Germany.* Bern and Frankfurt: Herbert Lang, Peter Lang, 1972.

Scudder, Horace E. *Seven Little People and Their Friends.* New York: A. D. F. Randolf, 1862.

———. *Dream Children.* Cambridge, Mass.: Sever & Francis, 1864.

———. "Five-Sisters Court at Christmas-Tide." *Atlantic Monthly,* January 1865, 22–39.

———. "Patchwork." *Riverside Magazine,* November 1868, 527.

————. *Stories From My Attic.* New York: Hurd & Houghton, 1869.

————, ed. "Advertisement." In *Wonder Stories Told for Children,* by Hans Christian Andersen, vii. Author's Edition. Boston and New York: Hurd and Houghton, 1870.

————, ed. "Advertisement." In *Stories and Tales,* by Hans Christian Andersen, vii–xix. Author's Edition. Boston and New York: Hurd and Houghton, 1871.

————, ed. "Advertisement." In *The Story of My Life,* by Hans Christian Andersen. Author's Edition. Boston and New York: Hurd and Houghton, 1871.

————. *Doings of the Bodley Family in Town and Country.* New York: Hurd and Houghton, 1875.

————. *The Dwellers in Five-Sisters Court.* New York: Hurd and Houghton, 1876.

————. *The Bodleys Telling Stories.* New York: Hurd and Houghton, 1878.

————. *The Bodleys on Wheels.* Boston: Houghton Osgood, 1879.

————. *The Bodleys Afoot.* Boston: Houghton Osgood, 1880.

————. *Stories and Romances.* Boston: Houghton Mifflin, 1880.

————. *Boston Town.* Boston: Houghton Mifflin, 1881.

————. *Mr. Bodley Abroad.* Boston: Houghton Mifflin, 1881.

————. *The Bodley Grandchildren and their Journey in Holland.* Boston: Houghton Mifflin, 1882.

————. *The English Bodley Family.* Boston: Houghton Mifflin, 1884.

————. *The Viking Bodleys: An Excursion into Norway and Denmark.* Boston: Houghton Mifflin, 1885.

————. *Men and Letters: Essays in Characterization and Criticism.* Boston and New York: Houghton Mifflin, 1887.

————. *The Atlantic Index, 1857–1888.* Boston: Houghton Mifflin, 1889.

————. *Childhood in Literature and Art.* Boston and New York: Houghton Mifflin, 1894.

————. *James Russell Lowell: A Biography.* 2 vols. Boston: Houghton Mifflin, 1901.

Sedgwick, Ellery. *The Atlantic Monthly, 1857–1909: Yankee Humanism at High Tide and Ebb.* Amherst: University of Massachusetts Press, 1994.

Seyersted, Per. *Hjalmar Hjorth Boyesen: From Norwegian Romantic to American Realist.* Oslo: Solum Forlag; Atlantic Highlands, N.J.: Humanities Press, 1984.

Spassky, Natalie. *American Paintings in the Metropolitan Museum of Art.* Vol. 2. New York: Metropolitan Museum of Art, 1985.

Spencer, Benjamin T. *The Quest for Nationality: An American Literary Campaign.* Syracuse, N.Y.: Syracuse University Press, 1957.

Stedman, Edmund Clarence. Introduction. In *Recollections Personal and Literary,* by Richard Henry Stoddard. New York: A. S. Barnes, 1903.

Steiner, Wendy. *The Colors of Rhetoric: Problems in the Relation between Modern Literature and Painting.* Chicago: University of Chicago Press, 1982.

Stoddard, Richard Henry. *Adventures in Fairyland.* Boston: Ticknor, Reed, and Fields, 1853.

————. *Recollections Personal and Literary.* New York: A. S. Barnes, 1903.

Swift, Lindsay. *Brook Farm: Its Members, Scholars, and Visitors.* New York: Macmillan, 1900.

Taft, Kendall B. Preface and "Minor Knickerbockers" [Introduction]. In *Minor Knickerbockers*, v–vi and xiii–cx. New York: American Book Company, 1947.

Tebbel, John. *A History of Book Publishing in the United States.* Vol. 1. New York: R. R. Bowker, 1972.

———, and Mary Ellen Zuckerman. *The Magazine in America, 1741–1990.* New York: Oxford University Press, 1991.

Tomsich, John. *A Genteel Endeavor: American Culture and Politics in the Gilded Age.* Stanford, Calif.: Stanford University Press, 1971.

Topsøe-Jensen, Helge. "The Background of the Letters." In *The Andersen-Scudder Letters: Hans Christian Andersen's Correspondence with Horace Elisha Scudder,* ed. Jean Hersholt and Waldemar Westergaard, xix–xxxiv. Berkeley and Los Angeles: University of California Press, 1949.

"Værkregister til bind I-VII." In *H. C. Andersens Eventyr,* ed. Erik Dal, Erling Nielsen, and Flemming Hovmann, 7:395–404. Copenhagen: C. A. Reitzels Forlag, 1963–1990.

Vogel, Stanley M. *German Literary Influences on the American Transcendentalists.* New Haven: Yale University Press, 1955.

Wermuth, Paul C. *Bayard Taylor.* New York: Twayne, 1973.

———. "Bayard Taylor." In *Antebellum Writers in New York and the South,* ed. Joel Myerson, 326–30. Vol. 3 of *Dictionary of Literary Biography.* Detroit: Gale Research, 1998.

West, Mark Irwin. "Horace E. Scudder." In *American Writers for Children Before 1900,* ed. Perry J. Ashley, 318–21. Vol. 42 of *Dictionary of Literary Biography.* Detroit: Gale Research, 1986.

Westbrook, Perry D. *Acres of Flint: Sarah Orne Jewett and Her Contemporaries.* Revised ed. Metuchen, N.J.: Scarecrow Press, 1981.

Westergaard, Waldemar. "Notes." *The Andersen-Scudder Letters: Hans Christian Andersen's Correspondence with Horace Elisha Scudder.* Ed. Jean Hersholt and Westergaard. Berkeley and Los Angeles: University of California Press, 1949.

White, Jr., Ronald C., and C. Howard Hopkins. *The Social Gospel: Religion and Reform in Changing America.* Philadelphia: Temple University Press, 1976.

Wilson, James Harrison. *The Life of Charles A. Dana.* New York: Harper and Brothers, 1907.

Wullschlager, Jackie. *Hans Christian Andersen: The Life of a Storyteller.* New York: Knopf, 2001.

Zipes, Jack. *When Dreams Came True: Classical Fairy Tales and Their Tradition.* New York: Routledge, 1999.

General Index

Abbot, Jacob, 154, 200
Addison, Joseph, 58
Alden, Henry Mills, 95, 150, 153, 155, 237 n. 20
Alden, John, 150–51
Aldrich, Thomas Bailey, 97, 160, 229 nn. 72 and 73
Alger, Horatio, Jr., 79, 225 n. 111
Allen, Alexander V. G., 167, 237 n. 13, 239 n. 63
American Historical Record, 77
American Memory: Historical Collections for the National Digital Library (Library of Congress), 13
American Periodical Series, The, 12
American Renaissance, 30
Andersen, Vilhelm, 234 n. 108
Antipas, 239 n. 71
Appleton's Journal, 27–28, 35–36, 95, 99–101, 103, 120–22, 197
Arcturus, 85
Ariosto, 96
Arnim, Achim von, 204
Arnold, Matthew, 174
Åström, Harald, 15, 201–3, 213 n. 26, 244 n. 30
Atheneum, 206
Atlantic Index, The, 51
Atlantic Monthly, 27–28, 34, 37, 39, 41–42, 49, 51, 53–54, 66, 71–73, 78, 80, 94–95, 98, 103, 150, 154, 159–60, 165–67, 171–72, 176, 183, 188, 197, 216 nn. 14 and 20, 240 nn. 77 and 86, 241 n. 108, 243 n. 13
Auerbach, Berthold, 107
Aulnoy, Madame d', 96

Author's Edition, The, 12, 20, 22, 33–34, 39, 51, 54, 66, 71, 80, 96–98, 120, 138, 155, 177, 186, 196–97, 200, 204, 215 n. 15, 216 n. 14, 229 n. 74, 236 n. 173
Avery, Gillian, 230 n. 2, 244 n. 26

Bagby, George William, 90–92, 227 n. 48
Bagger, Louis, 120–24, 143, 192, 194, 233 n. 82
Bain, Robert Nisbet, 197
Bancroft, George, 63, 173, 220 n. 103, 222 n. 29, 241 n. 94
Barnett, John, 163
Barrett, Samuel, 222 n. 29
Bartlett, W. C., 98
Baym, Nina, 167, 195, 213 n. 24
Beatty, Richard Croom, 232 n. 54
Beaty, John O., 228 n. 48
Beckwith-Lohmeyer, Charles, 81, 226 n. 7
Bell, Michael Davitt, 219 n. 84
Bentham, Jeremy, 86
Biedermeier culture, 202–3
Bille, C. St. A., 209–10
Bjørnson, Bjørnstjerne, 40–41, 86, 95
Blackwood's Edinburgh Magazine, 39, 43, 206
Blake, William, 151, 159, 165
Blicher, Steen Steensen, 221 n. 127
Boner, Charles, 83, 192
Boyesen, Hjalmar Hjorth, 51–52, 54, 131–44, 148, 191–93, 198, 235 n. 139, 236 n. 173, 245 n. 66
Braddon, Mary Elizabeth, 40–41, 218 n. 52

Index of Works by Hans Christian Andersen

269

NOVELS

PLAYS

POETRY

Index of Works by Horace E. Scudder